P9-CAS-581

LEADERSHIP FOR THE FUTURE

Core Competencies in Healthcare

AUPHA

HAP Editorial Board

Beaufort B. Longest, Ph.D., FACHE, Chair
University of Pittsburgh

Janet R. Buelow, Ph.D.
University of South Dakota School of Business

Lawton R. Burns, Ph.D.
University of Pennsylvania

Jeptha W. Dalston, Ph.D., FACHE
AUPHA

Myron D. Fottler, Ph.D.
University of Central Florida

Robert E. Hurley, Ph.D.
Virginia Commonwealth University

Arnold Kaluzny, Ph.D.
University of North Carolina

Kerry E. Kilpatrick, Ph.D.
University of North Carolina

Stephen F. Loebs, Ph.D.
Ohio State University

Brian T. Malec, Ph.D.
CA State University-Northridge

Kenneth M. Miller, Ph.D.
College of West Virginia

Michael A. Morrisey, Ph.D.
University of Alabama @ Birmingham

Anne Walsh, Ph.D.
La Salle University

Bryan J. Weiner, Ph.D.
University of North Carolina

Kenneth R. White, Ph.D., FACHE
Virginia Commonwealth University

LEADERSHIP FOR THE FUTURE

Core Competencies in Healthcare

Austin Ross, Frederick J. Wenzel,
and Joseph W. Mitlyng

Health Administration Press, Chicago, Illinois
AUPHA Press, Washington, D.C.

AUPHA
HAP

Your board, staff, or clients may also benefit from this book's insight. For more information on quantity discounts, contact the Health Administration Press Marketing Manager at (312) 424-9470.

This publication is intended to provide accurate and authoritative information in regard to the subject matter covered. It is sold, or otherwise provided, with the understanding that the publisher is not engaged in rendering professional services. If professional advice or other expert assistance is required, the services of a competent professional should be sought.

The statements and opinions contained in this book are strictly those of the author(s) and do not represent the official positions of the American College of the Healthcare Executives or of the Foundation of the American College of Healthcare Executives.

Copyright © 2002 by the Foundation of the American College of Healthcare Executives. Printed in the United States of America. All rights reserved. This book or parts thereof may not be reproduced in any form without written permission of the publisher.

06   05   04   03   02   5   4   3   2   1

Library of Congress Cataloging-in-Publication Data

Ross, Austin.
  Leadership for the future : core competencies in healthcare / by Austin Ross,
  Frederick J. Wenzel, Joseph W. Mitlyng, Jr.
    p. ; cm.
  Includes bibliographical references and index.
  ISBN 1-56793-160-X (alk. paper)
    1. Health services administration. 2. Core competencies. I. Wenzel, Frederick J.
  II. Mitlyng, Joseph W. III. Title.
    [DNLM: 1. Health Services Administration. 2. Health Facilities—organization &
  administration. 3. Health Facility Administrators. 4. Leadership. 5. Organizational
  Innovation. W 84.1 R823L 2001]
  RA394 .R674 2001
  362.1'068—dc21

                                                                    2001039322

The paper used in this publication meets the minimum requirements of American National Standard for Information Sciences—Permanence of Paper for Printed Library Materials, ANSI Z39.48-1984. ∞ ™

Acquisitions manager: Audrey Kaufman; Project manager: Cami Cacciatore; Text and cover designer: Matt Avery

Health Administration Press
A division of the Foundation of the
  American College of Healthcare Executives
1 North Franklin Street, Suite 1700
Chicago, IL 60606-3491
(312) 424-2800

Table of Contents

Foreword

FOR SEVERAL DECADES, the environment of healthcare has been undergoing continuous change, characterized by turbulence, volatility, and uncertainty. In this environment, the challenges facing organizations are complex and often contradictory. For example, concern continues about the rate of increase in healthcare costs and the about the long-term viability of major programs such as Medicare and Medicaid. Nevertheless, over 40 million Americans remain uninsured or underinsured. Technological advances in medicine and management, while highly promising, also serve to heighten these already serious concerns about cost. Consumers are becoming more informed and knowledgeable, accompanied by growing demands for professional, organizational, financial, social, and political accountability. In many parts of the country, we face shortages of critical health professionals, notably but not limited to nursing. The growth of managed care, and especially capitation, argued by some to be the answer to many of our problems, has slowed. Stimulated by recent reports from the Institute of Medicine, we are witnessing a reemergence of employer activity, with a strong focus on quality and patient safety. Unfulfilled promises from an array of organizational strategies—mergers and consolidations, physician practice acquisitions, entry into insurance—have only added to the turbulence.

In the face of these and other challenges, many observers are underscoring the importance of leaders and managers. In addressing the role of leadership, Austin Ross, Frederick "Fritz" Wenzel, and Joseph Mitlyng have taken a particularly useful approach, centering their attention on competencies. The authors recognize that management exists only in the context of organizations; thus, the competencies of leaders must be framed within the larger context of the competencies of the organization. To support their work, the authors wisely use and apply the literature and experience of management theory and behavior in other industries as well as their own, seeking key learnings to enhance management practices within healthcare.

After an introduction and discussion of healthcare perspectives, the authors organize their views of competencies into three levels of analysis. Essential system competencies address the competencies of the organization within its environment, while personal leadership competencies explore the individual level. Finally, leadership and management competencies define specific knowledge areas that effectively sustain leadership over time.

Essential system competencies are defined as the capabilities of the organization itself in relationship to its environment, its competitors, and its constituencies. These competencies include governance, strategic development (including vision and values), physician relationships, ethics and values, quality and value enhancement, public health and community involvement, health policy and law, and alternative, complementary, and integrative medicine. The chapter in this section on quality and value enhancement is especially timely in light of the recent reports from the Institute of Medicine. The exploration of public health and community improvement and health policy underscores the broadening role of healthcare organizations as they move beyond traditional models toward greater focus on population health. Likewise, discussion of alternative and complementary medicine acknowledges changing modalities of care and the changing expectations of consumers.

Moving to core competencies of personal leadership, the authors identify decision making, risk taking, team building and evaluation, managing conflict, professional mentoring, and managing your career as necessary to build an effective management team and an effective organization. On the basis of these competencies the authors urge continuing and life-long learning. Reemphasizing the contingent nature of their perspective, the personal competencies are viewed as those especially relevant in a complex, uncertain, volatile environment.

The final section of the book examines ten specific knowledge areas for organizational leadership in a complex environment, including governance and organizational dynamics (behavior); human resources; financial management and economics; strategic planning and marketing; information and information systems; communications and public relations; quantitative analysis and modeling; organizational and healthcare policy; and legal and ethical issues.

Throughout the book, Ross, Wenzel, and Mitlyng not only raise issues and challenges, but also offer an array of ideas, concepts, and specific suggestions to enhance performance of the organization and its leadership within each of the respective areas of competency. The book is quite user friendly; each chapter opens with a mini-case and question to serve as a starting point for the discussion to follow and to provide focus and practicality to the material. In addition, the authors draw extensively from the practice and academic literature, providing examples and illustrations to breathe life into their material. Questions at the end of each chapter offer practitioners the opportunity for self-assessment and exploration of their respective strengths and weaknesses against the ideas and concepts presented in the book, and provide students with a stimulus for discussion and debate.

Finally, the underlying philosophy of this book should be of special interest to educators and academics. The framework begins with an assessment of the current and likely external environment, follows with a characterization of the kinds of organizations most able to adapt to such environmental conditions, elaborates the core competencies of such organizations, identifies the core competencies of leaders of such organizations, and specifies the leader's requisite knowledge and skills. Such an approach is an appropriate basis for educational programming aimed at developing the core competencies for successful organizations and organizational leadership. Austin Ross, Frederick Wenzel, and Joseph Mitlyng have provided us with a valuable resource and an intriguing roadmap for our journey toward organization and leadership improvement.

—*Howard S. Zuckerman, Ph.D., University of Washington*

Preface

ESTABLISHING THE FRAMEWORK

Clearly, the healthcare environment has shifted from a level of reasonable predictability to one that is unpredictable and highly volatile. The rank ordering of core competencies for healthcare executives might be expected to change as a result of system volatility, and so it does. Our plan in developing this book was to lay out several of the determinants of change, to identify and classify key competencies most useful in coping with these volatile times, and, finally, to offer an inventory useful to several audiences.

DEFINING COMPETENCY

What exactly is a core competence? Which core competencies are most important from an organizational viewpoint? Do essential core competencies change based on environmental and organizational shifts or are they constant? How do you identify an organization's core competencies? Does a difference exist between organizational core competencies and those associated with personal and professional behavior, and if so, what is this difference? Do academicians and practitioners have a common understanding concerning the relative value of those competencies? How do these competencies relate to accepted behavior associated with management theory?

The purist may define *core competencies* as a set of skills that differentiates one individual from another. In this sense the set of core competencies is unique to the individual and specialized to the setting. An example of this core competency framework would be the unique leadership characteristics of Winston Churchill (vision) or General George Patton (dogged determination).

This book takes a slightly broader view of the definition of core competency. Core competencies refer to a set of interrelated skills that can be defined and categorized. These competencies transcend unique organizational settings and are applicable across the environment. An example might be the skills of an accomplished symphony director who builds core competencies by understanding not only the technical aspects of music but also how to convey that understanding and rally the musicians to produce the performance. Chapter 2 addresses in detail the historical background associated with identifying competencies.

INTENT AND APPROACH

This book is designed to provide the framework for identifying and assessing competencies of particular value to the healthcare executive. The intended audiences include the executive or clinician professional in practice, the student aiming for a health services management career, those moving into management positions, and members of boards who have a vested interest in identifying the core competencies of their executives.

We will dissect executive core competencies at three levels. Part II, "System Competencies," addresses competencies of the organization. These broader competencies establish the operating culture of the organization. Typically, team efforts are required to produce results based on these competencies. Part III, "Personal Leadership Competencies," delves into those competencies required at the personal executive level and deals with issues of leadership. Part IV, "Leadership Competency Knowledge Areas," defines a set of ten personal skills that are used by executives to lead and manage organizations. Finally, in the Epilogue, we will forecast about the future of leadership.

USING THE BOOK

Each part of the book begins with a brief description of the material covered in that part; therefore, not only is it unnecessary to start at the beginning of the book, but the reader is encouraged to skip around. Each chapter begins with a "Case in Point" to lay the foundation for the discussion to follow. The skills and competencies are outlined and a "Practical Application" section is followed by a series of self-assessment questions. The practical application section describes issues that are very difficult—if not impossible—to teach in the classroom. Exposure to such issues can be difficult, even in a formal residency or internship program, unless the programs have a strong mentorship component. The practical application sections present truths that the authors have found to be effective in their years of experience in leading and managing healthcare organizations.

This book is about self-assessment, and it presents the reader with opportunities to check his or her competencies against an inventory of competencies. Readers will need to ponder the content and form their own conclusions. They will receive the most value by mentally listing the competencies and evaluating their own performance. Readers will have to decide on the competency's usefulness in the context of their own organization.

REFLECTIONS

One of the tragedies of the day is the alleged inability of leaders to adapt quickly enough to change. The industry is littered with stories of executives who flounder when confronted with sudden organizational change—for example, the hospital-based professional who ventures into providing an insurance product or who moves into the acquisition and management of group practices. Focusing on identifying and strengthening the set of competencies may make that difference for executives trying to cope with the changing times.

Acknowledgments

WE WOULD LIKE to express our appreciation to Rob Fromberg, Audrey Kaufman, Marcy McKay, and Cami Cacciatore of Health Administration Press for their constant encouragement and assistance. We are grateful also to a number of others who contributed their ideas and research efforts to the project. These include Theresa Ryan-Mitlyng, M.D., Jane M. Wenzel, Ph.D., Jan Malcolm, B.A., and Mark Young, M.D. Thanks also to members of the faculty of the department of health services at the University of Washington for their enthusiastic support.

Part I: Healthcare Perspectives

THE CHARACTERISTICS OF leadership vary according to the environment. Keeping up to date requires acknowledging certain characteristics and then placing these characteristics in the context of the historical and current assessment of competencies. Chapter 1 sets the stage for subsequent discussions relating to system competencies, personal leadership competencies, and personal skills. Topics discussed include executive priorities, past and present management characteristics, special tasks for the reinvention of the healthcare executive, and characteristics of success for organizations and their leaders.

Chapter 2 provides the essential historical review of different aspects of core competencies, definitions of competencies, competency research, and a special emphasis on competencies within the management domain. The importance of developing an ongoing in-depth study and evaluation of competencies needed for success is stressed.

CHAPTER 1

The Challenge to Contemporary Leaders in Healthcare

CASE IN POINT: As a healthcare executive, you know the importance of keeping up to date and you recognize the difficulty of doing that in these turbulent times. You have assessed your abilities in technical competencies and have identified a number of areas that need some improvement. The problem you face is finding time to address these deficiencies.

Your board chair, sympathetic to your concerns, suggests that you set aside time out of the office to develop and implement a plan to improve your abilities. You are concerned that this approach will send a bad message to your core management team—why should you disappear from the office and leave your key managers to cover for you?

After much reflection you decide the best approach is to address team deficiencies and create a master plan that will help improve the competencies of the entire leadership group.

QUESTION: How would you go about designing a competency development plan for your management staff?

INTRODUCTION

Keeping up to date is a challenge for health services executives. This chapter addresses and identifies leadership and organizational characteristics that matter.

Clearly the healthcare system needs some serious overhauling. Increasingly, young families are opting to forego health insurance because of the costs, and the number of uninsured is rising. Managed care plans are not succeeding financially and the public is becoming disenchanted with such plans. Interested in serving only the well, some insurance plans are denying patients considered to be poor risks. The elderly are very concerned about gaps in Medicare coverage and the high costs of prescription drugs. The Medicaid system is underfunded. The administrative costs associated with managing the healthcare system are far too high. Hospitals, healthcare systems, physicians, and other providers of care have fallen on hard times.

When reform is implemented the effect will be substantial. Healthcare executives will be on the front lines. Healthcare leaders must consider what can be done to retool to embrace such change.

THE EVOLUTION OF HEALTHCARE MANAGEMENT

Professional management of healthcare surfaced in the early 1900s when structures were simpler and the "boss" was readily identified. As society expanded, the ever-increasing enhancement of technology required more organizational structures. Subsequent generations of executives witnessed the following eras.

1. *Initial organization and structure: 1910 to 1935.* This 25-year period was an era of new industries and entrepreneurship, of preregulation and high risk. The health industry was in its organizational infancy. Hospitals were individual units, physicians were individual entrepreneurs, and group practices were few in number.
2. *Productivity: 1935 to 1955.* A science of management began to develop. Units were counted and factories mechanized. World

War II profoundly affected how medicine was practiced and delivered. The concept of integrated hospital care matured and physician practitioners began to focus on activities closer to the hospital.

3. *Systems movement and management control: 1955 to 1970.* Technology continued to advance and society responded with an endless appetite and a new expectation that medicine and the health system could deliver quality care in limitless quantities. Management engineers were employed within hospitals to further operational effectiveness.

4. *System networking: 1970 to 1980.* Hospitals, group practices, and other providers began to network and link, initially sharing resources and services. The links took on a more significant role as financial restraints and regulation of the health industry began to limit decision-making flexibility. Joining forces allowed economies of scale and mutual protection. For-profit hospital systems flourished, existing nonprofit systems adopted corporate structure formats and outlooks, and independent institutions formed new alliances and consortia.

5. *The new competition: 1980 to 1995.* This era signaled shakedown and survival of the fittest. High technology, high expectations, and high costs were the drivers for change. Competition tested the traditional organizational climate. Hospital and group practice leaders learned how to downsize operations, diversify to protect revenue bases, and build management teams capable of rapid decision making. Organizations found new ways to reward innovators.

6. *Reinvention: 1995 to the present.* The health industry began to reinvent itself as it became clearer that previous approaches to cost control and maximization of revenue were not going to do the job in an environment where net revenue slices were too small to adequately sustain the organization. The hoped-for economy of scale associated with increasing the size of an organization to capture more market share failed to pay off for many, prompting unit divestiture of loss-leader units and services. New mergers between healthcare organizations diminished in

number. Healthcare leaders, board members, and stakeholders struggled to develop new strategies that would improve their organizations and allow them to continue meeting their missions. One such strategy led organizations and their leaders to explore executive competencies to forge new decision-making practices.

REINVENTING HEALTHCARE LEADERS AND MANAGEMENT TEAMS

The healthcare executive who is designing management teams for the future must:

1. enhance leadership practices;
2. upgrade technical expertise; and
3. enrich the team's sense of social accountability.

All three tasks are interrelated. The characteristics associated with outstanding leadership are not easily defined. Leadership competency requirements are subject to variables such as the culture of the organization, the stage in life of the organization, and its viability and the elements of change associated with a turbulent environment. A single correct approach to leadership does not exist, which creates challenges for those who aspire to lead.

These challenges are further complicated when a leader must somehow integrate personal style and characteristics with organizational need. Sometimes the match is not a good one and the tenure of the executive is shortened. At other times an executive is a solid match, and organizational movement and change take place.

Beneath the leadership style—which comes from years of experience and is an aging process requiring testing and modification along the way—are the technical skills required to sort and process information to validate decision making. These are not so much personal skills of the executive, but skills recognized by the executive as important pieces in support of leadership applications.

An executive's sense of social responsibility comes into the equation as the means by which values are identified and reinforced. As conditions change—perhaps financial setbacks for the organization—unique pressures placed on executives can distort or displace value systems important to the organization and to those served by the organization.

Of necessity, core competencies must recognize these leadership variables, the technical aspects in support of decision making, and the essential aspects of maintaining organizational perspective in support of the mission.

Building Blocks

In his five-year research on *Level Five Leadership,* Jim Collins (2001) makes a strong case for a building block approach to leadership development. He suggests that the truly great organization will have executives functioning at all five levels:

- *Level 1: Highly Capable Individual.* Makes contributions through talent, knowledge, skills, and good work habits.
- *Level 2: Contributing Team Member.* Contributes to the achievement of group objectives; works effectively with others in group settings.
- *Level 3: Competent Manager.* Organizes people and resources toward the effective and efficient pursuit of predetermined objectives.
- *Level 4: Effective Leader.* Catalyzes commitment to and vigorous pursuit of a clear and compelling vision; stimulates the group to high performance standards.
- *Level 5: Executive.* Builds enduring greatness through a paradoxical combination of personal humility and professional will.

A Level 5 executive has not necessarily moved through the stages sequentially; however, a Level 5 team must possess the capabilities of the lower four levels, plus the special characteristics of Level 5. Each level requires a set of core competencies that stretch across leadership practices, technical expertise, and social and system accountability.

Assessing Professional Competencies

Perhaps the best advice for the leader who wishes to strengthen team competency is to suggest first that sufficient thought be allocated to the process of assessing, strengthening, and testing the leader's personal competencies. This stretching process requires a developed degree of self-perception, an awareness of values, and sensitivity to basic human relationships. Once this has been accomplished, the stage is set to strengthen team competencies. Executives who fall by the wayside probably have a common weakness: they become so singularly focused on limited goals that they ignore the importance of keeping current.

Successful leaders will find that their success is not based solely on maintaining their technical skills. They will prosper because they have learned to rely on their intuition, an understanding of the need to take risks, and a full appreciation of the importance of adhering to a strong ethical and value-oriented base. These leaders will not derive power from an organizational chart but from a strong base of healthy interpersonal relationships. They will learn from their setbacks and will have staying power. These leaders will be skillful at networking and will seek counsel from specialists and others as a means of incorporating new ideas and concepts.

CHARACTERISTICS OF SUCCESSFUL CORPORATIONS AND THEIR LEADERS

Peters, Peters, and Waterman (1982) determined that highly successful business corporations have a number of common characteristics. Shortell et al.'s study (2000) followed with a focus on the characteristics of high-performing organizations and leaders in the healthcare field. According to Shortell, these organizations and leaders are willing to:

1. *Stretch themselves.* High-performing healthcare organizations commit to the extraordinary. Never satisfied, they are always striving for improvement.
2. *Maximize learning.* Top organizations learn quickly and do not reinvent the wheel. They continually search their environments for both opportunities and hidden threats. Learning is facilitated by channeling information down to the lowest possible level in the organization.
3. *Take risks.* Such organizations are risk takers and are meticulous in learning from their mistakes. To keep tuned into the new environment, they classify problems as challenges and consider that excellence is not perfection. These organizations are willing to change patterns of operation in the way they work with physicians, trustees, staff, and patients.
4. *Transform leaders.* Transformational leaders provide people with meaning because they integrate personal values and goals with those of the organization. These leaders continually keep the values of the organization before people in a visible and tangible way to develop a strong organizational culture.
5. *Be action oriented.* These organizations do not view their environment in a passive fashion. Rather than complaining, they believe they can influence events.
6. *Balance their teams.* A matching of "left brain" thinkers with "right brain" thinkers allows these organizations to successfully balance between the qualitative and quantitative aspects of management.
7. *Manage uncertainty and ambiguity.* In our current environment it is easier to focus on more comfortable operational issues than to deal with uncertainty and ambiguity and reflect on what it takes to modify the behavior of those people who resist innovation. Shortell notes, "High performing healthcare organizations are change makers. They create problems for others. Others do not create problems for them, only opportunities" (Shortell et al. 2000).

8. *Exhibit loose coherence.* In their book *In Search of Excellence,* Peters, Peters, and Waterman (1982) note that high-performing industrial companies exhibit simultaneously tight and loose control practices. When people buy into overall goals, values, and philosophies of an organization, they require less supervision than those who have not been given that opportunity. Shortell supports this and suggests that some operational "looseness" is useful. This does not imply that control systems should be ignored, but simply suggests that these high-performing organizations provide some freedom in the decision-making processes.

9. *Create a strong culture.* While all organizations have a culture, the strong ones have an ability to articulate their culture. They "live" their culture and personalize their approaches to its issues.

10. *Be spiritual.* Spirituality does not refer to religious affiliation or sponsorship, but rather to the ability to give meaning and purpose to people's lives. Organizations that perform well seem to recognize spirituality and capitalize on it.

PERSONAL ATTRIBUTES FOR SUCCESS

Some years ago, David Kinser (then president of the Massachusetts Hospital Association) studied ten hospital CEOs he knew well who had been in their institutions long enough for him to make judgments about their accomplishments. He sifted through their management operating characteristics and identified some common traits of success.

1. *They radiated value systems.* Highly successful CEOs had value systems that were evident to those with whom they worked. They were respected for their honesty and for keeping the commitments they made.

2. *They knew where they wanted to go.* They all had a clear perception of where they wanted to take their institutions.

3. *They often led from behind.* They were not necessarily frontline crusaders, but they functioned as very effective

change agents and had infinite amounts of patience and per-sistence.

4. *They knew how to manage stress.* They had learned to "leave it at the office" and did not take their daily problems home with them.
5. *They were modest salesmen.* None of them acted like high-pressure salespeople. Instead, they were viewed as very thoughtful and wise people.
6. *They were not all alike.* While all of the leaders differed extremely in their managing style, they knew how to delegate. Each of them demonstrated loyalty to the people who worked for them.
7. *They were career learners.* Finally, all had strong personal drives to keep learning.

While these various studies do not represent an all-inclusive list, they highlight characteristics useful to the executive who is building a successful team for the future.

AREAS OF EXPERTISE

Focus has shifted and the pressure of the day requires that executives be particularly familiar with a number of competencies. The executive does not have to be personally competent in all these areas, but rather he or she must have an awareness of their importance to a well-balanced team and have an understanding about how to acquire these skills for the organization. (Part IV of the book will discuss these and other important skills in more detail.)

Financial Management

Because of the pressures associated with federal and insurance in-dustry reimbursement practices, hospital leaders may have had a head start over executives in physician group practices and other organi-zations in cost containment and matters of resource consumption. But today the financial pressures facing the health provider and the in-tense competition, regardless of organizational base, have leveled the playing field. Today's executive must ensure that the organization excels in financial matters. Their management teams must be well equipped to work on forecasting, revenue enhancement, budgeting, and cost containment.

Negotiating Skills

One of the most highly valued team competencies will be the ability to negotiate tough deals with payers, competitors, or members of the internal staffs.

Information Systems

Of critical importance will be the team's ability to understand and use sophisticated data. Understanding information systems is essential to monitoring the quality of care and appropriately using resources. A very capable information systems team is necessary to engineer the linking of payer systems. Leadership teams must also display competency in tracking and evaluating the development of technology.

Human Resources

In addition to increasing the team's knowledge base about finances and information systems, the healthcare executive team will need to excel in the management of human resources. With the overload in the healthcare system and the push to become even more cost effective, the way that human resources are employed becomes crucial.

Patient Services

Changes in the healthcare system will bring about changes in the way organizations deliver patient services. In the era of intense competition and an enlightened patient group, enlightened in part through the use of the Internet, providers will need to spend time really understanding how the patient assesses service. The role of the ombudsman to quickly resolve patient concerns becomes very important.

Organizations will need to ensure that their quality-of-care mechanisms are effective and relate closely to patient expectations of service.

Broader Health Systems Orientation

New systems emphasizing integrated care will require leaders with a broader orientation to healthcare delivery. For example, leaders will need to understand the role of public health entities. Understanding how the pieces of the healthcare system fit together will be important to ensure a seamless delivery system.

ENHANCE THE TEAM'S SENSE OF SOCIAL RESPONSIBILITY

As the health system staggers under the weight of accumulated problems (aging population, federal budget problems, and access issues), the role of the healthcare executive as a spokesperson will assume more importance. Executives may begin by trying to justify what is taking place, to protect the status quo, or to minimize the shock that change will bring to the organization; however, eventually they will need to become very skilled advocates for change. Healthcare leaders should start now by making an investment in additional training to develop communication skills and by spending more time on networking with community leaders and others to increase their understanding of public policy issues.

Leaders will need to become much more visible and more articulate on health issues. Executives will focus less on addressing the interests of single organizations and more on resolving public health issues such as disease prevention or improved home care. For executives who have been immersed in managing internal affairs and have devoted little effort to outside issues, this change will require a major shift in orientation.

An understanding of bioethics is becoming increasingly important in an environment in which courts struggle to resolve issues such as the right to die and the right to life. The technical competence of professionals and the advancement of science and technology continue to raise new questions about the manipulation of human genes to improve resistance to chronic diseases. As scientists push to improve the quality and longevity of life through the rearrangement of genetic structures, their research will ultimately raise the question of "How much is enough?" As organ and body part transplants become more common, the healthcare executive and others in healthcare will face the ever more complicated decisions about the responsibility of the health services organization in response to these new technologies. Understanding bioethics should be high on healthcare leaders' list of competencies.

CONCLUSION

The healthcare leader is responsible for sponsoring team-wide development processes that are focused, sensitive to the environment, and conducive to maximizing individual commitment and involvement. The leader is also responsible for monitoring value systems and promoting and protecting an appropriate organizational culture.

Finally, the leader is responsible for creating user-friendly executive teams to ensure that the organization truly functions to meet its organizational and societal objectives.

DISCUSSION

1. Which organizational competencies will be particularly important in the future and why?
2. Identify several of the organizational and societal objectives associated with a high-performing healthcare organization and explain why they are important.
3. How will management styles change in the future?
4. Why are hospital and practice mergers diminishing in number?

REFERENCES

Collins, J. 2001. "Level 5 Leadership—The Triumph of Humility and Fierce Resolve." *Harvard Business Review* 79 (1): 70–71.

Peters, T. K., T. Peters, and R. A. Waterman. 1982. *In Search of Excellence.* New York: Harper and Row.

Shortell, S., R. Gillies, D. Anderson, K. Erickson, and J. Mitchell. 2000. *Remaking Healthcare in America: The Evolution of Organized Delivery Systems,* 2nd edition. San Francisco: Jossey-Bass.

CHAPTER 2

Historical Overview of Essential Core Competencies

CASE IN POINT: Dr. Strong and the clinic administrator, Ms. Adams, were discussing their new relationship since Dr. Strong was elected president of the Middleboro Community Clinic. They decided the first thing on their agenda was to define the major tasks necessary to successfully lead and manage the clinic and what each of them could contribute to that success. They asked a professor from an area university to help them with this identification. Professor Johns, a longtime friend of the clinic, agreed to help Dr. Strong and Ms. Adams define the competencies the organization needed as well as to identify their individual competencies to ensure a good match. The professor also shared a review of the literature on the topic with Dr. Strong and Ms. Adams.

QUESTION: Why is it important for Dr. Strong and Ms. Adams to identify their core competencies and understand how they relate to those needed by the organization?

INTRODUCTION

This section deals with three different aspects of core competencies. First, a review of core competency studies since the time it became a topic of interest to leadership and management researchers will be presented. Second, the many different definitions of competency as they relate to leadership and management will be examined by answering the following questions:

- What are the areas of competency?
- What are domains?
- What is a core competence?
- What is leadership?
- What is management?
- Are leadership and management the same?

The third aspect will focus on the application of core competencies to healthcare management with some emphasis on the ambulatory care setting.

HISTORICAL PERSPECTIVE

The origin of the phrase *management competency* goes back to the early 1980s when interest was renewed in the work done in the early part of the 1900s by some of the brightest lights in management research. A book written in 1982 by Richard Boyatzis, *The Competent Manager*, sparked interest in the term competency, bringing it to the attention of those who were serious about describing what was needed for appropriate and adequate leadership and management. At that time, although the word was used frequently, few understood what the term really meant. Later in that decade a number of authors (Boyatzis 1982; Albanese 1989; and Fleishman and Quaintance 1984) acknowledged that defining competency was a most difficult task indeed, evidenced in the many definitions of competency today. Boyatzis (1982) may have created part of this confusion when he defined competency as an underlying characteristic of a person, a "motive, trait, aspect of one's image or social role, or a body of knowledge, which he or she uses." That definition, of course, covered a broad spectrum of activity in the life of the manager.

It is interesting to note that this occurred about the same time that Neuhauser (1983) and others were writing about the roots of hospital management practice, its orientation, and its relationship to graduate programs in healthcare administration. Green (1990) and Griffith (1995) took up the cause and attempted to describe the skills that would contribute to the successful management of an organization. Everyone seemed to agree that these contributions were a series of skills, especially those related to human services and analytical and quantitative skills. In 1990, Green suggested that these skills should have both a sound research base and a theoretical foundation, which shifted health-care management focus from the traditional emphasis on core values of the healing professions and relationship-building skills toward business-oriented, functional specialties such as financial management and operations research. The leaders and managers of most healthcare organizations were especially strong in these latter areas.

The significance of business-related functional skills and analytic abilities to modern health services management is without question. However, it has become apparent that an exclusive focus on the competencies on the analytical side of the organization—without regard to the visionary, adaptive, and collaborative team-building requirements of complex organizations—might not serve contemporary healthcare organizations well. Many authors (Griffith 1995; Dalston and Bishop 1995; Pew Health Professions Commission 1993; Richie, Tagliani, and Schmidt 1979; Schweirkart 1996; and Wenzel, Grady, and Freedman 1995) point out a significant and continuing increase in the recognition of the importance of the "human side of the enterprise," characterized by strong interpersonal communication and integrating skills described as necessary prerequisites for success in leading and managing complex organizations and their relationships with other complex organizations. It was suggested that a blurring of the relationship between physician and nonphysician managers exists, with the climate now favoring strong team interrelationships (O'Connor and Shewchuk 1993; Reinertsen 1995; and Williams 1996). In the mid-1990s, Hudson

(1995) and Pryor (1996) called attention to the inadequate emphasis on the core values of the healing profession as well as a general lack of superordinate themes of humanitarian service and the improvement of the status of the health of the population. They suggested that this left many healthcare executives ill prepared for the stresses and turbulence of institutional restructuring and consolidations. This may be one of the factors inherent in the increasing dissatisfaction among physicians with the environment in which they must practice medicine.

Hudak (1990) references several sources (Pew Health Professions Commission 1993; Coile 1995; Wenzel, Grady, and Freedman 1995; and Blair et al. 1995), stating that, "There seems to be a growing consensus that in a predictable future characterized by increased organizational complexity, heightened inter-professional tensions; radically redefined role relationships between managers and clinicians; the continuous reformulation of the bases for risk, reward and survival in the managed-care marketplace; interpersonal skills related to leadership, conflict management, team building and network integration; as well as a generalist understanding of the political complexity of stake-holder management, may be as important for management's success in health services delivery as the quantitative skills of the business model." Most academics, as well as practitioners, would agree with Hudak's assessment.

Although the overwhelming majority of the early historical perspectives have been based in hospital settings, there has been significant interest on the ambulatory side beginning in the 1970s. Several sources (Morita, Hodapp, and Slater 1976; Manning 1977; and Allcorn 1989) reported on the use of checklists for self-audits. These checklists could be used by medical group practice administrators to assess the quality of medical group management and to identify additional training requirements to meet the demands of increased complexity in organizations serving the ambulatory care population.

A study of management skills in the ambulatory environment conducted for the Department of Veterans Affairs identified the need for substantial improvements in managerial skills related to matrix management, leadership, management information, resource utilization, quality assurance, and personnel management (Nardone and Webb

1989). Tabenkin, Zyzanski, and Alemagno (1989) conducted a mail survey of physicians that looked at the variance in physician-manager roles, tasks and management characteristics, and various types of primary care organizational structures. The study suggested major differences in physician-manager levels of responsibility and management characteristics between different primary care organizations. They identified the need for more extensive management training of physician-managers in people-oriented and task-oriented skills. This was one of the first indications of the difference between managing patients and managing the organization.

Nash and Bryce (1996) pointed out that in order for healthcare providers to create value they must master core competencies that include effective management of health and wellness, effective care delivery, effective population enrollment, and effective management of financial risk. This is in contrast to how healthcare providers created value in the past by delivering care on demand to their patients.

Other authors, including Hudak (1990), Hudak and Mouritsen (1988), and Hill et al. (1994), addressed the need for an increase in academic preparation relating to skills and management competency necessary in all settings, especially ambulatory care, by both physicians and nonphysician leaders and managers. Blair and colleagues (1995) conducted a broad study among a large sample of medical group practice executives that raised concerns that the traditional curricular emphasis on hospital-based environments was not appropriate for the preparation of medical practice executives. They pointed out that there was significant complexity in dealing with the intraphysician issues not generally found in the hospital setting. A question was also raised about freestanding multispecialty complex organizations where the enterprise was not only staffed, but also owned, by the physicians themselves. The approach was significantly different from what was taught in the traditional academic hospital-related program. (An interesting aside related to these programs is that there are no longer graduate programs in Health Services Administration that carry the title Master's in Hospital Administration.)

Virtually all of the studies discussed here have been confirmed by work done in the latter half of the 1990s by the American College of

Medical Practice Executives and the Association of University Programs in Health Administration (AUPHA). The emphasis on the core competencies necessary to lead and manage in these most turbulent and white-water times continues. The leadership and management of healthcare organizations must pay a great deal of attention to the need for core competencies as they recruit and develop staff members who are capable of dealing with the complexities of modern healthcare. We have a long way to go and it will take significant and intense cooperative efforts between practitioners and academics to place the notion of core competency high on the list of priorities for healthcare organizations. The practitioners must provide the input for needed competence and the academics must teach not only the theories of healthcare leadership and management, but their relationship to the everyday practice as well. Although we may not need *more* leaders and managers, we must have leaders and managers who achieve a high degree of competence according to any one of the definitions that will be considered in the following discussion.

DEFINITIONS OF CORE COMPETENCIES

Interest in and discussions about core competencies began shortly after the development of significant interest in leadership and management as both an art and a science. However, the definition of core competencies and whether or not there are differences related to leadership and management continues to be debated both at the academic and practice levels. The most intense discussions about core competencies, especially in business, occurred early in the 1980s. Since that time there have been a number of reports in the leadership and management healthcare literature.

Before beginning an in-depth discussion of core competencies, it is necessary to have a common understanding of the definition of the terms *competency* and *performance*. In *Merriam-Webster's Collegiate Dictionary* (1998), the first definition for competency is "a sufficiency of means for the necessities and conveniences of life." The second definition is "the quality or state of being competent." The final definition is "the knowledge that enables a person to speak and understand a language." If we look at the definition of the word competent, the first definition states that it is being "proper or rightly pertinent" and the second is "having requisite or adequate ability or qualities." If we study these definitions, we come away with the conclusion that the principle meaning of the word competency relates to "a state in which the individual has the requisite or adequate ability or qualities to perform certain functions." The only liberty in this definition is the addition of the term "functions," which relates to performance.

Spencer and Spencer (1993) define competency as "an underlying characteristic of an individual that is causally related to criterion-referenced effective and/or superior performance in a job situation." Estes (1997) states that "implicit in the definition is the expectation that competency is part of a person's make-up and can predict behavior and ultimately performance in a given job. A characteristic of an individual is not competency unless it is a predictor of performance in the real world." For example, Barnett and Mayer (quoted in Estes 1997) stress that "physicians who are successful in practicing in a managed care environment must have many of the following attributes as assessed by performance: (1) be a team player; (2) work cooperatively with staff; (3) be adaptable; (4) possess or develop business acumen; (5) be able to ask for help; (6) have the necessary confidence to practice without undue consultation or ancillary studies; (7) be committed to serving patients; and (8) be genuinely committed to cost control and quality."

Woodruffe (1991) added to the definition of competence by stating, "While areas of competence can be used to refer to areas of work at which a person is competent, the word competency can be reserved for the dimensions of behavior that lie behind a competent performance. Areas of competence derived by functional analysis tend to be quite specific. However, an analysis of person-related competencies proceeds in the opposite direction to cluster the behaviors that differentiate a high performer. It is vital that a list of competencies be flexible and able to reflect changes in the organization's direction."

There is no other industry where the understanding of core competencies, as outlined by Woodruffe (1991), is as crucial as it is in healthcare today. His comments reflect exactly where we should be headed in our understanding of the need for focusing on core competencies.

A number of organizations have undertaken study of the core competencies for leadership and management in healthcare. Several of these studies will be cited to illustrate the term core competencies as well as the ways different organizations look at the same model. Existing differences are more related to focus than to foundation.

THE CORE ELEMENTS

Having introduced and discussed the term competencies, we now turn our attention to the term *core,* or those elements essential for an individual to perform his or her tasks. There appears to be general agreement among both academics and practitioners that these elements are key to a working definition of core competency. Considerable debate remains, however, especially in academic circles, as to whether different core competencies are needed for leadership than for management. Before launching into such a debate there must be agreement that differences between leadership and management exist. Leaders are those with the ability to create a vision, energize people and organizations, set direction, and choose the right course of action. Managers are those who ensure that short-range goals and targets are met, organize systems to accomplish the tasks of the organization, and seek to install control mechanisms that help people complete routine jobs successfully.

Having successfully differentiated between leaders and managers, we can now define the core competencies necessary for both leaders and managers to be successful. Writing in the *Harvard Business Review,* Heifitz and Laurie (1997) state that "changes, in society, markets, customers, competition and technology around the globe are forcing organizations to clarify their values, develop new strategies, and learn new ways of operating. One of the toughest tasks for leaders in effecting change is mobilizing people throughout the organization to do adaptive work."

Adaptive work is required when deeply held beliefs are challenged, when the values that made organizations successful become less relevant, and when legitimate yet competing perspectives emerge. Adaptive challenges can be seen every day at every level of the workplace when companies restructure, reengineer, develop or implement strategy, or merge businesses. Adaptive challenges are evident when marketing has difficulty working with operations, when cross-functional teams do not work well, or when senior executives complain, "We don't seem to be able to execute effectively." Adaptive problems are often systemic problems with no ready answers. While this discussion suggests that the main emphasis will be on leadership, the core competencies of the manager as well as the leader will be considered since there is significant overlap between these two functions. There will be special attention paid, however, to the differences.

To begin this discussion, consider the words of the ancient Chinese philosopher Lao-Tse, who stated:

The best leaders, the people do not notice.
The next best, the people honor and praise.
The next, the people fear;
and the next, the people hate.

When the best leader's work is done
the people say: "We did it ourselves!"

In an interesting study, Esque and Gilbert (1995) wrote: "The idea is to define a set of competencies for each job in the organization and develop a list of things that the job holder must be able to do. These job-specific competencies become the basis for hiring, developing, and compensating staff within those jobs. The danger is that the term competencies can lead people to err by focusing on behaviors instead of accomplishments." The authors then described a six-part process for ensuring that any barriers to success could be overcome, with heavy focus placed on outcomes. McClagan (1996) proposed a job competency model as a decision tool that described the key capabilities for performing a specific job. Competency models can be used as criteria for:

1. Training and curriculum design
2. Recruitment, selection, and assessment

3. Coaching, counseling, and mentoring
4. Career development and succession planning

McClagan suggested that competency models could be the principal way for describing what Drucker (1999) calls knowledge jobs: "jobs that require high levels of creativity, judgment, and tolerance for ambiguity and that can't be described adequately by tasks or activities. Knowledge jobs are defined by their capability requirements." Esque and Gilbert (1995) suggested a process for identifying competencies that, if acquired, will help overcome known barriers to success:

1. Define the mission of the job.
2. Describe the major outcomes required to achieve the mission.
3. Define performance standards for each major outcome.
4. Identify known barriers to achieving the performance standards.
5. Determine which barriers will be best overcome by training the performer.
6. Develop and deliver training.

It is apparent that little use of this model has been made in recruiting and training healthcare leaders and managers.

THE RESEARCH

In the early in 1990s the American College of Medical Practice Executives (ACMPE) began a study entitled "The Body of Knowledge for Medical Practice Managers." The main conclusion of that study was that core competencies are key and critical to the success not only of the individual, but of the organization as well. The ACMPE continued the study in 1998 through the use of expert panels, and major performance domains were defined along with the tasks associated with successful performance in each domain. *Domain* is defined as a coherent subset of a body of knowledge or, according to *Merriam-Webster's Collegiate Dictionary* (1998), "the set on which a function is defined." The study further described the knowledge, skills, and abilities required for completing each of the tasks identified by ACMPE. An advisory group was used and a consultant conducted a psychometric and editorial review of the knowledge and skill elements. A national sample of practicing executives was then asked to evaluate, validate, and provide feedback on the domains and the tasks identified by the panel.

Hudak et al. (1997) reported on the ACMPE studies and listed the following critical core competency domains:

- Leadership and strategic management
- Relationships management
- Resource management
- Functional management
- Stakeholder management
- Patient care management

The most frequent responses within these management domains will be found in Table 2.1, which reflects significant relationships between the domains and within the elements of those domains.

PHYSICIAN STUDIES

In October 1998, with the assistance of Columbia Assessment Services, Inc., ACMPE developed and validated the scope of practice for medical practice executive studies (ACMPE 1999). The focus was on the major performance domains, the tasks associated with successful performance in the domains, and the knowledge, skills, and abilities required for completing each task. Advisory panels were appointed and a questionnaire was distributed to a national sample of practicing executives who were asked to evaluate, validate, and provide feedback on the domains and tasks developed by the panel. The primary purpose of the analysis was to assess the validity of domains and tasks in terms of importance, criticality, and frequency.

The major performance domains identified in the study were:

- Financial management
- Human resources management
- Planning and marketing

Table 2.1. Examples of Unique Competencies Listed Within Management Domains and Associated Frequencies of Response

Competency (Within Management Domain)	Frequency (%)
Leadership and strategic management	
Leadership	44
Strategic planning/management	26
Flexibility	15
Visionary	13
Adapt to changes	11
Manage change	9
Critical thinking	8
Governance	7
Strategic thinking	7
Decision making	6
Risk management	6
Awareness of the environment	5
Ethical/values	5
Executive development	5
Relationships management	
Communications	22
Interpersonal skills	9
Physician relations	9
Human resources management	7
Networking	6
People skills	5
Team-building skills	5
Resource management	
Management information systems	28
Financial (finance)	24
Financial management	16
Capitation and reimbursement	13
Cost accounting	8
Physician compensation	8
Computer skills	7
Cost containment	6
Legal competency	6
Information management	5

(continued)

Table 2.1.   (continued)

Functional management
Organizational knowledge	9
Operations management	7

Stakeholder management
Negotiation skills	34
Managed care	23
Contracting	7
Knowledge of acquisitions and mergers	5

Patient care management
Outcomes analysis	5

Source: Hudak, R. P., P. P. Brooke, K. Finstuen, and J. Trounson. 1997. "Management Competencies for Medical Practice Executives: Skills, Knowledge and Abilities Required for the Future." *Journal of Health Administration Education* 15 (4): 220–39.

- Information management
- Risk management
- Governance and organizational dynamics
- Business and clinical operations
- Professional responsibility

The domains were defined by the specific tasks inherent to each. The intent of the study was to provide a research base for medical organizations to use in the development of professional staffing and for academic programs to use as they develop their core curriculum in health services management education programs.

MANAGEMENT COMPETENCIES IN THE AMBULATORY SETTING

In 1997, Hudak et al. reported additional findings from the ACMPE study relating to the needed competencies of physicians in management roles. There is little question about the relative scarcity of physicians with the necessary education, skills, and competencies to successfully assume expanded clinical leader and manager roles in complex delivery systems. Other authors suggested that the competencies required of physician executives in these new roles differ substantially from the informal and highly collegial roles of the past (Kindig and Lastivi-Queros 1989; and Schneller et al. 1997). Brooke and Hudak (1998) asked physicians who participated in the ACMPE studies to identify the top five competencies that medical practice physicians will need to be successful. The physician participants were also asked to describe the specific management skills, knowledge, and abilities medical practice physicians will need to achieve the referent competency. The 13 most frequently identified were:

- Managing healthcare resources to create quality and value
- Fundamentals of business and finance
- Leadership and management competencies
- Development of vision and strategic planning for healthcare delivery systems
- Communications/interpersonal skills
- Human resources and performance management
- Negotiating and contracting
- Change management
- Governance and policy development
- Defining, servicing, and growing your market
- Applying electronic communications to medical practice
- Ethics (medical, business, legal)
- Maintaining your competency for the future

A report by Kindig and Lastivi-Queros (1989) found that the tasks most frequently encountered by physician executives were "managing internal clinical operations, other physicians, and quality." These authors focused on the growing importance of "boundary-spanning roles for physician executives between general management responsibilities and managing clinical activities and professionals."

Brooke and Hudak (1998) concluded that "medical practice physicians require a large array of competencies involving managing clinical quality, as well as business and finance issues. In addition irrespective of competency 'domain' there are skills, knowledge, and abilities that are extremely important and involve issues of credibility, trust, honesty, and interpersonal communications. As physician executive roles continue to expand to include managing other physician clinical activities, such skills, knowledge, and abilities will assume even greater importance. On the other hand, less significance appears to be placed on physicians possessing such skills, knowledge, and the ability to know practice valuation techniques and to evaluate software."

Rossiter, Greene, and Kralewski (2000) made a number of interesting observations based on studies conducted by the ACMPE. These findings state that, "While administrators and physician executives envision a far-reaching role for group practice managers in the increasingly competitive healthcare system when they participated in the development of the management process model, in reality they identified needs, skills and knowledge competencies that are more narrowly focused. Little emphasis is placed on clinical management of population health by either administrators or physician executives. Governance, internal administration, financial management, and strategic planning all received higher ratings than the skills needed to manage population health in a cost-effective manner. The high scores given to skills related to conflict resolution may be an indication of the many problems that management in those practices encounter as the practices shift to managed care."

They also observed that "administrators and physician executives display a relatively high degree of agreement on the specific knowledge and skill competencies needed in the evolving systems, with the exception of the information systems domain where physician executives perceive only minimal needs compared with extensive needs reported by the administrators. Little disagreement exists on the overall weighting of the domains or on the nature of the specific competencies within the domains."

This is a very interesting and useful study that demonstrates the effect of the changes in physician and administrator views of competencies and skills in the light of the changing environment in which they work. Their final conclusion was that "the need for a broad perspective on healthcare, strong planning and leadership skills, and the need to be able to communicate effectively are the themes that exist in all of the administrative domains included in the study. Also, it is clear that strong quantitative methods skills are essential to the roles identified in the study." Students of skills and competencies should take careful note of these findings.

Academic Studies

The AUPHA task force undertook an extensive study, the results of which are being prepared for publication. Preliminary reports on the "Outcome Approach" were presented at the National Summit on the Future of Education and Practice in Health Management and Policy (AUPHA 2001). Four of AUPHA's forums reported on their progress in the form of white papers. The data are already being used by academic programs in health administration to develop their own series of competency domains. St. Louis University has six domains under study by its National Advisory Council (Campbell 2000):

1. Leadership: the ability to define a vision and guide individuals and groups toward the vision while maintaining group cohesiveness, motivation, commitment, and effectiveness.
2. Critical thinking: the ability to ask the right questions, to conceptualize and problem solve in an unstructured environment, and to think logically and independently.
3. Scientific/analytic competence: the ability to use data management and analytic skills to understand and to resolve management issues.
4. Management competence: the ability to plan, make decisions, organize, lead, and control an organization's human, financial, physical, and information resources to achieve organizational goals in an efficient and effective manner.
5. Political and community development competence: the ability to understand the needs and expectations of groups of major stakeholders, their implications for institutional and community policy formulation, and the importance of effectively representing the organization within the greater community.

6. Communication competence: the ability to effectively transfer information in oral, written, and nonverbal form to others and to understand what needs to be communicated, when, how, to whom, and how much.

THE TRANSFORMATIONAL LEADER

Another consideration as we continue our review of definitions of leadership and management is the concept of the transformational leader. A transformational leader is a master of change, a visionary, and a public and community servant who is quality conscious and capable of systems thinking. This extends and expands our definition of leadership and leads to those core competencies that will contribute to the development of a transformational leader. Certain aspects of the competencies of leadership, especially those related to skills and knowledge, can be easily observed, while those that are based in values, social role, self-image, traits, motives, and self-confidence cannot.

In a 1988 article in *Fortune Magazine,* Labich and Ballen suggested that there are seven keys to leadership:

1. Trusting one's subordinates
2. Developing a vision
3. Keeping one's cool
4. Encouraging risk
5. Being an expert
6. Inviting dissent
7. Working toward simplification

Again we find a number of themes running through the discussions of many experts across the management and leadership spectrum. If we return to core competencies and their behavioral foundations, we see those elements that have been described as characteristics of the effective executive:

- A high degree of self-awareness
- A tolerance for ambiguity and complexity

- A willingness to take risks
- A low need for public approbation
- A set of intellectual traits by training and temperament
- A low-key manner
- A tendency to avoid absolute positions
- An ability to listen
- A prudent attitude toward optimism
- An ability to accept conflict and enjoy managerial challenges

Consider for a moment the environment in which the leader or manager must work on a daily basis. To be successful, a leader must think about the long term; grasp the organization's relationship to larger realities; reach and influence constituencies beyond their jurisdiction; put heavy emphasis on vision, values, and motivation; understand intuitively the nonrational and unconscious elements of leader-constituent interaction; possess political skills to cope with conflicting requirements of multiple constituencies; and think in terms of renewal and the core competencies. There also exists a need to build trust, balance ambition with ethics, and to develop significant expertise with a deep foundation in integrity and morality. Even with the idea of a model that represents these traits, the question still remains: "Is this the right model?"

In an article entitled "The Health Services Environment—Competencies for Health Management Practice: A Practitioners Perspective," Wenzel, Grady, and Freedman (1995) suggest that leaders should be required to master the universal management skills of planning, organizing, directing, controlling, and staffing resources. The authors also recommend that leaders have the ability to employ technical, human relationship, and conceptual skills. Additional areas of competency discussed included communication, lifelong learning, conceptual skills, results management, resource management, compliance to standards, political and health environment awareness, and consumer/community responsiveness and public relations. Wenzel suggested that a core curriculum—which stresses the human skills cited by Grady and the team orientation described by Freedman—will play a crucial role in the development of the successful healthcare organization of the future. Graduate education programs must be prepared to provide a learning environment for the professional (i.e., the physician previously trained in one-on-one interactions) as well as an environment where team building assumes a prominent role (Wenzel, Grady, and Freedman 1995).

The Manager's Role

Although a manager may not be in a top leadership position, he or she must possess many of the same characteristics outlined above. A manager must, at a very basic level, keep informed, have the ability to focus on key issues as outlined by the leadership, know how hard both the organization and his or her staff can be pushed, and provide the organization with a sense of direction from their level. They must also recognize those opportunities that might escape the view of the leadership. The competencies necessary to fulfill these criteria are significant, and while they may vary by environment, many of the key core competencies are related to the "human side" of the enterprise. Communication obviously tops the list of core competencies.

On the other hand, certain characteristics can be observed in leadership failure, including tunnel vision, an inability to communicate, the confusion of assertiveness with aggressiveness, and mediocrity. Even a strong leader can fall into mediocrity, especially a leader in a rapidly growing organization who does not possess the ability to delegate and insists on hands-on operational management. Such a leader does not have a sense as to when the organization should be observed from an objective distance.

The Physician-administrator Team

Since we are dealing principally with healthcare and medical organizations, it is appropriate to mention the competencies that are necessary for the development of the physician-administrator team. Many of the competencies that the physician and the nonphysician manager should possess to build and manage a team are based in trust and compatibility. Balance is a key factor as well. Roles are clearly defined; each team member has his or her own core competencies, yet all work together to build a successful team. Credibility must be established between the members of the team by openly sharing information that enables the team to carry out its duties. The leader will also understand the power of politics and not allow that element to come between the members of the team.

CONCLUSION

The discussion from both the leadership and managerial perspective demonstrates that it is critical for an organization to have an ongoing, in-depth study of the competencies needed to make the organization successful. These competencies, which should be based on the vision, mission, and goals of the organization, should be matched with the competencies of individuals who are seeking positions on the leadership and management team.

An excellent example is the recent work done at the Marshfield Clinic (Liss 2001) as they developed a new regional management structure. The leadership of the clinic first studied the divisional medical directorship needs and the competencies necessary to meet those needs. In doing so, they determined the following competencies as necessary to achieve their organizational goals: business knowledge; the ability to develop teams and encourage professionalism; strong personal performance; efficient use of resources; the ability to partner with customers; and the ability to effectively manage change. All too frequently, organizations needlessly use scarce resources attempting to develop competencies that an individual joining the organization does not possess. It has been suggested by Drucker (1999) that both individuals and organizations should not expend their efforts making incompetent individuals mediocre—they should place strong emphasis on helping competent individuals reach even higher levels of competency.

DISCUSSION

1. Why is it important to understand the definition of core competencies?
2. Are core competencies the same for leaders and managers?
3. In a typical clinical setting, should the physician leader and the nonphysician manager have the same or complementary competencies?
4. Will the same set of competencies serve the leader or manager in all types of organizational environments?

REFERENCES

Albanese, R. 1989. "Competency-based Management Education." *Journal of Management Development* 8 (2): 66–76.

Allcorn, S. 1989. "Self-audit: A Path to Excellence." *Medical Group Management Journal* 36 (4): 54–60.

American College of Medical Practice Executives. 1999. *The Body of Knowledge for Medical Practice Managers.* Englewood, CO: ACMPE.

Association of University Programs in Health Administration. 2001. "Outcome Approach." Preliminary Report by the Task Force on Leadership Competencies at the National Summit on the Future of Education and Practice in Health Management and Policy. Orlando, FL, February 8–10.

Barnett, A. E. and T. Mayer. 1993. "HMO Performance Assessment: Group Practice Strategies and Considerations." *Managed Care Quarterly* 9 (1): 1–18.

Blair, J. M., M. Fottler, S. Lazarus, A. Paolino, and T. Rotarius. 1995. "Strategic Stakeholder Management: First Round Results from 'Facing an Uncertain Future.' *Medical Group Management Journal* 42 (3): 17–21.

Boyatzis, R. E. 1982. *The Competent Manager: A Model for Effective Performance.* New York: John Wiley & Sons.

Brooke, P. P. and R. P. Hudak. 1998. "Management Competencies Required in Ambulatory Care Settings." *Physician Executive* 24 (5): 32–38.

Campbell, C. 2000. *Personal Communication.* June.

Coile, R. 1995. "Assessing Healthcare Market Trends and Capital Needs: 1996–2000." *Healthcare Financial Management* 49 (8): 60–65.

Dalston, J. W. and P. Bishop. 1995. "Healthcare Executive Education and Training." *Journal of Health Administration Education* 13 (3): 437–52.

Drucker, P. F. 1999. "Managing Oneself." *Harvard Business Review* 77 (2): 65–74.

Esque, T. J. and T. F. Gilbert. 1995. "Making Competencies Pay Off." *Training* 32 (1): 44.

Estes, M. L. 1997. "Core Competencies for Physician Practice Success." *Physician Executive* 23 (1): 9–14.

Fleishman, E. A. and M. K. Quaintance. 1984. *Taxonomics of Human Performance: The Description of Human Tasks.* New York: Academic Press.

Green, J. 1990. "Graduate Programs Get Back to Basics." *Modern Healthcare* 20 (34): 28–37.

Griffith, J. R. 1995. *The Well-managed Health Care Organization,* 3rd edition. Chicago: Health Administration Press.

Heifitz, R. A. and D. L. Laurie. 1997. "The Work of Leadership." *Harvard Business Review* 75 (1): 124–35.

Hill, C., J. Kimball, J. Lineberger, and R. Hudak. 1994. "Factors Influencing Provider Productivity in a Public Sector Primary Care Walk-in Clinic." *Medical Group Management Journal* 41 (5): 84–95.

Hudak, R. 1990. "Physician Productivity in Ambulatory Care: For Profit and Military Primary Care Health Clinics." *Journal of Ambulatory Care Management* 13 (3): 7–16.

Hudak, R. P., P. P. Brooke, K. Finstuen, and J. Trounson. 1997. "Management Competencies for Medical Practice Executives: Skills, Knowledge and Abilities Required for the Future." *Journal of Health Administration Education* 15 (4): 219–39.

Hudak, R. and P. Mouritsen. 1988. "Improving the Army's Primary Care Delivery System." *Military Medicine* 153 (6): 282–86.

Hudson, T. 1995. "Ex-hospital CEOs: Where Are They Now?" *Hospitals and Health Networks* 69 (24): 31–42.

Kindig, D. and S. Lastivi-Queros. 1989. "The Changing Managerial Role of Physician Executives." *Journal of Health Administration Education* 7 (1): 36–46.

Labich, K. and K. Ballen. 1988. "The Seven Keys to Business Leadership." *Fortune Magazine* 118 (9): 58–64.

Liss, P. L., Medical Director of Marshfield Clinic. *Personal communication.* January 2001.

Manning, F. F. 1977. *Group Practice Management, Monograph.* Englewood, CO: Center for Research in Ambulatory Care Administration.

McClagan, P. 1996. "Great Ideas Revisited: Competency Training Models." *Training and Development* 50 (1): 50.

Merriam-Webster's Collegiate Dictionary, 10th edition. 1999. Springfield, MA: Merriam-Webster.

Morita, E. K., R. P. Hodapp, and C. H. Slater. 1976. *Group Practice Administration: Current and Future Roles: Technical Report.* Englewood, CO: Center for Research in Ambulatory Care Administration.

Nardone, D. and D. Webb. 1989. Administration in Ambulatory Care. *Academic Medicine* 64 (10): S28–34.

Nash, R. K. and D. J. Bryce. 1996. "Core Competencies Create Value." *Healthcare Financial Management* 50 (10): 35–38.

Neuhauser, D. 1989. *Coming of Age: A 50 Year History of The American College of Hospital Administrators and the Profession It Serves.* Chicago: Pluribus Press.

O'Conner, S. and R. Shewchuck. 1993. "Enhancing Administrator-clinician Relationships: The Role of Psychological Type." *Health Care Management Review* 18 (2): 57–65.

Pew Health Professions Commission. 1993. *Health Professions Education for the Future: Schools in Service to the Nation.* San Francisco: PHPC.

Pryor, K. 1996. "Take this Job and Love It." *Hospitals and Health Networks* 70 (8): 28–29.

Reinertsen, J. 1995. "Transformation: The New Knowledge Needed for Health Care Administrators." *Journal of Health Administration Education* 13 (1): 39–51.

Richie, N., J. Tagliani, and J. Schmidt. 1979. "Identifying Health Administration Competencies Via a Delphi Survey." *Association of University Programs in Health Administration Program Notes* 82 (1): 8–18.

Rossiter, A. M., B. R. Greene, and J. E. Kralewski. 2000. "The American College of Medical Practice Executives' Competency Study." *Journal of Ambulatory Care Management* 23 (4): 1–8.

Schneller, E., H. Greenwald, M. Richardson, and J. Ott. 1997. "The Physician Executive: Role in the Adaptation of American Medicine." *Health Care Management Review* 22 (2): 90–96.

Schweirkart, S. 1996. "Reengineering the Work of Caregivers: Role Redefinition, Team Structure and Organizational Redesign." *Health Services Administration* 41(1): 19–36.

Spencer, L. M. and S. M. Spencer. 1993. *Competence at Work: Models for Superior Performance.* New York: John Wiley & Sons.

Tabenkin, H., S. J. Zyzanski, and S. A. Alemagno. 1989. "Physician Managers: Personal Characteristics Versus Institutional Demands." *Healthcare Management Review* 14 (2): 7–12.

Wenzel, F. J., R. Grady, and T. J. Freedman. 1995. "The Health Services Delivery Environment." *Journal of Health Administration Education* 13 (4): 611–30.

Williams, A. 1996. "Health Services Administration Education: Meeting the Challenge of a Culturally Diverse Workforce." *Journal of Health Administration Education* 14 (3): 315–26.

Woodruffe, C. 1991. "Competent by Any Other Name." *Personnel Management* 23 (9): 30.

Part II: System Competencies

SYSTEM COMPETENCIES, ALSO called organizational competencies, are the competencies of the organization as it relates to its environment, its competitors, and its constituencies (physicians, patients, the community, payers, employers, and the government). Organizational core competencies define the organization's culture—how things are done. The leader can affect the culture over time, but at any point in time the organization's core competencies provide the framework within which the leader exercises his or her leadership competencies.

This part of the book presents the elements of essential system competencies in the areas of governance, strategic development, physician relationships, ethics and values, quality and value enhancement, public health and community involvement, health policy and law, and complementary medicine. An organization that develops competencies in each of these areas as outlined in the following chapters will be a formidable competitor in any market. The organization is not dependent on the leader for its basic functioning, but is a high-performance vehicle that extends the capabilities of effective leadership.

CHAPTER 3

Governance

CASE IN POINT: Ray Paulson is the board chair of Memorial Hospital. He is a successful banker and investor, and he is widely recognized as the wealthiest person in the community. His banks are tightly managed. Much of his wealth has come from acquiring other banks, pruning their operations, and consolidating them as added branch offices in his banking network. He is a major financial contributor to the hospital and has been board chair for the past 20 years. He approves all changes in board membership, and most members of the board are business associates and personal friends.

John Bradford has been president of Memorial Hospital for the past seven years. Four years ago, he and the board chair had heard a presentation by The Advisory Board in which the speaker talked about how the future of medicine was going to be managed care. To be successful in a managed care environment, hospitals would need to acquire physician practices to be able to provide and manage the continuum of care. Ray was very excited by the presentation and told John, "I have reduced costs at the banks I have acquired by a minimum of 20 percent. We both know that physicians are terrible business people. I'll bet we can reduce costs in physician practices by at least that much. And when the physicians are employed, you can just tell them to practice in the most efficient way. Healthcare costs are a major concern for the employers in this community, as you well know. Acquiring physician practices will be a good thing for both Memorial and the community. Develop a plan for the next board meeting that outlines how many physician practices you can acquire in the next two years, how much investment will be required, and the payback period. I suggest you assume at least a 20 percent reduction in the physicians' practice costs in the first year."

It is now four years later, and costs for the physicians' practices actually increased by 10 percent in the first full year. Major efforts to control costs have reduced the operating loss to $50,000 per physician per year, about at the "best practice" level for hospital-owned practices. Losses continue and seem to be irreducible. The physicians, angry at the changes in their practices that the hospital has made to reduce the operating losses, are unwilling to make any changes in how they practice. John's relationship with Ray has become very strained over the past year.

The presentation of the monthly financial statement at each month's board meeting has called attention to the continuing losses on the owned physician practices. Individual board members have also heard from physician friends who are dissatisfied with the owned physician practices. The idea of divesting the owned practices has been raised a few times, but Ray has continued to support retaining the practices, stating: "Owning these practices was, and still is, a good idea. The problem is with management that is not up to the task." Each month, the meeting has moved on to other agenda items—with little debate and no decision on a new course of action.

Ray announced at the end of last month's board meeting that he was going to retire, and recommended the board elect Rusty Black as his successor. John was glad to hear that Rusty was likely to be the new board chair. Rusty has been on the board for only three years, but after Ray, is the most respected member of the board. He is a very successful businessman, asks good questions, and is interested in learning John's perspective on the issues facing the hospital. At yesterday's board meeting, as expected, Rusty was confirmed as the new chair.

John and Rusty speak briefly after the meeting and Rusty comments: "I have wondered for some time if the board is doing what it should be doing. We spend a lot of time in meetings going over the same issues. I suspect we are going to see a lot of turnover on the board. What can we do to make the board more effective?" John is pleased with Rusty's interest in change and is eager to work with Rusty to find the best solutions for Memorial Hospital's current situation.

QUESTION: What changes should be made to make the governance of Memorial Hospital more effective?

INTRODUCTION

Governance pertains to the actions and responsibilities of the governing board of the organization. The board's primary responsibility is the same for both for-profit (commercial) and nonprofit organizations: to see that the interests of the commercial shareholders (or the nonprofit stakeholders) are met. In their book, *Board Work,* Orlikoff and Pointer (1999) draw an interesting comparison between the governance of commercial corporations and the governance of not-for-profit (nonprofit) organizations. Commercial corporations have shareholders who own shares in the corporation. These individuals are easily identified and their interests are similar. Nonprofit organizations, in contrast, "... have stakeholders, not shareholders, who have a collective and indivisible interest in the organization but do not own it. These stakeholders are often difficult to identify and typically want very different things" (Orlikoff and Pointer 1999).

The specific stakeholders and their relative importance are different for each organization, and the first step for each board—or for individuals responsible for organizing a board—is to identify the stakeholders, their interest, and their relative importance. The differences between hospitals and health systems, medical groups, and health maintenance organizations (HMO) are reflected in their governance.

This chapter suggests ways of identifying stakeholders, presents sample lists of stakeholders for different healthcare organizations, and describes the responsibilities and roles of governance. This chapter addresses board composition (size, term limits, and legal restrictions); board structure (the question of centralized versus decentralized governance powers); challenges that face governance in all organizations; and the role of committees and ideas to improve the effectiveness of committees. The chapter concludes with a comparison showing general differences between the governance of hospitals and medical groups.

STAKEHOLDERS

Stakeholders are those who make the delivery of services possible, who benefit from those services, or who have clout affecting the decisions of an organization. A first step should be to identify the core suppliers and users of services. Orlikoff and Pointer (1999) provide an example of the separate groups that might be considered as stakeholders for a Catholic acute care hospital:

- The sponsoring religious congregation
- Purchasers and insurers
- Underinsured and uninsured customers
- Medical groups owned by the hospital or tightly affiliated with it
- Physicians and medical groups loosely affiliated with the hospital
- The community that forms the hospital's primary service area

This is not a prescriptive list. The key stakeholders may be best identified as the groupings the board wants to consider in evaluating the effects of proposed decisions. Patients, employees, financial contributors, and government regulators are examples of additional groupings that the board might consider as key stakeholders.

Medical groups tend to see the following as key stakeholders when the possible effects of decisions are evaluated:

- Patients
- Physicians
- Staff
- Referring physicians
- Hospitals
- Community
- Purchasers and insurers
- Government regulators

Key stakeholders for not-for-profit HMOs might include:

- Employers/purchasers
- Enrollees
- The community
- Physicians
- Hospitals
- Government regulators

The interests of one group of stakeholders may be opposed to the interests of another group. The physicians may want to add new services to provide better care for their patients, and the payers may want to limit the proliferation of new services as a way to control costs. In practice, the board must come to an understanding of the relative importance of each stakeholder group to the organization. Decisions may support the interests of one stakeholder group at the expense of another.

The idea of serving the interests of groups of stakeholders is a useful framework for thinking about the various interests the board must address. If a stakeholder group's interests are not being met over time, and the stakeholder has an opportunity to go elsewhere—or to take actions to see that its interests are addressed—it will do so. If a stake-holder group is important to the organization, care must be taken over time to see that at least some of the group's interests are being met.

An organization with a board that is both efficient and effective—in knowing who the stakeholders are, knowing their interests, and in seeing that the organization's resources are deployed in ways that most benefit the stakeholders—will have developed a core competence in governance.

RESPONSIBILITIES OF GOVERNANCE

Orlikoff and Pointer (1999) make a useful distinction between "what" governance should do (responsibilities) and "how" governance should function (roles). This section addresses the "what" of governance.

Developing Mission and Vision Statements

The mission statement describes the basic purpose of the organization and answers the question "Why are we here?" That purpose can change over time, but the board is responsible for determining the organization's purpose. The mission statement outlines how the organization intends to meet stakeholder interests.

The vision statement is a vision of what the organization can and should become. But in the words of Orlikoff and Pointer, "Visions are vivid dreams, not hallucinations" (1999). Sound visions are based on a thorough understanding of the organization's capabilities and values, its environment, and an assessment of the role the organization should play in that environment.

Although the final affirmation of the vision is the board's responsibility, the development of a vision that engages the commitment of the people in the organization to achieving the vision is a process that involves the entire organization.

The board chair may have a thorough understanding of healthcare and take the lead in identifying elements of the vision for the organization. The organization's CEO is often the source for new ideas on what the organization can become. The board chair and the CEO must share a vision if the organization is to have a single vision. The CEO must have a mental model (Senge 1990) of the organization, of how it works and serves customers in its environment. In an effective governance/leadership relationship, the board chair and the CEO share this mental model. Peter Drucker (1994) calls this mental model "the theory of the business." That mental model is employed as the CEO recommends decisions and sees the success or lack of success with those decisions. Unexpected success or lack of success—by the organization or its competitors—is a clear signal that something significant has changed and the organization's vision must be reconsidered. Sputnik was a clear signal for a new mental model, a new vision of what we could do: put a man on the moon.

Agreement by the leader and the board on a new vision is necessary but not sufficient. The accomplishment of the vision is not just a leadership activity, it is the result of a commitment to achieving a vision that is widely shared within the organization. One turning point in an organization turnaround is when the leader sees opportunities to substantially improve the organization's performance. Another turning point is when the people in the organization begin to share the vision of what can be done. The whole organization becomes energized. People become committed to achieving the vision of a successful organization, and they put their minds and energies to work on achieving that vision.

In his book *The Fifth Discipline* (1990), Peter Senge writes:

In a corporation, a shared vision changes people's relationship with the company. It is no longer "their" company; it becomes "our" company. A shared vision is the first step in allowing people who mistrusted each other to work together. It creates a common identity .... Late in his career, the psychologist Abraham Maslow studied high-performing teams. One of their most striking characteristics was shared vision and purpose.

In the book's chapter on "Shared Vision," Senge offers a rich set of ideas for creating a shared vision in the organization. One key is for leaders—the board chair and CEO—to recognize that their vision is their personal vision. It does not become a shared vision until it is tested and enriched by the personal visions of others in the organization.

The monthly board meetings, and informal meetings around the board meetings, offer an excellent opportunity for the leader to keep the board informed on the evolution of the shared vision and the changes that are occurring as the vision does become truly "shared." The board affirms the shared vision that results.

Developing the Strategic Plan

The strategic plan identifies the short-term and long-term goals that move the organization toward its vision. The strategic planning process, presented in the next chapter, is an excellent opportunity to bring together the knowledge, skills, and experience of top management and the board members. Issue papers prepared by management and reviewed by appropriate board committees provide the core of the background material to be discussed at the strategic planning retreat.

Choosing the Organization's Leader

Board members have only a part-time commitment to the organization; therefore, the board's most important activity is the recruiting and evaluation of the organization's full-time leader. The leader is accountable to the board for the performance of the organization. An effective leader can make an organization more successful than previously envisioned; an ineffective leader can drive the organization into the ground. The question is, "How can the board increase its chances of hiring an effective CEO?"

In their article "Don't Hire the Wrong CEO," Warren Bennis and James O'Toole (2000) observe that leadership is a "combination of personal behaviors that allow an individual to enlist dedicated followers and create other leaders in the process." Boards go wrong when they look solely for hard facts like increases in market share, increases in revenue, and decreases in costs and headcount. It is not that hard measures of performance are not important—they are. But hard facts are not sufficient. Real leaders are great because they "demonstrate integrity, provide meaning, generate trust, and communicate values. In doing so, they energize their followers, humanely push people to meet challenging business goals, and all the while develop leadership skills in others. Real leaders, in a phrase, move the human heart" (Bennis and O'Toole 2000). Effective leaders build organizations that are capable of sustained success. Therefore, Bennis and O'Toole recommend that boards take the following steps to hire the right CEO.

- *Come to a shared definition of leadership.* The process of coming to a shared definition of leadership is important in bringing the board to a common understanding. To find the leader it needs, the board must understand what it is looking for in a leader. Consultants can provide a definition of leadership, but not the actual leader.
- *Resolve strategic and political conflicts.* The board chair is primarily responsible for the resolving of conflicts. The CEO is accountable to the board and is in a relatively weak position to resolve these issues. However, differences do exist on boards, and dealing with those differences in a productive way is part of the CEO's challenge.
- *Actively measure the soft qualities in CEO candidates.* The hard numbers are easy to measure, but assessing the soft qualities is as important when considering a CEO. Interviews with prior associates are an effective way to obtain this information.
- *Beware of candidates that look like CEOs.* Looking and sounding good in an interview is easy, and an inflated ego is too often confused with charisma. Boards should look for an ability to energize followers, enable staff to achieve their potential, and achieve organizational goals.
- *Recognize that real leaders are threatening.* Real leaders will be looking for ways to improve the organization, and those improvements will involve change.

- *Know that insider heirs are not apparent.* To assume that all insiders are not qualified or that an "heir apparent" should be given the position are both mistakes. Consideration of both outside and inside candidates demonstrates the board's interest in choosing the most qualified candidate.
- *Do not rush to judgment.* Take time to be thorough.

An organization that considers each of these points will demonstrate competence in hiring a CEO. The following section addresses effectively evaluating the leader.

Evaluating the Organization's Leader

The effort that goes into the selection process pays dividends when evaluating the leader's performance. The board and the leader know what performance has been expected, and those expectations provide the framework for evaluating performance.

A subcommittee of the board is often charged with the responsibility of evaluating the CEO's performance. Two ideas are helpful to any such committee to supplement a quantitative analysis of performance against hard number objectives: a self-appraisal and a "360-degree" performance appraisal. The self-assessment gives leaders an opportunity to highlight their accomplishments and any insights for improvement. The 360-degree assessment is completed by members of the executive team and selected employees in the organization, as well as by members of the board. The 360-degree assessment is confidential and presents a blind compilation of the survey results and comments. It provides invaluable feedback to the leader by identifying and affirming strengths, yet also identifies areas to improve. The wise leader sees and uses this information to make midcourse corrections.

Ensure Quality of Care

The governance team is responsible for ensuring quality of care. Credentialing of physicians is the front-end of quality control for all healthcare organizations. The credentialing process verifies that the physician's stated training and experience is a sound basis for the board to offer employment, grant privileges to practice, or to be enrolled as a health plan provider. The board is responsible for authorizing hiring based on the individual's credentials.

Physicians are accountable, by law, for the quality of the care they provide. Medical groups are typically responsible financially for each physician's performance as well as the performance of the organization as a whole. Hospitals are accountable for the quality of care the hospital staff provides. HMOs perform under a strong public pressure to be responsible for the medical outcomes of decisions made by their staff, and some states are now allowing HMOs to be sued for questionable clinical decision making.

Boards are encouraged to establish a system for ongoing monitoring of the quality of care provided. Data on patient satisfaction (i.e., "Would recommend this organization to a friend") are common measures in all healthcare organizations. "Readmission rate" is a common hospital quality measure. "Disenrollment rate" is a common HMO quality measure. The monitoring of these measures provides the board with information to identify trends. Sharp drops in performance or negative trends provide the board with the information it needs to ask "Why?" and to see that corrective action is taken.

Assume Fiduciary Responsibility for the Success of the Organization

The board must provide for appropriate accumulation and preservation of reserves. The organization answers to the interests of shareholders, and it must be sufficiently successful financially to continue to meet those interests. It is important to recognize, however, that the organization is a *means* to address shareholder interests and not an *end* in itself (Orlikoff and Pointer 1999). At a time when hospitals and health systems have been burning through tens of millions of dollars in reserve to fund current operating losses, it is difficult to see the overaccumulation of reserves as a problem, but the overaccumulation of reserves is a risk for the organization. The overaccumulation of reserves has, arguably, led to less rigorous decision making, substantial losses, and the depletion of reserves.

Ensure the Effective and Efficient Functioning of the Board

To be effective in carrying out its responsibilities, and efficient in using its members' time, several policies can be implemented.

Identify board member performance expectations

New members need to know what is expected of them. Board candidates may have been informed of requirements before accepting the position, but board memberships are seen as prestigious positions, and some members may accept the position without appreciating the amount of work required. Orientation to the board should include coverage of:

- The meeting attendance policy
- Expected performance (i.e., preparation, participation, perspective, and decision making based on the interests of the organization as a whole)
- The conflict of interest policy
- A sample annual board member evaluation by others on the board

Organizations that have explicit performance expectations for board members find that members who are not meeting those expectations will choose to leave voluntarily.

Orient new members

New members come with a wide range of knowledge about healthcare and the organization. New member orientation is an opportunity for all members to receive a base-level introduction to:

- The organization's mission, vision, and values
- Healthcare trends and issues such as managed care and reimbursement levels
- The organization's strategic plan and financial performance

- Governance responsibilities and roles
- Governance structure and accountabilities
- Leadership and management structure and accountabilities
- Board member performance expectations

Develop agendas that are focused on what the board must do

Agenda development is a primary responsibility of the board chair and the CEO in a hospital. In a medical group, the board chair is often also the president of the medical group, and leadership is referred to as a "physician/administrator team." The administrator may hold a title of executive vice president/COO, executive director, or administrator. In both hospitals and medical groups, control of the agenda is a core strength of leadership. Decisions on agenda items and the order of the items included—along with the following points—have much to do with the effectiveness of the meeting.

- *Time allotments and presenter responsibilities.* The board agenda should show the time allotted for each topic. That information enables the board members to participate in managing the agenda. Listing the presenter forces the decision on who will be prepared to lead the discussion on each item.
- *Use of consent agenda.* Some items, such as "review of minutes" are necessary, but warrant minimal discussion. Place these items on a "consent agenda" to allow them to be approved as a group unless someone chooses to raise a question.
- *Agenda distribution.* Board members are part time. In most cases, their board duties must fit around their other responsibilities. Because members sometimes have the most discretionary time on weekends, the board packet should be in their hands by Friday of the week prior to the meeting.

Create committees and task forces

Committees and task forces enable a subset of the board to focus their efforts on issues that are detailed and too time consuming to be considered by the full board. Task forces are ad hoc committees formed to consider one-time or major projects such as a new building program or a new computer system. The committee/task force report should be a summary presentation covering an overview of the issue, a discussion of the alternatives considered, and the committee's recommendations.

The productivity of the ensuing discussion is a test of the board's sophistication. An effective board and board chair will decide to "call the question" when they see the board rethinking the committee's work.

Perform board evaluations

The board should evaluate its performance, perhaps as often as each meeting, but at least annually. The evaluation is designed to assess performance on the basics:

- What are we doing well?
- What could we be doing better?
- What specific recommendations do you have to improve board performance?

The brevity of this approach lends itself to more frequent assessment, which allows the board chair and the CEO to make mid-year changes as issues and improvements are identified.

Board Roles

Board roles include policy formulation, decision making, and oversight (Orlikoff and Pointer 1999). The board also serves as a touchstone for leadership—a resource for reviewing and providing insights related to proposed decisions.

Policy Formulation

Board policies provide guidelines and constraints for decision making in the organization. They also formalize the delegation of decision making within the organization. Policy formation is the most important board role because it is the way the board expresses its expectations in the organization.

Orlikoff and Pointer (1999) provide a detailed description of policy formulation. In their experience, most boards spend upwards of 50 percent of their time listening to reports. The typical board spends 70 percent of the remaining time making decisions, about 20 percent in oversight, and 10 percent formulating policy. In contrast, the best boards spend less than 20 percent of the time making decisions, about 30 percent on oversight, and more than half their time formulating policy.

Decision making is a major board role. The board can and should use policy formulation to provide guidance or delegation of decision making within the organization, and thus minimize the number of decisions that come to the board for review or approval (Orlikoff and Pointer 1999).

Decision Making

Decision making is the most visible board role. If the board allows itself to be drawn into making a broad range of decisions, including reviewing the decisions of others, it runs the risk of:

- Making decisions with less than complete information
- Making decisions with less than adequate time for the decision
- Making decisions without the direct input of those affected
- Undermining the leadership of those who should be making the decisions
- Being seen as coercive—the least effective form of leadership (Goleman 2000)

Goleman (2000) points out that the most effective leaders use a range of leadership styles in making decisions—authoritative, affiliative, democratic, and coaching—but leading with such a versatile range of styles is virtually impossible for a board.

Orlikoff and Pointer (1999) provide a list of key principles for boards to follow that enhance their decision-making role.

- Make as few decisions as possible.
- Do not ratify decisions that are appropriately within the domain of management and the medical staff.
- Subject proposals to committee review before placing them on the board's agenda for action.
- Retain control over only the most important and potentially most risky decisions.
- At the end of the year, review a representative sampling of board decisions.

The year-end review enables the board to ask and answer the questions: Are these decisions we should be making? Did we follow the above principles?

Oversight of Leadership and Operations

The board's responsibility is to monitor indicators of organizational performance, that is, to know that the organization is performing well or to be aware of which areas require further attention. The "dashboard" model, constructed like the dashboard in an automobile, is a useful way of identifying and presenting the significant few measures that give a quick, summary overview of how well the organization is performing. Examples of dashboard indicators might be percent operating margin, days in accounts receivable, occupancy rate, average length of stay, and—for ambulatory care—number of patients seen. For organizations with significant managed care involvement, bed days per 1,000 enrollees is an important measure.

The concepts of statistical quality control are important in understanding the dashboard indicators. On an actual dashboard, a sharp drop in miles per gallon may mean that something is seriously wrong with the car or may also mean that the car has been climbing a steep hill. The monitoring of current results in the context of longer-term trends is important.

Review Proposed Decisions

Board members bring special skills, knowledge, and experience to the organization. Some may be specialists in law and finance, some may have special knowledge of community and physician interests, and others may be successful leaders of other organizations.

The board's responsibilities for selection and evaluation of the CEO, and for operations oversight, do present an opportunity for the board to closely monitor and control CEO performance. Monitoring of the organization's performance is another core board responsibility. If the part-time board finds it must monitor and control the CEO closely to ensure effective performance by that CEO, it has the wrong CEO.

The best organizations have a strong, collegial relationship between their CEO and the board, and the CEO is a voting member of the board. Orlikoff and Pointer (1999) cite a study of 90 California acute care hospitals that revealed that "CEO participation on the board as a voting member significantly enhanced hospital performance." The CEO and the board chair, in particular, must see each other as colleagues. If the CEO is effective, the opportunity exists to make the organization even more successful by teaming the skills, knowledge, and experience of the CEO with the skills, knowledge, and experience of the board members.

Developing and refining the vision, devising strategy, formulating policy, and making decisions are all areas where the organization will benefit from a strong, collegial relationship between the board members and the CEO. Such a relationship is marked by a joint sharing of ideas, knowledge, skills, and experience in making decisions. The CEO takes the lead in bringing ideas and decisions to the board for consideration, but the CEO also looks to the board to contribute their perspectives through a dialog that develops the ideas and reaches decisions.

In this process, the board must always remember that it is finally accountable for the organization's performance. The CEO is accountable to the board, and the board must maintain that accountability. The directors and officers policy will protect individual board members from the financial consequences of their decisions, but it will not protect them from public embarrassment, as demonstrated in the AHERF bankruptcy (Friedman 1999). The directors and officers policy will also not protect members from possible legal action if the Medicare and Medicaid compliance regulations, or the statutes governing referrals and other relationships between healthcare providers, are violated (Tyler and Biggs 2000).

BOARD COMPOSITION AND STRUCTURE

Membership on the governing board is the highest form of stakeholder recognition because it brings stakeholders directly into the decision-making process. Stakeholders are important to a nonprofit organization—it exists to serve their interests—and the most important interests are represented on the board. Given that importance, board members regard their primary responsibilities to be to reflect their stakeholders' interests. This tendency conflicts with the fundamental responsibility of all individual board members to act in ways that most benefit the organization as a whole. That fundamental responsibility merits emphasis and reaffirmation on both an annual and as-needed basis.

Board Composition

Hospital boards have historically been self-perpetuating boards and represent primarily the community served. On self-perpetuating boards, the nominating committee chooses candidates to nominate from lists of possible candidates suggested by the present members of the board. Medical groups, in contrast, have historically had 100 percent physician membership elected by members of the group. As integrated systems have brought physicians and hospitals together, the challenge has been to develop governance models that creatively meet the interests of stakeholders. Board composition in a nonprofit organization is a balancing act. The stakeholders must see board composition as providing a reasonably appropriate representation of all interests.

Physicians are in a unique position on a healthcare board. Their services are, in significant ways, the "product" the organization delivers.

They are expected to be concerned for patients and for the quality of care delivered, as well as their own interests. Orlikoff and Pointer (1999) observe: "Physicians on boards tend to vote in favor of the physicians' interests." The broad range of physician interests (as discussed in chapter 5) begs the question: "Who else is prepared to speak to those interests?"

Health system boards continue to choose members by the self-perpetuating process. One or more major stakeholders may be allowed to nominate or appoint other candidates. If the process is one of nomination, the full board may have the right to affirm or reject the nominees. Physician interests can be met, in part, by being able to appoint to system board seats physicians who do not practice in the organization. Concerns about control can be addressed by requiring a "super-majority," that is, the support of members representing different groups for a vote to pass.

A board member's responsibility to act in the interests of the whole is supported by the fact that, at some level, nonprofit organizations are voluntary relationships. If a member perceives that their stakeholders' interests are not served in an adequate way, they can choose to leave the organization.

In addition to specific stakeholder representation, the criteria for membership may include special skills, knowledge, and experience that will be valuable to have on the board. Some boards elect an attorney, certified public accountant, or a member with special knowledge in information systems.

Size

A board of 10 to 15 members is large enough to represent diverse interests and yet small enough for effective discussions and decision making. That number is large enough to include representation of the major stakeholder interests. It is also small enough for the members to each participate in the discussion, see their contribution to the organization as significant, and become engaged in the success of the organization. Larger boards can appear to provide more opportunity for stakeholder representation, but most members become mere observers of the process rather than contributing board members. Board meetings become forums for presentations rather than the needed opportunity for effective dialog between the board members and the organization's leadership.

Term Limits

Term limits are designed to provide members with enough time on the board to learn the work to be done and to be productive, and yet to allow new board members to be recruited to bring fresh ideas to the board. Experience has demonstrated that "3/3"—a maximum of three successive terms of three years each—is a good model. The board chair is expected to work through the positions of vice chair and chair with, at most, a one-year extension on a three-year term.

Legal Restrictions

A definitive legal analysis of the board composition that will qualify for tax-exempt status is a "facts and circumstances" situation that is beyond the scope of this book. A "rule-of-thumb" restriction states that no more than 49 percent of a tax-exempt organization board can be interested parties, the definition of which includes management and physicians who practice in the organization. The IRS refers to this rule as the "community board" standard. This rule also requires "that the board has adopted and operates under a conflicts of interest policy, and that all components of the organization conduct periodic activity reviews to ensure the organization operates in a charitable manner" (IRS 1997).

The 49 percent rule of thumb can be overridden based on the facts and circumstances. "Where facts and circumstances, such as a long history of substantial community service and the absence of inurement or private benefit, provide assurance that the community benefit standard is satisfied, the community board standard may not be required. On the other hand, the Service will consider whether the 20 percent safe harbor guideline should be applied in situations where an existing exempt healthcare organization has a record of problems with its charitable operations or a history of inurement or private benefit. In any event, the organization should adopt a substantial conflicts of interest policy" (IRS 1997).

BOARD STRUCTURE

As integrated healthcare systems have brought previously independent organizations together in a single organization, the question of how to deal with governance of the total organization has been one of the first addressed. The component organization boards have wanted to know their future role in the new organization. Most systems have maintained some form of governance at the level of the individual components (such as community relations and credentialing at hospital A, hospital B, etc.). As large physician groups have been acquired or merged with hospitals, many have continued to have a predominantly physician operating board that is accountable to a mixed-composition system board.

Governance powers at the component level should parallel the management style the system chooses. A highly centralized management structure, with centralized decision making, will have a highly centralized governance structure. Decentralized management will work best with a decentralized governance structure.

Some have argued that the best form is a highly centralized structure to facilitate timely and efficient decision making and to help ensure that the system functions as an integrated whole (Orlikoff and Pointer 1999). Others argue that the challenge is not so much decision making as it is "insuring the system functions as an integrated whole" (Mitlyng and Wenzel 1999). The effectiveness of the governance decision making is related to how to the organization will effectively empower the governance of component entities consistent with the risks they assume. Component entities can be viewed as "agents" of the total organization. As noted by Alexander, Zuckerman, and Pointer (1995), "Agency theory tells us that if the transfer of risk to agents is not accompanied by effective control over outcomes on the part of the agent, dysfunctional behavior will result."

Although some acquired physician groups have continued to function with a physician-controlled operating board, the effectiveness of that control remains in question. The governance and management staffs of component entities can be asked to identify specific ways in which the present allocation of governance power limits their ability to produce desired outcomes. The system board can use this information to help decide to keep—or change—the present allocation of governance power. Identifying ways to improve the performance of integrated systems is critical. Moody's recently reported that of the 500 hospitals they rate, the largest 50—which typically have acquired physician practices—have less operating income than the smallest 50 (Jaklevic 2000).

GOVERNANCE CHALLENGES

Some principal healthcare governance challenges can be identified.

Consider Stakeholder Interests

The challenge of identifying stakeholders and their interests was noted at the beginning of this chapter. Given that difficulty, keeping the interests of stakeholders foremost as decisions are made is a particular challenge. The board should review its list of shareholder interests on at least an annual basis to assess how the organization's performance is meeting stakeholder interests.

Evaluate the Decision-making Process Continually

Consensus decision making is critical to the success of a nonprofit organization. In this way decisions are seen to represent all interests. A shift to pure majority voting will predictably have the immediate effect of polarizing the board.

In the context of consensus decision making, the concept of board control, although critical in a for-profit organization, is not an effective way to look at a nonprofit board. Adequate representation—the ability to speak and influence decisions—is what counts. Minimum adequate representation is sometimes thought of as two voices: one to speak and the second to support what is said. But all of this requires representatives who do speak, are heard, and who do influence decisions.

Consensus decision making does not require a unanimous vote, but it does require a visible effort to meet the concerns of all involved. People need to sense that their concerns have been heard and considered in the final decision. The sense of being heard by their board colleagues is the basis for the board to expect that all members of the board will publicly support the decision once the decision is made.

Certain voting situations can signal specific issues, however, and the board should be aware of what these situations can mean. A continuous pattern of unanimous voting can indicate that the board is extraordinarily effective in reaching consensus on all issues. It may also mean that some board members are "coasting" and not critically examining the issues. A close vote, in the context of an organization that normally decides issues by consensus, is unambiguous. It indicates significant, unresolved issues. Dealing with those issues through more dialog may be thought to be impossible, but if the objective is to continue to have an effective, functioning board, taking time to work through the issues before making a final decision is required.

Observing the Line Between Governance and Management

When board members see an underperforming area of the organization in an area in which they have special skills, they are often tempted to step in and deal with the problem themselves. The problem may be with the CEO or a member of their staff. It is important to remember that the CEO is hired and paid to lead and run the organization. If the CEO is unable to lead the organization, and achieve expected performance targets, the board must replace the CEO.

ROLE OF BOARD COMMITTEES

The role of committees is to make better use of board members' time by allowing some portion of the board to become its "experts" in the area covered by the committee. The concept of a task force is closely related. Committees tend to serve ongoing functions while task forces tend to be ad hoc. Board decision making should be minimized, as noted earlier, and reserved for only the most significant decisions. Effective boards will make decisions based only on the recommendation of a committee or task force. Some common committees follow.

- *Executive committee:* empowered to act on behalf of the board, within limits, between board meetings
- *Personnel committee:* coordinates and conducts CEO and board evaluation processes; recommends any changes in CEO compensation and benefits
- *Nominating committee:* coordinates selection process for new board members and prepares slate of candidates
- *Finance committee:* performs a detailed review of organization's financials on a monthly basis; also reviews the audit report in a medical group; hospitals may assign audit to a separate audit committee
- *Information systems committee:* acquires and develops computer systems
- *Strategic planning committee:* oversees the annual strategic planning process
- *Facilities committee:* responsible for oversight of any major building program
- *Quality assurance committee:* oversees the clinical quality assurance process

Committees and task forces can be established for any purpose. With the time they require, a zero-based committee structure that requires annual justification to continue a committee has been recommended (Orlikoff and Pointer 1999). Regardless of how the committees are established, some basic elements will substantially improve committee performance:

- A committee charge that specifies what is to be done
- A committee chair appointed by and accountable to the board chair

- Administrative support staff as necessary
- Committee process expectations that obtain and incorporate the views of stakeholders
- A deadline for presenting recommendations to the board
- A summary format for presenting recommendations

Hospital vs. Physician Group Governance

A comparison of hospital and physician group governance is summarized in Figure 3.1. The points shown have been addressed in the previous sections of this chapter and are included here for easy reference.

CONCLUSION

Effective governance is critically important to the functioning of healthcare organizations today. The responsibilities and roles of the board presented in this chapter are ample testimony to that importance. Those responsible for the governance of a not-for-profit organization are accountable to stakeholders for identifying and serving their needs. Arguably, meeting those needs is important in for-profit organizations as well. Patients of for-profit organizations can choose to go elsewhere for care. An organization with a board that is both efficient and effective—and a board that knows who the stakeholders are, knows their interests, and sees that the organization's resources are deployed in ways that most benefit the stakeholders—will have developed a competence in governance.

DISCUSSION

1. What are the elements of effective governance?
2. How are stakeholders in a not-for-profit organization like shareholders in a for-profit corporation? How are they different?
3. What is the difference between a mission statement and a vision statement? What is the board's role in developing a "shared" vision statement? Why is a shared vision statement important to the organization?

Figure 3.1. Comparison of Hospital and Physician Group Governance

	Hospital	Physician Group
Stakeholders	Community that forms the hospital's primary service area	Community
		Employees
	Employees	Government regulators
	Financial contributors	Hospitals
	Government regulators	Patients
	Medical groups owned by the hospital or tightly affiliated with it	Physicians
		Purchasers and insurers
	Patients	Referring physicians
	Physicians and medical groups loosely affiliated with the hospital	
	Purchasers and insurers	
	Sponsoring religious congregation	
	Underinsured and uninsured customers	
Membership	Primarily external	All physicians
Board chair	Elected by board	Elected by group or board
Member selection criteria	Stakeholder representation; special skills, knowledge, and experience	Member of the group
Selection process	Self-perpetuating and appointed	Election by the group

4. Identify four board responsibilities.
5. What is the board's most important role? Why?
6. Identify five ways that a board can improve its performance.

REFERENCES

Alexander, J. A., H. S. Zuckerman, and D. D. Pointer. 1995. "The Challenges of Governing Integrated Health Care Systems." *Health Care Management Review* 20 (4): 69–81; discussion 82–92.

Bennis, W. and J. O'Toole. 2000. "Don't Hire the Wrong CEO." *Harvard Business Review* 78 (3): 171–76.

Drucker, P. 1994. "The Theory of the Business." *Harvard Business Review* 72 (5): 95.

Friedman, E. 1999. "Where Was the Board?" *Health Forum Journal* 42 (5): 10–13.

Goleman, D. 2000. "Leadership that Gets Results." *Harvard Business Review* 7 8 (2): 81.

Internal Revenue Service. 1997. *Continuing Professional Education—Exempt Organizations—Technical Instruction Program for* FY 1997. Washington, DC: Internal Revenue Service Exempt Organizations Division.

Jaklevic, M. 2000. "Profit Decline." *Modern Healthcare* 30 (34): 3, 16.

Mitlyng, J. W., and F. J. Wenzel. 1999. "It Takes More than Money—Keys to Success in Leading and Managing Physician Groups." *MGM Journal* 46 (2): A30–38.

Orlikoff, J. E., and D. D. Pointer. 1999. *Board Work: Governing Health Care Organizations*. San Francisco: Jossey-Bass.

Senge, P. 1990. *The Fifth Discipline: The Art and Practice of the Learning Organization*. New York: Currency/Doubleday.

Tyler, J. L. and E. L. Biggs. 2000. *Practical Governance for Healthcare Executives*. Chicago: Health Administration Press.

CHAPTER 4

Strategy Development

CASE IN POINT: Jack Mason was hired as CEO of Strong Memorial Hospital in 1992. Don Alford, the board chair, was elected the year before. Don Alford was particularly pleased that Jack Mason agreed to take the CEO position. He had a solid record of financial performance and high levels of patient satisfaction in his previous hospitals; he also had strong support of the physician staff.

In 1993, Don and Jack heard a presentation sponsored by The Advisory Board based on findings in its recently published report "The Grand Alliance—Vertical Integration Strategies for Physicians and Health Systems" (1993). The presentation outlined the qualities of a stable, successful, integrated system. Two conclusions were drawn: (1) closer alignment of hospitals and physicians is a requisite for prosperity if not survival; and (2) a rich primary care base is a central ingredient to a viable system.

The presentation also identified several "Herculean" tasks to be accomplished, including:

1. Addressing cultural issues in converting from fee-for-service to capitated-lives care
2. Winning a population of capitated lives

3. Building a primary care network in which the physicians are tied to the system in some way that they are not free to move for a higher offer

The tasks were difficult, but future success depended on successfully accomplishing these tasks.

After the presentation of The Advisory Board on integrated delivery systems in 1993, the mandate seemed clear: acquire as many primary care physician practices as possible. The strategy was likely to cost tens of millions of dollars, but there was no choice. Jack and Don made an oral report to the board about the need for a physician acquisition strategy. The strategy would cost $10 to 15 million to implement. The estimate of annual added operating costs was also $10 to 15 million, but they expected the hospital's management ability would enable it to reduce these costs to a breakeven point in two to three years. Once they had capitated contracts, the added margin from better management of care would turn the losses to profits. The board had given unanimous approval to their proposal.

It is now eight years later and Jack reflects that he and Don have been through a lot together. Since first acquiring the physician practices in 1994, the strategy has had total operating losses of $103 million. The divestment of these practices over the past year has meant an added operating loss of $12 million. The hospital's bond rating has dropped from a solid "A" rating to "Bbb–." Despite the cost of the divestment, many physicians who are now back in private practice are angry about the hospital's treatment of them and angry with Jack. Jack's relationship with Don is strained.

In looking back, Jack reflects that the easy agreement by the board to support the proposed strategy—with no consideration of alternatives—was not helpful to the organization. It was a high-risk strategy and alternatives should have been formally considered. Jack also observes that by 1995, the insurers were clearly showing no interest in moving to global capitation as a basis for paying health systems. Owning the practice network had no advantage and resulted in significant losses. Jack knew changes needed to be made in the way the organization makes major strategic decisions and asked himself: "What can be done to ensure more timely action to modify or discard decisions that are not working as intended?"

QUESTION: What techniques can Jack use to make it easier to modify or discard strategies that are no longer working as intended?

INTRODUCTION

Strategy development is an ongoing process of relating the vision, values, and capabilities of the organization to the needs and wants of customers. Strategy development occurs formally as part of the strategic planning process on an annual or other periodic basis. Strategy development also occurs informally as customers' needs and wants—and opportunities to satisfy those needs and wants—are identified. This chapter presents the elements of strategy development. An organization that can develop and implement strategies and continue to work on the established goals, objectives, and workplans as agreed in the absence of new information—but change if new information indicates that the strategy should be modified or discarded—will have developed an organizational competence in strategy development.

STRATEGY DEVELOPMENT AS A CONTINUOUS PROCESS

Strategy development identifies broad directions (goals) for the organization, and supportive actions (objectives) that enable the organization to achieve its goals.

Strategy development is often thought of in terms of an annual planning exercise that produces a strategic plan. It may be an annual update of a multiyear plan, but it is the point in time when the elements of strategy development are formally considered and a formal strategic plan developed.

An annual strategic planning process allows an organization to set aside a time to consciously stop, take stock, and decide if the organization's stated strategies should be reaffirmed or modified. The execution of strategy and feedback on the effectiveness of a particular strategy is, however, a continuous process. The governance and leadership of organizations are faced with decisions that were not foreseen in the strategic planning process. Decisions need to be made and actions taken based on the learning that occurs and the situations that arise in the course of the year. In practice, the elements of strategy development occur both formally on an annual or other periodic basis and continually as new opportunities and threats are identified. Effective strategy development is both a formal point-in-time process and an informal continuous process.

Figure 4.1 presents strategy development as a continuous process. The arrows show the sequential relationship between the steps in this process. The elements are defined in the points below the diagram. The annual strategic planning process is a snapshot of the elements shown in Figure 4.1. In practice, new opportunities and threats are identified in the day-to-day experiences and insights of leadership, management, governance, and staff. Effective leadership and governance will consider how the present strategic plan addresses the opportunities and threats, but, if necessary, will establish new goals, objectives, and workplans to deal with the opportunities and threats. The implementation (execution) of workplans to achieve goals and objectives occurs on a daily basis. Encountering either success or problems in executing strategic workplans provides experience and insights for those involved, as reflected in "Performance measurement" and "Reassessment" in Figure 4.1. Reassessment can question the validity of the vision: Are the goals appropriate? Are the objectives reasonable? Effective strategy development guides the work of the organization, but allows reassessment as new information is learned about the performance of existing strategic initiatives and/or the opportunities and threats facing the organization. The difficulty of reassessing strategies will be discussed later in this chapter.

Figure 4.1. Strategy Development

Vision. Who will our customers be in the future and how will we serve them?

Values. Inherent to the people involved: "What is important to the organization and the employees?"

Goals. Broad statements of purpose (e.g., "Increase referrals to the hospital")

Objectives. Specific accomplishments to be achieved by a certain date (e.g., "Increase referrals from the north suburb by 10 percent in the next 12 months")

Workplans. Identification of the multiple tasks required to achieve the objective, the individual with primary responsibility for each task, and the timeframe for accomplishing each task to meet the target date for the objective

Execution. The workplan is carried out

Performance measurement. A specific way to measure results (e.g., volume of referrals)

Reassessment. Is the vision realistic? Is the goal sound? What new objective(s) should be set?

Knowledge Necessary for Good Strategic Planning

Answers to the following questions provide the knowledge needed for good strategic planning.

What is our vision, what do we value, and what are our core competencies?

This question refers to the organization's *shared vision*—a common understanding by governance, leadership, management, and staff of the customers, environment, and the organization's role in serving those customers. Peter Senge (1990) noted the finding by psychologist Abraham Maslow on high-performing teams that, "One of their most striking characteristics was shared vision and purpose." The sense of just who our customers are can and should broaden over time as we identify other customers we can serve with our core competencies. At any point in time, though, the challenge is to know who our customers are and have a vision of how we can best serve our customers.

Values speak to who we are and what is intrinsically important to us as individuals. The individuals who choose to stay with an organization will be those who find the organization's vision is reasonably compatible with their values. We tend to want to be with people who share our values. In his research on long-lived companies, Arie de Geus (1997) found that successful organizations have a strong organizational culture: "Above all ... members know 'who is us' and they are aware that they hold values in common." The organization's vision and values determine, and reflect, the organization's core competencies. What are we really good at? Are we really good at providing access for patients to address their immediate concerns? Do we have the level of specialization to be a referral center in our area? How do we know? Where do we have, or can we develop, distinctive core competencies relative to our competition?

In what ways can we better serve the wants and needs of our present—and potential—customers?

Present customers will help with one major category of opportunity—improving existing services. Some may call or write with complaints or suggestions. Many will respond if asked. Ongoing patient and internal customer satisfaction surveys are the best source of this information. It is important to recognize that very few people go out of their way to complain—less than one in ten, and a satisfaction survey re-sponse of one in four is considered acceptable. Most people "vote with their feet" by seeking service elsewhere. All comments must be taken as an accurate reflection of how the organization's services are per-ceived.

Potential customers represent a substantial opportunity for most businesses. The challenge for leadership and others in the organiza-tion is to understand wants and needs of "noncustomers" (Drucker 1994). A large market share in many communities is in the range of 20 to 30 percent. That means 70 to 80 percent of the market consists of customers who obtain services elsewhere. Understanding why these noncustomers choose to do so can identify opportunities to improve present services and grow market share.

A third opportunity is to identify wants or needs in the market that are not now being met by anyone. The development of new products such as electronic medical records and knowledge-based decision sup-port systems are examples of products that meet needs for access to people and information that were not being met.

What present and possible actions of competitors represent threats to the organization?

Competitors are individuals and organizations that provide the same services, or services that can substitute for the services, of the organi-zation. Competitors look for ways to provide products and services that customers will see as better than the products and services they have been buying.

Answering the following questions will help identify the opportu-nities for competitors:

- In what areas are our services just average or below average?
- Are there areas where patient complaints over several years have not resulted in significant improvements (i.e., billing, telephone access, and appointment access)?
- If patients are leaving the organization, why are they leaving?

The last question is too important to leave to a paper survey only. Telephone follow-up with "nonresponders" is important to verify that the reasons provided by the paper responders are a valid indicator of the reasons for all persons leaving the organization.

Trends elsewhere in the country also provide insights into the actions local competitors will take in the future. A colleague from Indiana once said, "We do not need to be all that insightful. All we need to do is pay attention." Some areas always seem to be on the leading edge of change. The late 90s taught many health services leaders to be more critical as they considered national trends and the applicability to their market.

A sense of organizational will—what do we as an organization want to do?

Vision, values, and an assessment of organizational competencies identify the organization's capabilities. The assessments of opportunities and threats identify opportunities for success. Collectively, the above points identify a range of possible strategies that the organization can undertake and that have a high potential for success.

The difference between a high potential for success and actual success is often a great deal of work. Those developing the strategies must assess for themselves, and for those who will be carrying out the strategy, "What do we want to do?" It is what the individuals involved want to do that will make the difference as they work through the inevitable difficulties of change.

DEVELOPING THE STRATEGIC PLAN

The following points are not intended to be a detailed description of the strategic planning process. They highlight the importance of the organization's leaders leading the strategic planning process themselves. The points also present the value of engaging a broad range of participants in the planning process as part of effective preparation for a strategic planning retreat.

Leaders' Role

Strategic planning sets the direction for the organization. The organization's top leadership—the board chair and the CEO in a hospital or health system, and the president and COO in a medical group—must provide the leadership for the strategic planning process. Other leaders in line positions who will be responsible for carrying out a part of the strategic plan must also lead the development of strategy for their areas of responsibility. The purpose of strategic planning is to accomplish productive change. The active involvement and commitment of the organization's leaders to accomplishing that change is critical to its success.

Retreat Participants

Strategy development is an important opportunity to engage a broad range of people in the organization:

- Organization's top leadership (board chair/CEO/COO)
- Board members with specific area responsibility (e.g., information systems)
- Managers of areas that will be considered in the strategy planning process
- Individuals with specific knowledge of areas to be included in the strategic plan
- Other stakeholders (those who would be affected by possible changes)
- Community members (both customers and non-customers)

A strategic planning retreat should include the board members, members of top management, and others with specific knowledge of the topics to be addressed. It is the preparation for the retreat that provides the opportunity to involve many people, and it is important that the preparation include input from the above groups of individuals.

That input enables the board members and others at the retreat to make informed decisions.

Retreat Preparation

The organization's leaders must take responsibility for overseeing the development of background issue papers that frame the issues for consideration at the strategic planning retreat. Examples of issues might include:

- Should we consider dropping a payer that provides 10 percent of our volume, but at rates that are 10 percent less than our other major payers?
- Should we sell our HMO? If so, what relationship should we seek to have with the new owner of the HMO?
- Should we develop a stronger relationship with the local public health and community services agencies? What should that relationship be?

Staff planners can help to assemble information and facilitate the planning process, but they cannot be expected to do the work of the organization's leaders. The background issue papers should include:

- A brief summary of the present situation
- Alternatives to the present situation that can be implemented and the expected costs and benefits of each, including the effect of implementing the change on people in the organization
- A recommended alternative and basis for the recommendation

Obtaining the input of those possibly affected, prior to the retreat and any decisions, pays significant benefits. It helps ensure that the implications of a change are thoroughly considered before the change is proposed for implementation. If the leaders see obtaining this input as a benefit to making more informed, better decisions, those affected will see that their concerns are heard and taken seriously. The resulting decision may still involve disruptive change, but those involved will know the issues and be well on their way to resolving the issues. In most instances of proposed change, the fundamental question is one of "When do you want to pay your dues?" Paying on the front end, before change is decided and position modifications are relatively easy, gives leaders the greatest flexibility. It also pays dividends in demonstrating the importance of people in the organization.

FORMAL VS. INFORMAL STRATEGY DEVELOPMENT

Informal strategy development is the way all strategy begins. Effective leaders need a mental model of their organization, of how it works and serves customers in its environment, just to make decisions. The process of applying that mental model develops ideas of how to better meet the wants and needs of both present and potential customers. Observation of the actions and experience of immediate competitors and others in the industry also provides ideas.

In some situations, informal strategy development is sufficient. If the stakes for the organization are small, and few people beyond those making the decision are affected, informal decision making is sufficient. Leaders just decide what to do and a new or revised strategy is implemented.

Formal strategy development is the full process of reviewing the organization's vision, values, present opportunities and threats, and experience with current strategic initiatives as outlined in Figure 4.1. The formal process is done on an annual or periodic basis, but the process can also be used to identify and evaluate options as new opportunities or threats are identified.

Formal strategy development is required when:

- Many people beyond those making the decision are affected
- The stakes for the organization are high
- Stakeholders need to get on board and be committed to the decision

When an issue arises that involves one or more of the above conditions, the process can be expedited, but it is unwise to shortcut the process. Taking time for review is often difficult for leaders. They know the issue, have the information, and have an idea of what should be done. The decision does not need to be made right now, but a timely decision is required. Why should they not just make the decision? Making the decision under one or more of the above conditions is unwise, precisely because it does not have to be made right now. Given the conditions outlined above, at best the least significant downside is the question of "When do they want to pay the dues in dealing with those affected?" At worst, the decision is "betting the organization" and the leader's decision has damaging effects.

The board chair and the CEO/COO may be together on a decision, but if they just make a decision, they are not using and building the organization's competency in strategy development. They are minimizing the chances for a successful strategy. The board chair, as chair of the organization's governance, must be certain that the board meets its responsibility to ask the tough questions of management.

CREATING STRATEGY IN A RAPIDLY CHANGING ENVIRONMENT

Strategy is based on assumptions about the environment: assumptions about customers' needs and wants, assumptions about new services that can be developed, and assumptions about how competitors will react. The assumptions may be based on thorough analysis, but there is always an element of uncertainty. An expectation that the uncertainty will play out in a specific way is an assumption.

Assumptions about customers' wants and needs were discussed in an earlier section of this chapter. The following points illustrate the risks of assuming that competitors will not react and outline a conceptual approach to developing strategy under uncertainty.

Risks in Assuming that Competitors Will Not React

As noted in the previous section, all strategy begins with an individual idea on how to better meet the wants and needs of present and potential customers. Those ideas occur in the context of the present environment: the perceived wants and needs of competitors, the products and services that are available, and the current actions of competitors. It is natural to begin analyzing the potential for a new idea in the context of the present environment. The risk is in not going beyond the present environment and analyzing the probable actions and reactions of competitors.

The potential for a new idea is critically dependent on assumptions about unit price, unit costs, and volume. What if competitors match the price? Will the volume increase as projected? What other actions can competitors take to minimize the loss of their volume? If the volume does not increase, what will happen to the profit margin? The fundamental question is the "product plus" features of the idea—what features are both valuable to customers and not easily copied by competitors? The assumption must be that competitors will react to efforts to take their patients and prices are easily copied by competitors. Unless the organization has a sustainable cost advantage, cutting price is more likely to cut the profit margin than it is to increase volume (and margin). Consider the following examples.

Acquiring physician practices

Some hospital CEOs initially thought they could grow their hospital volume by acquiring the practices of physicians who practiced at a competing hospital. The competing hospital typically responded with the same or higher bid to retain their physicians. The end result for most hospitals is that they paid significant sums just to retain the physicians they had on their staff.

HMO pricing

When HMOs began, their competitors were the large indemnity insurers. The HMOs had a price advantage with their provider contracts, and the initial strategy was to "cut price and grow volume." This strategy worked well in Minneapolis until the early 1980s when the HMOs reached a market share of 25 percent, at which point they began to try to underprice each other. Prices in the mid-80s were well below cost.

By 1987, the health plans were in a weak financial condition, physician reimbursement was well below cost, and physician groups began legal action to raise fees. Finally, as one HMO raised its price, the others followed and prices increased to profitable levels.

The lesson is that cutting price as a stand-alone strategy is one of the easiest to employ, and the easiest to defend—unless the organization first cutting the price has a significant price advantage. The best defense against a price cut is a matching price cut because little or no volume changes hands, and the initial organization cutting price is not rewarded with increased volume. When the organization cutting its price is not rewarded, it eventually realizes it is in its best interest to raise prices back to a level that the competitors will support.

The points in this section are not meant to be a complete discussion of pricing strategy or other actions that competitors can take. The above examples illustrate pure price competition between products that customers view as "like" products. Price is often not a stand-alone strategy. The above examples illustrate, however, the risks in assuming competitors will not react to price changes.

DEALING WITH UNCERTAINTY

The potential effect of uncertainty can be evaluated by considering the effect of a range of probable assumptions about the environment. There is value in assuming what "cannot happen" as a test of strategy. A leader cannot be faulted for bad circumstances—only for failing to see the possibility of bad circumstances. The effect of differing assumptions on the assessment of "best strategy" shows the sensitivity of best strategy to a particular set of assumptions.

In the article "Strategy Under Uncertainty," Courtney, Kirkland, and Viguerie (1997) outline a three-dimensional framework for developing strategy in an uncertain environment. Their observation is that strategy has traditionally been thought of as binary: either the situation is seen as so predictable that strategic decision making is a question of choosing between the discounted cash flows of alternatives, or it is seen as totally unpredictable and strategic decision making is a question of acting on gut instinct. The analytical rigor of traditional strategic planning processes is abandoned entirely: "This 'just do it' approach to strategy can cause executives to place misinformed bets on emerging products or markets that result in record write-offs" (Courtney, Kirkland, and Viguerie 1997).

Rethinking the development of an integrated delivery system illustrates the three dimensions of the framework, as follows.

Dimension I. Levels of Uncertainty

The first dimension is an assessment of the future environment. What likely future or futures can be identified? Courtney, Kirkland, and Viguerie (1997) identify four groupings of future environments: a clear-enough future, alternate futures, range of futures, and true ambiguity.

Level 1: A clear-enough future

In the early 1990s, many viewed the future healthcare environment as having only one likely outcome, with a single forecast of what was going to happen. The predominant form of future healthcare coverage would be capitated care, and physicians and hospitals had to come together in integrated delivery systems in order to survive and prosper.

Level 2: Alternate futures

Another view of the healthcare environment was to see a set of discrete alternatives. If national health insurance was established, the predominant form of healthcare coverage would be capitated care. If national health insurance was not established, the existing mix of capitated and noncapitated care would not change. In most areas of the country, capitated care would be only a minor form of coverage.

Level 3: Range of futures

This view of the healthcare environment presented a range of futures, with national health insurance and virtually full capitated care at one end of the spectrum, and the existing level of capitated care at the other.

The range of futures within the spectrum would be determined by the future growth of capitated care.

Level 4: True ambiguity

True ambiguity is an environment where multiple uncertainties come together in ways that make the future totally impossible to predict. Courtney, Kirkland, and Viguerie (1997) use the example of companies making market-entry investments in post-Communist Russia in 1992 as an example of operating in an environment of true ambiguity. Level 4 tends to occur at times of transition. The admonition of Courtney, Kirkland, and Viguerie (1997) is that even at level 4, "It is critical to avoid the urge to throw one's hands up and act purely on gut instinct." Even in these market environments, it is possible to identify variables to watch, such as the growth of capitation volume, that will be key indicators of the best strategic choices as the market evolves.

Dimension II. Strategic Postures

The second dimension identifies strategic intent. Courtney, Kirkland, and Viguerie (1997) identify three distinct strategic postures: shape the future, adapt to the future, and reserve the right to play.

Posture 1: Shape the future

Those hospitals and health systems that saw developing an integrated delivery system as a way to become the competitive model in their community were taking a "shape the future" strategic posture. They were going to set the standards for healthcare delivery and create demand. The idea was to create the most desirable place for employers, insurers, and government to purchase healthcare.

Posture 2: Adapt to the future

Those hospitals and health systems that decided to position themselves as a preferred source of care in any future system, by becoming even better at their basic strength, were taking an "adapt to the future" strategy. Those who continued to focus on providing "lowest cost high quality care" or "best place for specialty care" strategies in this period as stand-alone strategies were following a basic "adapter" strategy.

The challenge in this strategy is to identify market changes as they occur and to react quickly enough to meet the competitive market needs. An example is the University of Minnesota, which continued to focus on being the "best place for specialty care" as Abbott Northwestern and others became highly competitive places for specialty care. By the time the university realized the need for a primary care referral network, the opportunity was gone and the university had to merge with Fairview, one of the community-based hospital systems.

Posture 3: Reserve the right to play

By buying options to purchase physicians' practices in the future, many hospitals and insurance companies "reserved" their right to make future decisions. This strategy was a middle ground between the high costs and commitment of a shape-the-future strategy and the risk of not being able to develop stronger relations with primary care physicians in the future if needed. The strategy was to keep the option of a stronger primary care relationship open at less cost than moving ahead immediately with a shape the future strategy.

Dimension III. Portfolio of Actions

This posture identifies strategic intent. The portfolio of actions identifies the size of the bet or the action that implements the strategic intent. Courtney, Kirkland, and Viguerie (1997) identify three sizes of the bet: big bets, options, and no-regrets moves.

Action I: Big bets

Hospitals and health systems that purchased physician practices to move directly to a fully integrated delivery system were making a big bet. Those who refused to compete in any way, when the practices of physicians practicing in their hospital were being purchased, were also making a big bet.

Action II: Options

Those who acquired options to purchase physician practices in the future were choosing this action that allowed them to remain relatively uncommitted at the time, but left them choices for the future. This action implemented the strategic posture of reserving the right to play.

Action III: No-regrets moves

No-regrets moves are those that will pay off in any scenario. Actions to reduce costs or to develop a unique competence in the market are examples of such moves that usually have no negative—but possibly very positive—effects.

These three dimensions provide a framework for evaluating the level of uncertainty and for identifying and considering alternatives. This framework provides options and alternatives to the binary view that either the strategic situation is known and the best choices can be determined, or the situation is totally unknown and the best choice is a "gut" decision. The framework emphasizes making use of whatever is known or thought about the market to at least identify variables, such as the growth of capitation, that will, over time, determine the market and the best strategies.

Flexibility in Using the Organizations' Core Competencies as a Strategy

In a rapidly changing environment, opportunities are often only potential opportunities. The online medical record has been a potential opportunity for years. Some organizations have invested heavily in the development of a complete medical record—a shaper strategy that involves a big bet. Others have invested in the elements that will eventually tie into such a record such as online test results and transcription. Moving the organization thorough individual steps, valuable in themselves, are some no-regrets moves.

Flexible use of core competencies also recognizes that opportunities and threats can be identified at any time during the year. The success or lack of success of current strategic initiatives is also learned during the year. This is the reverse side of staying the course. There is a role for an opportunistic flexible strategy that frees the organization to make changes as new information is learned.

IMPLEMENTING STRATEGY IN A CHANGING ENVIRONMENT

The best leaders for a strategy will be different people in different situations. The strategy may require a visionary, charismatic leader to bring two organizations together in a merger. Once a merger is formally complete, a more operations-oriented leader may be needed to implement the merger. An organization's formal leaders may have particular strengths as visionaries, but they may not have particular strengths in operations. The implementation of complex strategies requires a team with competencies in all areas.

Implementing strategy is always difficult. It involves change, and implementing change is always a challenge. To accomplish change, the leader must be able to make a convincing case that the old ways cannot continue (sometimes referred to as a "burning platform") and/or communicate the desirability of the new ways. The difficulties of change are compounded in a changing environment. In a changing environment, it is more difficult to make a convincing case for the change, as the value of the change itself may be uncertain.

When implementing strategy in a changing environment, it is helpful to:

- *Maintain a bias toward action.* The lack of clear certainty of the course to be pursued can be a drag on any change. A bias toward action is acting on the best information available while recognizing that it is not perfect. Good ideas come out of the change process itself as those involved identify and address issues.

- *Look for early feedback on strategy performance.* Those involved in implementing the strategy will be focused on implementing the strategy itself. As an example, implementing a centralized nurse triage line is a major organizational challenge. Staff are relocated and hired, and physician relationships with their patients are disrupted. It is difficult for the people who are implementing a strategy to also focus on how well the strategy is performing. The organizational competence is to establish early performance targets that must be met if the process is to be successful, and to hold the leaders accountable for meeting the performance targets. Examples of performance targets include call response time, length of triage call, patient satisfaction, physician satisfaction, and cost of the triage process versus the dollars expected to be saved elsewhere in the system. The performance targets measure the value of the strategy in meeting the organization's needs to serve its stakeholders.

REASSESSING STRATEGIES CAN BE DIFFICULT

Organizations tend to build up and retain strategies that are not working as intended. In the words of Thomas Priselac (2000), CEO of Cedars-Sinai Medical Center in Los Angeles, "All of us have undertaken initiatives that haven't worked to the degree planned. Pruning and/or eliminating programs, both recent and long-standing, is a must." The question is: "Why is the process of pruning and/or eliminating programs so difficult?"

Leaders are champions of change. They must have a mental model of how the organization fits with its environment in order to lead the organization. Ideas for new strategies often come out of the experience of making decisions and seeing the organization's success or lack of success in comparison with competitors. Research by Joel Barker (1993) on paradigms (mental models of what we believe to be true) has shown that people tend to ignore, minimize, or literally not see information that conflicts with their assumptions.

Comparisons can be made between leaders and combat fighter pilots. Like pilots, leaders are flying: they can take the organization up, down, and sideways. They continually scan the horizon, looking for opportunities to make the organization and themselves successful while avoiding threats. They also face significant risks. One risk faced by combat fighter pilots is called "target fixation," when pilots become so focused on a target that they lose perspective. They lose sight of the choices available to them and fly right into the target. The decisions that leaders make are not as time critical, and a single decision rarely results in being "shot down." However, leaders can still fly into the target and, subsequently, be relieved of their duties. Leaders can choose to support strategies long after the signals are calling for change (Mitlyng and Wenzel 2001).

What is different about leaders and organizations that are most able to discontinue strategies that are no longer effective? One difference is that they have a clear understanding that strategies are not "forever." These leaders and organizations use the following techniques to evaluate and change strategies that are not working as intended.

1. All new strategic initiatives are treated as "pilots" until they are clearly successful.
2. A review of all strategic initiatives is a routine part of the annual strategic planning process.
3. If the CEO receives information that a strategic initiative is not working as intended, the CEO talks with board members, physicians, and staff to learn their perspectives on the performance and what should be done.
4. If the situation is highly political, a consultant is used to facilitate and legitimize the review.

Technique number three provides significant benefits for the CEO and the organization. It alerts the organization that the strategy is under review, it engages the organization in the process of deciding what to do, and, if change is necessary, it builds understanding of the need for change.

CONCLUSION

Strategy development is a continuous process. Conscious or otherwise, decisions that have strategic implications are made continually. This chapter has presented the elements of effective strategy development, a three-dimensional technique for dealing with levels of uncertainty, and techniques for modifying and/or eliminating strategic initiatives that are no longer working as intended. This chapter has emphasized the importance of monitoring the performance of strategic initiatives and being open to changing strategic direction as new information is obtained. An organization that is able to develop and implement strategies and continue to work on the established goals, objectives, and workplans as agreed in the absence of new information—but change if new information indicates that the strategy should be modified or discarded—will have developed an organizational competence in strategy development.

DISCUSSION

1. What are the elements of an effective process for strategy development?
2. Identify and describe two ways in which strategy development is a continuous process.
3. What is the role of governance in strategy development?
4. Identify four areas of knowledge required for good strategic planning and describe their importance.
5. Identify the three dimensions of a framework that leaders can use to help avoid viewing strategy development as a binary process.
6. Why is the reassessment of strategies so difficult? Identify three techniques that leaders can use to make the reassessment of strategies easier.

REFERENCES

The Advisory Board. 1993. *The Grand Alliance—Vertical Integration Strategies for Physicians and Health Systems.* Washington, DC: The Advisory Board.

Barker, J. K. 1993. *Paradigms.* New York: HarperCollins Publishers, Inc.

Courtney, H., J. Kirkland, and P. Viguerie. 1997. "Strategy Under Uncertainty." *Harvard Business Review* 75 (6): 67–79.

de Geus, A. 1997. "The Living Company." *Harvard Business Review* 75 (2): 51–59.

Drucker, P. F. 1994. "Theory of the Business." *Harvard Business Review* 72 (5): 102.

Mitlyng, J. and F. Wenzel. 2001. "Leaders as Combat Fighter Pilots." *Physician Executive* 27 (6): in press.

Priselac, T. 2000. "Do-it-yourself Budget Relief." *Modern Healthcare* 29 (30): 26.

Senge, P. 1990. *The Fifth Discipline: The Art and Practice of the Learning Organization.* New York: Currency/Doubleday.

CHAPTER 5

Physician Relationships

CASE IN POINT: James Lynn is CEO of Johnsville Community Hospital, a position he has held for the past ten years. He is thinking about the hospital board meeting that is scheduled for tomorrow evening. The hospital's financial performance is on or ahead of budget in all areas but the employed physician practice. The losses on the physician practice are going to produce a loss on operations again this year.

The hospital purchased the assets of Johnsville Clinic, a highly regarded, 50-physician multispecialty group, five years ago. The physician practice is going to lose about $3 million as it has for each of the past three years. The loss is down from the initial $5 million, but the ongoing loss is a serious problem. A local businessman, who became board chair a year ago, is becoming increasingly agitated about the continuing losses. He is beginning to suggest that it is time for new hospital leadership.

James has always felt he had reasonably good relationships with the physicians. The hospital department administrator he appointed to lead the group, when it was purchased, had a good track record of cost management and a good history of working with physicians. Two days ago, Dan Palmer, M.D., the physician leader in the group, mentioned to James that morale in the group is terrible and several of the most productive physicians were looking at other positions.

James reflects that purchasing the clinic seemed like such a good idea five years ago: it made them an integrated delivery system and gave them the opportunity to better manage care. The mass shift to capitated care has not occurred, however, and better management of care is often penalized as lower charges produce less revenue. Better management of care still seems like a good idea for the community.

QUESTION: What skills and knowledge of how to work with physicians will help James Lynn understand the present issues and identify the actions he should take?

INTRODUCTION

Working with physicians has been compared to herding cats. Whether the relationship is between a hospital leadership team and the hospital's medical staff, or between the leadership of a medical group and the physician members of that group, the challenges are significant. There are differences and similarities in a hospital setting as compared to a medical group. The keys to successfully working with physicians are, however, fundamentally the same and are based on understanding and working with the interests and values of physicians.

This chapter identifies similarities and differences in physician relationships within hospital and medical group settings, describes typical physician leadership positions in hospitals and medical groups, presents the concept of the physician-administrator team, outlines the particular challenges that physicians face as CEOs, and summarizes the interests and values of physicians. The final section presents seven keys to success based on the interests and values of physicians.

The organization that understands the interests and values of physicians and uses that understanding to work well with physicians will have developed a significant competence in physician relations.

DIFFERENCES AND SIMILARITIES BETWEEN PHYSICIAN RELATIONSHIPS WITHIN A MEDICAL GROUP PRACTICE AND WITHIN A HOSPITAL

In a group practice, the physicians are the engine that produces financial success or loss. As the members of the group, they have total financial responsibility for the group's performance. In a hospital, physicians are visitors that use the facility, but they are not "members" of the hospital. Physicians have no direct financial responsibility for the hospital, seeing the hospital only as a place to work and earn income.

A hospital is paid for the services it provides: the facility and the work of its staff. Hospitals can be helped or hurt by the way physicians practice if the financial payment for the service is fixed, as it is with diagnosis-related group payments. An orthopedic surgeon who insists on using the most expensive implants, or an internist who tends to discharge patients early, will incur financial losses or gains on those patients for the hospital. Physicians also affect hospital revenue by the decisions they make to admit patients and the services they prescribe. Physicians affect costs by the services they require in caring for the patients. While physicians influence the size of the hospital's revenue and expense streams, the revenue and expense streams for physicians and hospitals are separate.

Hospital-physician relationships are fraught with issues of co-dependency.

- Hospitals depend on physicians to admit patients to the hospital; the physician depends on the hospital's efforts to continue to be seen as a preferred hospital for care.
- Hospitals are dependent on physicians to order and use services; physicians are dependent on hospitals to provide the services their patients need.
- Physicians are dependent on hospitals to invest in state-of-art equipment; hospitals are dependent on physicians to use and justify the investment in that equipment.

- If a situation of possible malpractice that involves a physician occurs in the hospital, it is likely that both the hospital and the physician will be named in the lawsuit.

The medical group and individual physician relationships are also codependent. The medical group relies on the individual to provide high-quality care and be a productive member of the group. The individual relies on the group to manage revenues and costs and provide the facilities, equipment, and staff required for a successful practice environment. If an individual is sued for malpractice, the group and the physician are named in the suit. The medical group is typically liable for all defense costs and the costs of any settlement.

There are differences, but in both physician medical groups and in hospitals and health systems, the relationship is significantly codependent. The ability of the physicians and organization leadership to work together well is a key determinant of organizational success.

PHYSICIANS IN LEADERSHIP POSITIONS

This section identifies several physician leadership positions, the qualifications required, the typical selection process, and responsibilities of the position.

Chief Medical Officer

The chief medical officer is a licensed physician who typically has several years of experience on the hospital's medical staff. They are hired by the hospital CEO, for an indefinite term, to be a member of the hospital/health system's senior management team. Responsibilities include credentialing and quality assurance/quality improvement.

Chief of Staff

The chief of staff is a licensed physician who also typically has years of experience on the hospital's medical staff. They are elected by members of the medical staff for a one-year period, although they may precede that year with one or two years as an "associate" chief of staff as they assist with and learn the responsibilities of the chief of staff. The chief of staff represents the hospital staff in working with hospital leadership to address mutual concerns.

Department Chair

The department chair is a licensed physician who is the organization's formal leader of the physicians in their department. Internal medicine, surgery, obstetrics/gynecology, pediatrics, and family medicine are typical departments. This position exists in both hospitals and medical groups. Hospital department chairs are appointed by the hospital CEO for an indefinite term. Medical group chairs are typically elected by the physicians in the department for a defined period of one to three years, but they can be reelected for subsequent terms. In hospitals and medical groups, the department chair is responsible for recruiting, performance review, educational programs (although another member of the department may be the primary leader in a medical group), financial performance, relations with the organization's leadership, and the development of the department's skills and capabilities.

Physician Leader of Medical Group

The physician leader of the medical group is a licensed physician with several years of experience in the medical group. Their title may be chairman of the board or president, and they are the political leader of the medical group. They are elected by the physician members of the group for a defined period—typically one to three years—often with an opportunity to be reelected. They are practicing physicians who continue to practice while they are in these elected positions, although the actual practice time is reduced to provide time for the elected position responsibilities. This position is responsible to individual physicians to see that their concerns are heard and addressed, for addressing performance issues of individual physicians as a last step prior to bringing recommendations for action to the group's governing board, and for the strategic development of the medical group. The physician leader represents the medical group in relations with the hospitals they use, the media, the government, and other outside organizations.

Medical Director of Medical Group

Groups that have reached the size of about 30 physicians and larger find that the daily clinical issues are more than the elected physician leader can personally handle. The position of medical director is established, and a physician member of the group is selected by the leader of the group and confirmed by the group's governing board. The individual in this position is appointed for an indefinite term. The primary requirement for this position is that the other physicians in the group see this individual as a very competent physician—a "clinician's clinician." The medical director's responsibilities include recruiting, quality assurance, and dealing with individual physician performance issues.

WHAT PHYSICIANS ADD TO ORGANIZATIONAL CORE COMPETENCIES

In health services organizations where the core business is providing physician-based clinical practice—in office or inpatient settings—the physician's knowledge of clinical practice is an organizational core competence.

Physicians in clinical practice will accept the leadership of people who are not physicians in those areas where they feel physicians do not have a particular skill. Some examples are finance, billing and collecting, managed care contracting, and information systems. In the area of clinical practice, however, physicians will only accept another physician as a clinical practice leader.

Understanding of physician interests and values is critical to success in leading and managing physicians. Physicians are often thought of as motivated only by money, but the reality is a far more complex set of interests and values. Leaders who are effective in leading physicians, whether they have a medical degree or not, understand and act based on their knowledge of physician interests and values. Physicians will expect that another physician knows and understands these interests and values. Someone who is not a physician will have to demonstrate such knowledge and understanding. The interests and values of physicians will be discussed in more detail later in this chapter.

RECOGNIZING PHYSICIAN AND ADMINISTRATOR DIFFERENCES AND SIMILARITIES

Physicians and administrators can both have extensive formal training, but the primary focus of their daily work is quite different. The physician's focus is a series of "right now" decisions on the care of individual patients. With the exception of those physicians treating chronic diseases, physicians expect to see the results of their treatment in a few hours, days, or weeks. The administrator's focus is primarily on the success and well-being of the organization as a whole, and the administrator's decision is rarely as time sensitive. The results of the administrator's decision may be known in a few weeks, as in the case of a managed care negotiation; but the results of other efforts, such as a merger with another organization, may not be known for years.

The Physician-administrator Team

Developing a leadership team that the physician group views as highly competent is the first key to success in leading and managing groups of physicians. Competence is measured in terms of physician leadership, which other physicians see as necessary for the medical group. Competence is also measured in terms of managing the "business affairs" of the medical group—areas where most physicians feel they are not competent. These areas include billing and collections, accounting and finance, computer systems, employee management, and contract negotiation. The physician-administrator team pairs the physician leader's clinical and leadership skills with the skills of the administrator in these other areas.

In effective teams, the "team" is a partnership where each respects and relies on the skills of the other. Decisions on all major issues are made after thorough discussion of the alternatives. Deference in making the decision is given to the individual with lead responsibility in the area (e.g., the administrator on which computer system to select or the physician leader on a decision to support recruiting a new specialist). Once decisions are made, each relies on the other to know the reasons for the decision and to support the decision made.

DEVELOPING PHYSICIAN LEADERSHIP SKILLS

Physicians are trained to be leaders of the healthcare team. There are differences in leading an organization, and it is important that physicians learn those differences in the context of what is appropriate and effective in leading the healthcare team versus leading the organization. The healthcare team expects the physician to decide on what should be done for a patient. The physician may ask for information to help them decide on a course of action, but the decision as to what should be done is clearly the physician's responsibility. In leading healthcare organizations, physicians—and other leaders—must consciously learn and follow a more participative style of leadership (discussed in the following section).

Some specialized education programs in management and leadership help to build on the skills of physicians. The American College of Physician Executives has a series of programs and offers fellowship in the American College of Physician Executives. The Medical Group Management Association has a Society for Physicians in Administration and offers fellowship in the American College of Medical Practice Executives.

Many physicians are enrolling in MBA programs to develop the skills and obtain the MBA credentials. Most programs offer working professionals flexibility in time commitments. The most popular way to earn a master's degree is through evening or weekend MBA or MHSA programs. National and international programs are also available on a distance-learning basis. Such programs have been structured to include both limited on-site work and computer-based learning that allow continued full-time work. Selection for a physician leadership position, and success in that position, is helped by the knowledge gained in earning an MBA or MHSA degree. An MBA degree is not generally required for a physician leadership position today, however, and the decision to seek an MBA is a personal decision. What is needed is a basic level of business skill understanding, developed either through formal training or work experience, to communicate with others in the organization who already have the skills and who are expected to be experts in applying those skills.

Regardless of a leader's personal knowledge of the subject, the leader must expect and require the experts in the organization to explain issues in terms the leader understands, whether the subject is medical records or computer information systems. Requiring such an explanation is often a good test of the soundness of an idea.

The challenge for leaders is twofold: (1) deciding how best to spend their time and (2) engaging the time and skills of others in the organization in accomplishing the organization's goals. In leading healthcare organizations, the physician leader brings status as a physician and knowledge of clinical practice to the leadership position. The physician leader is often the sole member, or at most one of a few, who has that knowledge. The leadership team looks to the physician leader for an understanding of how issues affect physicians and clinical care and of the best choices to be made from those perspectives.

PHYSICIANS AS CEOS

Physicians face special challenges in the role of CEO. The perspectives and behaviors that serve them well as a practicing physician may limit their effectiveness as a CEO. Functioning as an effective CEO may require learning new perspectives and behaviors.

Sharing Responsibilities with Teams

Individuals who are new to leadership positions often make the mistake of concluding that they alone are totally responsible for the success or failure of the organization. This is a particular risk for physicians who are new leaders. In their previous experience as a practicing physician, they have been the "captain of the ship" and totally responsible for their patients. A seasoned physician CEO of a large physician group, Henry Berman, M.D., speaks to this point and the importance of leaders seeing their role as part of a management team.

> Although CEOS must, of course, be willing to accept responsibility for all failures, they are hardly at fault, any more than they would be responsible for all successes. The recommendation to work closely with a highly effective management team is the best antidote to feeling so overwhelmingly responsible (Rubin and Fernandez 1991).

Having a Vision (But Not All the Answers)

Leaders must have a vision, a mental model of where they think the organization should go if they are to be effective. That vision is key to identifying opportunities, formulating alternatives, and assessing the pros and cons of the choices. There are times, however, when it is important for leaders to recognize and acknowledge that they do not have all the answers. And this, too, is a particular challenge for physicians.

Involving Others in Decision Making

A common trap for leaders is to think that once they have done all the work of the analysis, they should make the decision. There may be significant questions where judgment is needed, but they think the leader's job is to make the decision and "sell" it to the group. The thinking is perfectly logical: they have the best knowledge of the issues and the choices to be made. Why should they not make the decision?

If the decision can potentially affect the physician group, "followership" is a significant issue. The most significant judgment that has to be made is to determine what the group will support. Numerous decisions have been made with little or no involvement of the physician group—because it was best for the group and there was not time for involvement—with poor results. The energies of the physician group go into finding fault with the decision, and untold hours are spent later trying to convince individual physicians that the decision was "right."

A few years ago, the management committee at Park Nicollet Medical Center in Minneapolis decided to look back and analyze six decisions that had been made. In three cases the implementation had gone well, and in three the implementation had gone poorly. The question was: "What were the distinguishing characteristics between those that went well and those that did not?" They found that in the "good" cases—where the decisions were supported by the group—(1) the process for decision making was clearly identified at the beginning; (2) participation was widespread and open; and (3) the information obtained was fed back to the group so the participants would know their views had been taken into account in making the decision. The other three cases provided a marked contrast. In those cases, the process for making the decision was not clearly identified and feedback was not obtained from those involved. Because these decisions were not supported by those affected, there was resistance, resentment, and sabotage.

Using the Authoritative Leadership Style

It is better to have a process up front that engages individual physicians in the issues and gains their support for the decision that results (Delbecq and Gill 1985). It builds physician support for the decisions—even if they disagree, they will understand why the decision was made. Dr. Berman (Rubin and Fernandez 1991) has described this approach to leadership as the *authoritative* style:

> The authoritative style is not a compromise between the other two styles [autocratic and laissez faire] but a third, entirely different approach. Authoritative parents and leaders understand that they have knowledge and skills that are greater in certain areas, and responsibilities that they cannot shrug off. They also understand that wise leaders make most decisions after considerable consultation with those whom the decisions affects, that they hold as few decisions to themselves as possible, and that they encourage independent decision making .... Paradoxically,

when CEOS admit they are uncertain about the best course to take, the effect will be to energize other staff—in this case, physicians in particular—to take more responsibility for decision making.

The issue of overwhelming self-confidence and inability to hear and benefit from the perspectives of others is not solely a physician CEO issue. And in times of great transformation, the qualities of overwhelming self-confidence and inability to be distracted by the views of others can be an asset. The article "Narcissistic Leaders: The Incredible Pros, the Inevitable Cons" (Maccoby 2000) gives examples of people described as *productive narcissists*. "They are gifted and creative strategists who see the big picture and find meaning in the risky challenge of changing the world and leaving behind a legacy .... One reason we look to productive narcissists in times of great transition is that they have the audacity to push through the massive transformations that society periodically undertakes." They are charismatic leaders and people choose to follow them. The con is that narcissists can become unrealistic dreamers. "They nurture grand schemes and harbor the illusion that only circumstances or enemies block their success. This tendency toward grandiosity and distrust [of other's views] is the Achilles' heel of narcissists." He cites an example of a very successful leader who began to feel he could disregard the "concerns of his operational managers," pursuing high-risk deals until he was forced to resign (Maccoby 2000).

UNDERSTANDING PHYSICIAN VALUES AND INTERESTS

Physicians are commonly viewed as bright, highly educated, and motivated people. Another common view is that they are also highly motivated by money; however, the reality is a far more complex set of interests and values. Consider the following ten points.

1. *Providing the best care for their patients.* This is the fundamental value of physicians. It is the original drive that provides sustained satisfaction.

2. *Personal control over what they do and how they practice.* Physicians are trained to be "in charge." They are held responsible, both legally and by their profession, for what happens or does not happen to patients under their care.

3. *Limited control by others.* This is a corollary to the control issue above. Relinquishing control is acceptable only in areas where others clearly have the responsibility and more expertise. Decisions in other areas may be made with the best intentions, but until physicians understand and accept them, those decisions are seen as limits on points one and two.

4. *Doing well in comparison to peers.* Doing well on report cards is part of the experience of becoming a physician. Comparisons with others are always seen as "report cards."

5. *Sense of fairness in relationships.* Even tough decisions are acceptable if they result from an open and fair process. Arbitrary decisions based solely on the power of position, the "king's X," are unacceptable.

6. *Fostering an environment of clinical inquiry.* Physicians continue to learn from their experiences and those of others to keep current with best medical practice.

7. *Opportunity for dialog—ability to influence decisions that affect them.* Listening to and *hearing* the physician's perspective is critical. Data and real dialog are valued as the basis for reaching decisions.

8. *Maintaining collegial relations with peers.* Relationships are based on working together as professionals with special competencies.

9. *Choice of those they work with.* Physicians must rely on their colleagues and coworkers in caring for patients, and the quality of their colleagues and coworkers reflects on them.

10. *Partnership model.* The concept of equal partners, with each party contributing skills and efforts to the success of the whole, is valued. If you are seen as working in their interests, they will work in yours. However, if you are seen as working without regard to their interests, they will work without regard to yours.

With the above points in mind, it is particularly curious to see how many hospitals and physician practice management companies (PPMC) have focused on physicians' compensation as the sole motivation for physician behavior. Compensation is a report card—if it is less than acceptable, it is a "dissatisfier." If it is more than acceptable, it is a marginal plus. But the other interests and values are still there, regardless of compensation level. Each must be satisfied to have an effective, committed medical group and to be able to manage a physician group well. As in Maslow's hierarchy of needs (1970), financial security addresses only the most basic need.

Physician values are the central determinants of a physician group's culture, the "silent governor" of behavior in the group (Wenzel 1989). Any disparity between these values and the values of an owner hospital or PPMC poses significant challenges for the leaders and managers of these groups. An astute manager can use his or her understanding of corporate culture to effect changes, but in these composite organizations, a significant question is: "Which culture?" The corporate objective may be to reduce costs and improve financial performance. Success in achieving that objective depends on resolving the culture conflicts in ways that meet the strategic needs of the organization (Kornacki and Silversin 1998). It must build on the strengths of the physician culture. In groups that have been assembled by acquiring a number of practices in recent years, there may be several, distinct subculture differences that need to be resolved to develop a strong physician culture; however, the core physician values noted above are the common threads.

SEVEN KEYS TO WORKING WELL WITH PHYSICIANS

The following seven keys, however difficult, build on the interests and values of physicians. They apply to working with groups of physicians in all settings. Interesting parallels exist between these keys and those for success in very long-lived companies in other industries (de Geus 1997).

Key 1: Develop a Leadership Team that Is Considered as Highly Competent

Competence is measured in terms of physician leadership, which other physicians see as necessary for the medical group. Competence is also measured in terms of managing the "business affairs" of the medical group—those areas where most physicians feel they are not competent. The physician-administrator team pairs the physician leader's clinical and leadership skills with the skills of the administrator in the other areas.

The advantage of the physician-administrator team, however, is much more than a question of complementary skills. The challenges of leading a physician group are significant. There are always issues to address, and a single leader risks being held responsible for all problems that occur. Berman (Rubin and Fernandez 1991) describes this problem as "an unhealthy dependency" by the physician group on that leader. Distinct advantages in shared leadership exist if (1) each member of the team is seen as competent in their respective areas of expertise, and (2) the team is seen as bringing together the skills and perspectives of each individual to do what is best for the group.

- *Build performance on the basics.* Managing both the clinical and the business affairs well will result in continued bottom-line profitability, which will carry the leadership team a long way. Competency today is demonstrated by how well the leadership team works with the physicians (as outlined in these seven keys).
- *Focus on high-quality patient care.* Decision making that supports high-quality care is a necessity.
- *Understand the value of culture.* Culture is "the way we do things here"—how decisions are made, who is involved, and who makes the final decision. A leader or manager who is not sensitive to the culture of the medical group will not last long.
- *Understand the need to communicate.* The ability to have a "say" is highly valued by physicians. Significant dialog on issues that affect them is a core element of physician group culture.

- *Emphasize the need for trust.* Trust is the glue that holds the group together. The previous chapter identified ten interests and values of physicians. The label "democracy" is a good summary of these values. Trust is a critical element in the success of a democracy.

Democracy + Lack of Trust = Chaos

A democracy without a broad base of trust will not be successful. Without that trust, questioning an action leads to more questions and chaos. The group cannot decide on a common direction.

Democracy + Trust = A Rocky but Manageable Road

With trust, the questioning of direction occurs, but there is a basic trust in the integrity of the answers given. Questioning leads to resolution of concerns and agreement on a common direction.

Key 2: Develop a Physician Leadership and Governance Structure with Accountabilities that Include the Interests and Values of Individual Physicians

Physician leadership is important to the profession, but managing physician groups well requires more than a well-chosen leader. Even physicians have difficulty managing physician groups.

The leadership and governance members in independent groups are selected by the membership, from the membership. That leadership and governance is very attuned to the interests and values of the individual members of the group. Successful leadership listens, hears, and acknowledges the concerns of individuals. It also recognizes leadership's fundamental responsibility to ensure the long-term success of the group. To have an effective medical group, all members of the group's leadership and governance structure do not necessarily need to be elected by the group, but at least a majority must be. That majority gives those elected the "political legitimacy" that is the source of their power in leading the group. Whether elected or appointed, all members of the leadership and governance structure must act as if they are directly accountable to the group. They must be servant leaders.

There is much more to "structure and accountabilities" than listening to the concerns of individuals. It is an active process that engages members of the group in the issues facing the organization. The following points present the elements of an effective, active process.

Engage physicians in discussions of how decisions are to be made, and the accountabilities of organization and physician leadership

The challenge for leadership is to develop a process that (1) includes broad involvement of the physician group and (2) avoids the paralysis of being held hostage by a vocal minority. It is an opportunity to engage each member of the group in answering the question: "What does the group want the organization's leadership to do?" How should the organization establish priorities for future development? On the subject of physician recruiting, should each clinical area decide, alone, who to recruit to practice with them? Should each clinical area have to present their recommended candidate's qualifications to the organization's physician leadership for final approval? What is the process for terminating a physician's practice with the group? Leadership must highlight the issues and develop a balanced presentation of data and information on the issues that individual physicians can consider.

This can be an unsettling experience for leadership. "What if the members of the group (collectively) do not agree with what we think should be done?" They may not. But our experience is that physicians, when presented with data and information on an issue in a situation where they know that what they say will make a difference, will make productive and helpful recommendations.

Culture is often referred to as "the way we do things around here." The process of assessing and reestablishing the structure and accountabilities of leadership will examine the current culture. The process positions the group to change in ways the majority concludes that it should change, based on the data and analysis provided and the dialog that occurs. Some of the ideas will be incorporated in the bylaws, and other ideas will be recorded in new policies and procedures. Writing down how the organization should work is an important step because it defines the rituals of the organization, or "culture in action" in the words of Deal and Kennedy (1982). To be most effective, this process should include an open discussion of culture, the group's culture, and culture change.

Most healthcare organizations develop annual budgets. Many groups precede the budgeting process with a strategic planning process that identifies major strategic directions, goals, and objectives for the next year. The group developing the strategic plan is the organization's top leadership, often broadened to include other leaders in the organization. The group developing the budget may include administrative and physician leaders at all levels in the organization, with the final budget pulled together and presented to the governing board for approval.

If the planning and budgeting process is effective, it is a forecast of the leadership team's priorities in the coming year. The actions that result from the plan may affect each physician. The questions are: "What steps are taken to identify the priorities of the individual physician members, as part of the planning and budgeting process?" and "What steps are taken, in the process of approving the budget, to ensure that the plans are understood and supported by the physicians?"

Establish processes to involve physicians on issues they will see as significantly affecting them

Three processes have proven effective in involving physicians.

1. *Use the governing board in physician groups.* The members of the governing board, who are also practicing physicians in the group, can serve as a valuable sounding board for the leadership team. These physicians know the interests of their colleagues in the practice. The physician board members are the first contacted with concerns about the board's actions. It is particularly

important to gain their understanding and build their support in developing proposed recommendations that affect the physician group. The leadership team can be tempted to bring "final" recommendations to the board for its approval, as noted. While that may be the standard in other settings, in a physician group it is helpful to consciously include the board in the process of developing recommendations.

2. *In all groups, talk with formal and informal thought leaders.* Every group has both formal and informal leaders, people whom their colleagues look to for guidance when they want information on how the group is doing or they need to make a decision related to the group. This group is broader than the members of the governing board in a physician group. It serves the same purposes, however, in that it gains the insights of these individuals in developing recommended courses of action that affect the physician group, and builds support for the actions that are finally recommended.

3. *Meet with groups of individuals on major issues.* On major issues that affect the group, there is no substitute for meeting directly with small groups of individuals. The communication is direct and timely. The meetings can be scheduled on an ad hoc basis. Taking the time for these meetings, if the information gathered is used in the decision process, shows respect for these individuals and their opinions. It builds support for the resulting recommendations. Perhaps even more important, a practice of using these meetings as part of the leadership process will build a culture that says "we are a strong team."

Key 3: Work with the Governance Structure and the Physician Group to Develop Performance Expectations

Physicians who constructively contribute to the success of an organization do expect to be accountable for their decisions and for achieving reasonable, competitive performance expectations. Information and dialog are needed to develop and agree on performance expectations. As an example, comparative production data for similar specialties are integral components of dialog on productivity expectations.

Responsibility for meeting performance expectations is the reciprocal accountability of the individual to the group. In a small group, the individual physicians know their colleagues and their performance. In a larger group, individual physicians may not know all the other physicians in the group, and they know less about how well or poorly others are performing. When the physicians see the group's performance affecting their future, explicit performance expectations are an important component of their culture.

Key 4: Expect that Physicians Will Seek to Create a Community

Building for the future is an important part of healthcare leadership. As Arie de Geus put it in "The Living Company" (1997):

> To build a company that is profitable and will live long, managers take care to develop a community. Processes are in place to define membership, establish common values, recruit people, develop employees, assess individual potential, live up to a human contract, and establish policies for graceful exits from the company.

Successful medical groups and other healthcare organizations have similar characteristics. They focus on common values, recruit physicians and other staff who share those values, emphasize continuing education, give individuals the freedom to grow, live up to the spirit of commitments made, and provide opportunities for individuals to leave if they do not "work out" after a trial period. They have a strong organizational culture. Arie de Geus goes on to say, "Above all … members know 'who is us' and they are aware that they hold values in common."

Groups that have been drawn together in recent years, without regard to common values, can expect to fail or face periods of significant transition as they develop their culture. As common values are identified, some physicians may choose to leave while others may be asked to leave.

Key 5: Be Sure that Physicians Lead on All Issues that Primarily Affect Them or Where They Have to Initiate Change

Physicians are better directing themselves than following the direction of others. For example, while a group of physicians might develop and adopt a compensation system change that reduces their compensation, they would more than likely resist the same change if developed and suggested by others.

Structuring the process is critical. A physician project manager, chosen by the leader of the organization and supported with administrative staff analysis, is important. A reasonable deadline for presenting recommendations to the organization's leadership and/or the governing board is critical. A process that includes obtaining the ideas of those affected, as noted above, is also crucial.

Key 6: If an Issue Arises, Provide Information that Individuals Can Act on

The general statement that "productivity must be improved" will have little or no effect. And, while paying a financial incentive is often seen as the way to increase performance, financial incentives can have little effect if the performance that is being incented is in conflict with physicians' interests and values.

In contrast, information on an individual's clinical performance that shows it is in some way less than the specific (but unnamed) performance of other members of the group (e.g., mammography rates) is a powerful motivator. It can increase performance on whatever is being measured, even without a financial incentive. The report becomes a report card.

Key 7: Always View the Relationship as a Partnership—and Continue to Demonstrate Value

Partners do not "own" each other. Partners are drawn together and stay together based on mutual interests, mutual respect, and perceived benefit.

Managing physician relationships poorly produces a dispirited organization that loses money. The best people leave, and those who stay
will do so only as long as someone else pays the check. Leading and
managing a physician group well produces a powerful organization
that is profitable and that other physicians want to join. It engages the
interests of each physician in the success of the group. They see the
group's success as ensuring their individual, future success.

The current losses in owned medical practices are presenting a significant opportunity to reinvent these groups and transform them into
self-sustaining, physician-led medical groups. The losses are a crisis
that is becoming evident to all. Individual physicians are looking at
these losses, hearing that some owners are filing bankruptcy to deal
with these losses, and they are wondering: "How secure is my future?"

Crisis is a necessary prerequisite to fundamental change. It is the
"burning platform" that shows the current organization and relationships cannot continue. In his book *Crisis and Renewal—Meeting the
Challenge of Organizational Change,* David Hurst (1995) argues by anal-
ogy to ecosystem change that "renewal" cannot take place until the
crisis has effectively brought an end to the past. "The objective of creating a crisis is to break the harmful constraints that bind the organization in the final phase of the conventional life cycle." But the crisis
alone is not sufficient. By itself, it only adds to emotional stress. Values-
based leadership is needed to create "conditions under which self organization or learning can occur ... the objective of this leadership activity is to build a larger-scale, loosely connected network of talented
individuals who are held together by common values, a shared vision
of the future, and a unique sense of who they are as a people" (Hurst
1995).

CONCLUSION

Effective medical groups are those in which there is mutual accountability between the leadership and the individual members for the
success of the whole. Codependency, although an inherent part of

hospital or medical group and physician relationships, can be a strength or a weakness. If the physicians see that there is mutual accountability between the hospital or medical group leadership and the physicians for the success of the whole, codependency will be a strength. If that sense of mutual accountability is lacking, codependency will be a weakness.

The organization that (1) understands the interests and values of physicians and (2) uses that understanding to work well with physicians as outlined in the seven keys in this chapter will have developed a significant competence in physician relations.

DISCUSSION

1. What are the keys to developing an effective physician and hospital relationship?
2. What is the "authoritative" leadership style?
3. How do physicians assess the competency of the organization's leadership? Why is that assessment important?

NOTE

This chapter is adapted from Joseph W. Mitlyng and Frederick J. Wenzel, "It Takes More than Money—Keys to Success in Leading and Managing Physician Groups," MGM *Journal* 46 (2), 1999.

REFERENCES

Deal, T. E. and A. A. Kennedy. 1982. *Corporate Cultures.* New York: Addison Wesley.

de Geus, A. 1997. "The Living Company." *Harvard Business Review* 75 (2): 51–59.

Delbecq, A. L. and S. L. Gill. 1985. "Justice as a Prelude to Teamwork in Medical Centers." *Health Care Management Review* 10 (1): 45–51.

Hurst, D. K. 1995. *Crisis and Renewal—Meeting the Challenge of Organizational Change.* Boston: Harvard Business School Press.

Kornacki, M. J. and J. Silversin. 1998. "How Can IDSS Integrate Conflicting Cultures?" *Healthcare Financial Management* 52 (6): 34–36.

Maccoby, M. 2000. "Narcissistic Leaders: The Incredible Pros, the Inevitable Cons." *Harvard Business Review* 78 (1): 68–77.

Maslow, A. H. 1970. *Motivation and Personality,* 2nd edition. New York: Harper and Row.

Rubin, I. and C. Fernandez. 1991. "Commentary: Reflections of a Seasoned Veteran." In *My Pulse Is Not What it Used to Be.* Honolulu: The Temenos Foundation.

Wenzel, F. J. 1989. "Corporate Culture—The Silent Governor." *MGM Journal* 36 (3): 33–35, 38, 40–42.

CHAPTER 6

Ethics and Values

CASE IN POINT: It had not been a good year financially for Mid-Central Memorial. The bottom line was eroding and the net profit of this 500-bed hospital was 2 percent, down from the previous year's 3.4 percent. Although management staff had been working diligently to reduce expenses, fluctuations in volume were still causing a problem. Management of diagnosis-related groups was working well, thanks to a cooperative medical staff, but neighboring hospitals were cutting back in response to weakening patient volume. Charity care write-offs were increasing, although still at a manageable rate.

The hospital's CEO, Helen Weisman, was very concerned. At the most recent board of directors meeting, the chairman of the finance committee suggested it was time to eliminate a few of the hospital's low-margin programs. One of the programs that might be affected is the one supporting a newly opened 45-bed off-campus AIDS hospice unit, which Mid-Central Memorial operates as a community service. The unit has received widespread community support, but concerns surfaced that the sponsorship of the project might attract additional AIDS patients to the hospital, which would bring further financial strain.

The hospice unit was being subsidized by Mid-Central Memorial at only $120,000 per year. However, because of the perceived risks to the staff of providing care for additional AIDS patients, opponents of the unit were focusing on its financial viability as a means of urging Mid-Central out of this "loss leader."

Fortunately for both the hospital and the community, the board, medical staff, and management had recently updated the hospital's strategic plan, including a major rewriting (and adoption) of a mission statement stressing the hospital's commitment to meeting the needs of the underserved. AIDS patients obviously were part of this segment of the population.

Helen used this updated and well-endorsed mission statement to remind critics that continuing to support the AIDS hospice was essential to the hospital's mission—a position that was strongly supported by the entire hospital board and most of its medical staff. Helen knew that in the absence of this mission statement, the program might not have survived. Keeping the focus on the mission made the difference.

Helen reflected that the ethical issues facing her and the staff were much broader than the specific issue of treating AIDS patients.

QUESTION: What initiatives could Helen encourage that would further assist the board, management, and staff in addressing ethical issues? What more should be done?

INTRODUCTION

An organization's ethics and values are reflected in the general sense that individuals have of what is, and is not, acceptable behavior. That sense of appropriate behavior is what guides individual decision making at all levels, and in all contexts, in the organization. It applies as products and services are sold and as individuals serve customers, bill for services, and relate to others in the organization. An organization determines its ethics and values in part by the ethics and values of individuals who are recruited and hired, by the orientation of new employees to the organization, and, most importantly, by the decisions individuals see being made as they work in the organization.

This chapter describes the relationship between individual ethics and values and the organization's culture; identifies the connection between ethics and values and effective compliance programs; presents the two ethical frameworks that underlie much of American and Western thought; and shows the pervasive influence of ethics and values on individual decision making at all levels and in all contexts in the organization. This chapter also presents an approach to developing a written statement of ethics and values, the importance of developing a written statement, the leader's role and a set of questions to assist the leader in ethical decision making, and an approach to developing an effective ethics committee.

An organization that has a broadly understood and supported ethical approach to decision making will have an organizational competence in ethics and values.

ETHICS AND VALUES REFLECT THE CULTURE

The mission of the organization answers the question: Why are we here? What services and products do we provide? Who do we serve with our products and services? What do we want to accomplish with our organization (e.g., provide quality services and have a financially sound organization)? Ethics and values provide a framework for making all the decisions around competing objectives (e.g., what services to provide, at what price, how they are sold, and how we deal with customers, suppliers, and employees).

An organization's ethics reside in the sense that individuals have of what is acceptable and not acceptable behavior in the organization. The organization's ethics may be written down as a statement of ethical principles or as a "code of ethics," or they may be understood as the general "way we do things around here." It is important to write down the principles, as will be discussed later in this chapter, but it is most important that individual actions—at all levels in the organization—

reflect those ethics. Written statements reinforce individual assessments of what is right or wrong in a given situation, and they increase the likelihood that individual actions will reflect the organization's sense of what is ethical.

An organization with a strong culture will have a strong, consistent set of ethics and values. People in the organization have a sense of community. Individuals know and behave in ways that reflect respect for each other, pride and satisfaction in their work, and fair dealings with customers and suppliers. The challenge for leaders and managers is not only what should be done in a specific case, but how to "build an organization where more people do the best thing" (Griffith 1996).

The ethics that individuals live by reflect their values and what is important to them, whether they are leaders, managers, or employees (chapter 5, "Physician Relationships," discusses the values of physicians and the importance of those values in determining behavior). Individuals have an internal sense of the "right thing" to do, and organizations with a strong culture take care to hire employees with consistent values. In every organization, however, differences of opinion will exist on what should be done in specific cases. The issue is how to deal with these differences to ensure consistent, ethical behavior.

It is our values that we fall back on when faced with ethical decisions, and the development of a written statement of ethics should begin with an assessment of employee and organizational values. Individuals can identify ethical issues they find themselves faced with in the organization. They can also identify aspects of the organization's actions, as reflected in incentive and recognition systems and leadership decisions, that encourage or undermine ethical behavior (Perry 1993). Steps to developing an effective ethics program that builds on employee values will be presented later in this chapter.

Healthcare exists and functions as a trust relationship with patients and their families. It is more than a typical business relationship (e.g., "trust that we will do what we say"). It is trust that we will do what we can to care for them and their interests. Living up to and maintaining that trust should be a priority interest of all healthcare leaders. Instances where that trust has been lost have led to the passage of laws to protect the public interest. The challenge for healthcare organizations today is the same, whether the objective is to maintain the trust of patients or the objective is to simply meet the requirements of the office of the inspector general. Both objectives require an effective ethics program that builds on the values of individuals, explicitly identifies organizational values, and fosters ethical behavior at all levels in the organization.

ETHICS, VALUES, AND COMPLIANCE PROGRAMS

The development of federal sentencing guidelines in 1991 by the Federal Sentencing Commission established a set of incentives that encouraged organizations to create compliance programs. The commission outlined seven essential elements to be included in a compliance program (Worthley 1999):

1. Written standards and procedures
2. Designated high-level oversight
3. Due care in delegation of authority
4. Effective communication of standards
5. Monitoring and reporting systems
6. Disciplinary enforcement
7. Appropriate response after detection

Some organizations responded with a program developed by their corporate counsel with rulebooks of appropriate behavior designed to prevent, detect, and punish violators. Research has found that organizations with effective compliance programs go beyond the minimal requirements of compliance to make ethics a core part of the way they do business, as indicated in the following three excerpts.

- "In general, the enforcement approach assumes that the members of an organization cannot be trusted. It fails also to respect individuals, their autonomy and integrity, and their capacity to assume personal integrity for the actions they perform. Respecting these things has been identified as a major factor in an organization having a strong organizational culture ... used alone, enforcement fails to develop the motivational base for reliable compliance and is, ultimately, self defeating" (Brien 1996).

- "Overall ethical environment was the most consistent culture dimension to be associated with organizational commitment ... [in cases where the organization climate focused on employees and the community] employees were more likely to identify and feel a sense of shared values with organizations that supported and rewarded ethical conduct and that emphasized the good of employees, customers and the public ... a climate focused on self-interest not only appears to promote unethical conduct, it also has a negative influence on organizational commitment" (Trevino, Butterfield, and McCabe 1998).

- "Prompted by the prospect of leniency, many companies are rushing to implement compliance-based ethics programs. Designed by corporate legal counsel, the goal of these programs is to prevent, detect, and publish legal violations. But organizational ethics means more than avoiding illegal practice; and providing employees with a rule book will do little to address the problems underlying unlawful conduct ... An integrity-based approach to ethics management combines a concern for the law with an emphasis on managerial responsibility for ethical behavior. Though integrity strategies may vary in design and scope, all strive to define companies' guiding values, aspirations, and patterns of thought and conduct. When integrated into the day-to-day operations of an organization, such strategies can help prevent damaging ethical lapses while tapping into powerful human impulses for moral thought and action. Then an ethical framework becomes no longer a burdensome constraint within which companies must operate, but the governing ethos of an organization" (Paine 1994).

In his book *Organizational Ethics in the Compliance Context*, John Abbot Worthley (1999) presents findings from extensive research on organizational ethics and compliance. He concludes that, "Organizational ethics in healthcare has a lot to do with structurally and culturally developing behavior that respects and honors human dignity ... Organizational ethics is what organizations do to institutionalize and inculturate—in the routine of healthcare delivery—an awareness and behavioral appreciation of the dignity of all people involved with the organization."

AN ETHICAL FRAMEWORK

Acting ethically presupposes an ethical and values framework that provides guidance in making decisions. The golden rule—do unto others as you would have them do unto you—is one widely accepted and followed framework. Griffith (1996) notes that it dates back to the admonitions of Christ in Matthew 7:12 and Luke 6:31, and he cites several related statements of this framework. The one-sentence summary of the Torah attributed to Hillel is similar: "That which you would not welcome yourself, you must not do to your fellow man." The concept of *universalization* is a secular version of this framework—any action can be tested for fairness by reversing the positions of the parties involved or by considering the fairness when applied to different economic or social groups. Immanuel Kant's statement, "Act so as to treat humanity as an end and never only as a means," is the premise of Griffith's book, *The Moral Challenges of Health Care Management* (1996). Kant's statement is related to the basic idea of "Do unto others ...," but it highlights and answers the question of who the "others" are— the others are all of humanity. A second widely accepted framework for ethical decision making in American and Western thought is "The greatest good for the greatest number." This *utilitarian* view focuses on the end result. These two types of frameworks—"Do unto others ..." (universalization) and "The greatest good ..." (utilitarian)—govern much of the behavior of organizations (Griffith 1996).

A framework of belief that an individual can use to guide specific actions is also referred to as a theory of moral obligation. The idea of obligation is that a person with a framework of belief is compelled to act in a way outlined in that belief. Understanding the sources of theories of obligation is helpful in understanding the different views that individuals may have in a specific situation. Griffith (1996) notes that there are three sources of theories of obligation:

1. *Divine*: God told me so, it says in God's testament, or it is part of my religious beliefs.
2. *Personal:* I simply believe it is so.
3. *Utilitarian:* It promotes nonmoral goodness; the world will be a better place. (Note that *nonmoral* means not a question of right and wrong. It may be a question of "better or worse," but it is not of right or wrong.)

With the possible range of these sources, it is not surprising that people can and do have different views. Listening to the way individuals present their arguments will help to classify and understand their perspectives. Although beyond the scope of this book, Griffith presents a taxonomy, a system for classifying theories of moral obligation. Those interested in a more thorough description and understanding of the theories of moral obligation are referred to his book *The Moral Challenges of Health Care Management* (1996).

With the understanding of the two basic frameworks (universalization and utilitarian) that underlie much of American and Western thought, the elements included in statements of ethics can be better appreciated and understood. A group of 44 physicians, nurses, healthcare executives, ethicists, academic policy analysts, and religious leaders came together over a two-year period to consider ethical dilemmas in healthcare. The group concluded that healthcare providers are obligated to make decisions "within a basic ethical framework built on compassion and respect for human dignity, commitment to professional competence, spirit of service, honesty, confidentiality, good stewardship, and careful administration" (Dolan 1995). Paraphrased to apply more broadly: "a basic ethical framework built on compassion and respect for others, commitment to doing work competently with a spirit of service, honesty, confidentiality, and good stewardship of an individual's time and the resources assigned them." Which elements of this statement relate to "Do unto others?" or "The greatest good?" Which relate to a source that is divine, personal, or utilitarian?

Ethics and Values Are Shown at All Levels

Virtually everything that is done involves an element of ethics and values as it relates to others and the quality and value of the work. The following points provide some examples drawn from clinical care and administrative or support services. The third list identifies some ethical and value issues facing managed care organizations.

Clinical care

- Keeping patient records confidential
- Treating patients regardless of race, color, gender
- Giving emergency treatment to all individuals
- Complying with patients' advance directives
- Providing one standard of care for all patients
- Providing competent care for all patients
- Referring patients elsewhere, as necessary, to obtain the care they need
- Providing all appropriate and necessary care
- Providing the most appropriate care when providers profit from use of specific resources or when rules and regulations conflict with professional judgment
- Acting in the best interest of the patient when reporting requirements may be in conflict with patient confidentiality
- Using new or unproved technologies appropriately
- Documenting the services provided (basis for subsequent billing)

Administrative and support services

- Providing supportive environment for patients
- Creating teamwork with colleagues
- Providing timely and cost-effective support services
- Allocating limited capital resources
- Maintaining supplier relationships
- Building customer relationships
- Contracting of managed care

- Recruiting new employees
- Evaluating performance
- Discharging employees
- Downsizing
- Respecting all individuals
- Dealing with sexual harassment
- Advertising
- Billing for services

Managed care organizations

- Payment of appropriate treatment
- Timeliness of decision making
- Limits on decision making by nonphysicians
- Opportunities to appeal and affect decisions
- Exclusion of high-risk patients
- Patient confidentiality
- Percent of premium paid for medical care
- Percent of premium for administrative costs

The above examples are not meant to be a comprehensive list of the ethical issues faced by healthcare organizations. They do, however, show that ethical behavior is an issue that faces all employees in the organization, at all levels and in all areas.

ETHICS AND VALUES: TOUCHPOINTS FOR DECISION MAKING

The organization and its leader must rely on the ethical awareness of individuals in the organization as they make decisions and act on those decisions. What service is provided, how that service is coded, and how that bill is handled by the billing department as it deals with the insurers and patients—these details cannot be micromanaged in any productive way. Griffith (1996) concludes that the management style should be participative management: workers should be "empowered to the greatest extent possible," and management should establish an environment "where difficult issues can be discussed." To be effective at all levels and in all areas, ethical decision making must be based on the organization's values and embodied in the culture—it must be "the way we do things around here." Coupled with organization policies that reflect standard, good business practices—obtaining competitive bids, looking for and evaluating alternative courses of action, and promoting on demonstrated competence and ethical decision making— ethical principles are "the way we do things around here." Effective supporting policies are important. In the words of Griffith (1996), "Good policies promote strong wills."

Also to be considered are the major decisions made by the organization's top leadership. It might seem that while the organization's understanding of its ethics and values is sufficient for the decision making of others in the organization, top management and the organization's governance should have the power to decide issues on a case-by-case basis. The power is there, but two problems exist with this position. The first is that the most telling demonstration of organizational ethics is when the organization sees how top management and governance act. The second problem is that there may be little time for deliberation. Top management is faced with the same problem faced by those lower in the organization: the decision needs to be made *now*. The questions are: What is acceptable behavior? What is important?

CEO decisions can be highly visible with severe time limits, as illustrated in the classic decision of the then-CEO of Johnson & Johnson, James Burke. Based on evidence that tampering with some Tylenol packages had led to a death, Burke recalled all Tylenol packages from store shelves around the country. Although product recalls are now common, Johnson & Johnson's was the first, it was voluntary, it was complete, and it was immediate. Burke explained that Johnson & Johnson was a trusted family name and would do nothing to jeopardize that trust. This decision, while widely credited to Burke, was also consistent with, and dependent on, a deeply ingrained set of organizational values and guiding principles that made clear to everyone in the company why it was the right course of action (Paine 1994).

WRITTEN STATEMENTS OF ETHICS AND VALUES

Individuals have their own perceptions of what is acceptable behavior and what is important to them, and as they join the organization, they bring those perceptions with them. Written statements inform individuals of the organization's ethics and values, and they provide an opportunity for new individuals to compare their perceptions with the organization's ethics and values.

An "ethics audit"—an audit of the present state of ethical behavior in the organization—is a good place to start (Hofmann 1995).

1. Collect and analyze key documents, including the organization's mission, vision, and values statements. Also review policies and procedures-related issues such as uncompensated care, confidentiality, conflicts of interest, and sexual harassment.
2. Survey representative board members, management staff, physicians, employees, volunteers, and community residents and organizations. The survey is an opportunity to reinforce the organization's commitment to ethical behavior by highlighting what the organization considers its values and the significant ways that it demonstrates ethical behavior. The survey will provide feedback on the assessment of those surveyed: do the organization's actions reflect its stated values and intended ethical behavior? Where are the opportunities to do better? Are there major gaps, areas that the organization should be focusing on but apparently is not? The survey results will identify the values of employees (and others within the organization) as well as what they consider ethical behavior.
3. Review the results and identify opportunities for group discussions to come to a common understanding of what the organization's values and demonstrations of ethical behavior should be and as a basis for developing a code of ethics that engages individuals in the organization and builds on their values.

Perry (1993) provides some concise guidance for developing and communicating a code of ethics. The code should:

- Relate to management systems and practices
- Affirm a basic set of organization values, principles, or commitments
- Establish ground rules in areas where they are needed
- Provide illustrations and guidelines in some of the "gray" areas
- Explain how employees can obtain further advice and counsel without fear of retribution

New employees do bring their experience and perspectives to the organization, and new employee orientation is the time for a significant discussion of the organization's code of ethics. Ethics-related case studies provide valuable examples for the new employees to discuss. The discussion will likely turn to situations from the new employees' prior experiences, which offers an excellent opportunity to discuss how to handle such situations in their new organization's culture.

LEADER'S ROLE

Healthcare leaders must lead by example, and to do so they must set their own standards for proper conduct. They must know how far they are willing to stretch rules, for themselves and for others; what to do if and when organizational goals compromise their personal standards, and vice versa; and when to confront unethical personal and professional behavior in staff members. Executives must, for example, be careful to avoid preferential treatment of staff. In appreciation of services well-performed, some executives reward immediate subordinates very liberally, without realizing that other staff who are performing equally well in other parts of the organization might feel slighted. CEOS who are willing to undermine the equitable compensation of individuals throughout the organization have not fully accepted their overriding responsibility to act fairly. Compromising this responsibility might reflect, or be viewed by others, as an urge to purchase personal loyalty by granting special privileges. How leaders act shows the importance they place on organizational ethics. Reference to the organization's ethics, as a basis for decision making, builds credibility and support for ethical behavior in the organization. Acting without regard to such ethics undermines both the organization's and a leader's credibility.

If they have not examined their own expectations and standards on a personal level, healthcare executives will not be prepared for challenges with staff members. As the guardians of ethical conduct, healthcare leaders face daily decisions about how and when to address individuals' behavior and what measures to take. Consider, for example, the following scenarios.

1. A prominent member of your medical staff sends an insulting memo to one of your hospital managers. This physician is responsible for admitting many patients to your hospital each year. What should you do?
2. An administrative assistant who is responsible for physician recruitment quietly sets himself up in a real estate business. When showing prospective physician candidates around town, he refers them to specific realtors and receives part of the commission on sales in return. Why is this wrong?
3. A surgeon with a temper throws instruments in the operating room. The chief of surgery is unwilling to confront the situation. What do you do?
4. A board member who heads a large construction firm takes you aside quietly and tells you that he has worked very hard for years on behalf of the hospital and hopes that this will help you make the correct decision in selecting the contractor for the next hospital job. How do you deal with this?
5. You find that one of your administrators has pushed through a much larger salary increase for her secretary than the levels established through usual market surveys and that this has created an inequity for others in the same category. How do you resolve this?
6. You are the CEO in a major teaching hospital. You hear a rumor that there are so many "no codes" that the residents are fretting because they are not getting sufficient experience in resuscitating patients. You then receive a letter from a patient's family that indicates that in spite of their clearly documented wish that their

father not be resuscitated, the medical staff did resuscitate him and he was left to linger painfully for another 24 hours. Is this an ethical issue or just a matter of circumstance? What do you do about it?

A leader's inclination to look the other way on little things, even more than on larger organizational issues, contributes to declining staff confidence in ethics and values. A CEO who is unwilling to really confront poor behavior in others is putting both the leadership position and the internal structure of the organization at tremendous risk. In addition, executives who set one ethical standard for the organization and another for themselves will ultimately face the erosion of self-respect and, potentially, the loss of the privilege of leadership. When dealing with human life, these ethical considerations become increasingly complex, and the implications of ethical decision making are far reaching. It is imperative that healthcare leaders examine and define for themselves where they stand on ethical issues.

ETHICAL DECISION MAKING

When resolving ethical questions, you may not always know whether the decision you are making is the right one. There may come a point at which you cannot afford to deliberate any further, and you must make a decision and hope you can live with it. The questions listed below were designed by Laura Nash (1989) to assist with ethical decision making.

1. Have you defined the problem accurately?
2. How would you define the problem if you stood on the other side of the fence?
3. How did this situation occur in the first place?
4. To whom and to what do you give your loyalty as a person and as a member of the corporation?
5. What is your intention in making this decision?
6. How does this intention compare with the probable results?
7. Whom could your decision or action injure?

8. Can you discuss the decision with the affected parties before making the decision?
9. Are you confident that your decision will be as valid over a long period of time as it seems now?
10. Could you discuss without qualm your decision or action to your boss, your CEO, the board of directors, your family, and society as a whole?
11. What is the symbolic potential of your action if understood? If misunderstood?
12. Under what conditions would you allow exceptions to your stand?

Your responses may help you to clarify your reasons for making the decision you made. If you feel comfortable with your answers, you have probably made the best decision you can under the circumstances.

ETHICS OFFICER

The ethics officer is the full- or part-time individual whom the organization's leadership, governance, and staff look to for a continuing focus on the organization's ethical performance. This individual is responsible for managing internal reporting systems, assessing ethics risk areas, developing and distributing ethics policies and publications, investigating alleged violations, and designing training programs (Petry 1998). As noted earlier in this chapter, there are many commonalties with an effective ethics program and an effective compliance program. If the organization has two separate programs, the leadership should be combined.

ETHICS COMMITTEE

The role of the ethics committee has changed from its historic role of focusing on acute care, specifically end-of-life issues. Although it continues to be an independent, highly regarded committee that provides consultative advice on ethical issues, the issues it faces today include managed care and organizational ethical issues. The following points are drawn from William Nelson's (2000) article "Evaluating Your Ethics Committee."

Purpose and Functions

With the broadening of ethics committee responsibilities, a useful question to ask committee members is: "What is the purpose of the committee?" Once the purpose is agreed on, the committee members can address how the committee will perform its functions, including policy review, education, evaluation, and clinical/organizational ethics consultations.

Composition and Competencies of Members

Committee membership should be broad and balanced, reflecting both professional and community interests. Community representation should include members of any significant religious or ethnic group. To ensure active, interested committee members, most should be volunteers.

The American Society for Bioethics and Humanities (ASBH) report "Core Competencies for Health Care Ethics Consultation" (quoted in Nelson 2000) identifies needed competencies in three major areas:

- *Ethical assessment skills* enable individuals to identify the values underlying ethical conflicts. These skills include the ability to distinguish the ethical dimensions of a situation from other overlapping dimensions such as legal or medical; to access, critically evaluate, and use relevant knowledge; to identify and justify various morally acceptable options and their consequences; and to evaluate evidence and arguments for and against different solutions.
- *Process skills* focus on efforts to resolve uncertainty related to values that arises in healthcare settings. These skills include the ability to facilitate meetings, identify key decision makers, create an atmosphere of trust, negotiate between competing moral views, and engage in creative problem solving.

- *Interpersonal skills* include the ability to listen effectively, educate concerned parties about the ethical dimensions of their dilemma, and represent the views of concerned parties to others.

In addition to these general skills, the ASBH identified nine core knowledge areas that are required for competent ethical consultation (Nelson 2000).

- Moral reasoning and ethical theory
- Common bioethical issues and concepts
- Healthcare systems, including knowledge of managed care and governmental systems
- Clinical context
- Culture of the healthcare organization, including its mission statement and structure
- Policies of the healthcare organization
- Beliefs and perspectives of the local patient and staff population
- Relevant codes of ethics and professional conduct and guidelines of accrediting organizations
- Relevant health law

Leadership

The chairperson should be highly respected in the organization and open to input and feedback from committee members and staff. The leader should see that duties on the committee are fairly distributed and that all committee members contribute. There should also be a mechanism that ensures the chairperson does not become a "fixture." Time limits are an effective, nonconfrontational way of seeing periodic change in the position.

Organizational Support and Respect

It is crucial that the organization create a climate for the committee to carry out its activities with integrity. That integrity is required for an honest dialog to take place between the administration and the committee to enhance the overall ethical nature of the organization.

Nelson (2000) concludes: "Ethics committees that are well informed, representative, and motivated can be a healthcare organization's greatest resource for ethical guidance and support."

CONCLUSION

Ethics and values are internal to each individual. Individuals do have a common understanding of what is right, and organizations with a strong culture take care to hire individuals with similar values. Whether an organization wants to build a strong ethical culture as an effective way of relating to their customers, employees, and suppliers—or if they are concerned primarily about having an effective compliance program—the challenge is the same: to develop ethical guidelines that engage the interest and support of individual employees, and to have leaders that embody and reflect those guidelines in their actions. An organization that has a broadly understood and supported ethical approach to decision making will have an organizational competence in ethics and values.

DISCUSSION

1. How should an organization go about developing a code of ethics?
2. How are a code of ethics and the organization's culture similar? What is likely to happen if they are not?
3. Why is it important to have written statements of ethics and values?
4. Identify two common frameworks for ethical decision making. In what ways are these two frameworks complementary?
5. In what ways are an effective compliance program like an effective ethics program?
6. Outline the steps you would take to develop a code of ethics for your organization.

NOTE

The *American College of Healthcare Executives Ethics Self-Assessment* is a 53-question self-assessment that covers the areas of leadership and relationships. Relationships with the community, patients and their families, the board, colleagues and staff, clinicians, and buyers, payers and vendors are each separately addressed. *The Ethics Self-Assessment* is available in the March/April 2001 issue of *Healthcare Executive;* online at ache.org; and through ACHE FAX by calling (312) 424-9190 (ACHE FAX No. 7023).

REFERENCES

Brien, A. 1996. "Regulating Virtue: Formulating, Engendering and Enforcing Corporate Ethics Codes." *Business and Professional Ethics Journal* 15 (1): 21–52.

Dolan, T. C. 1995. "Ethics and the Business of Healthcare." *Healthcare Executive* 10 (5): 47.

Griffith, J. R. 1996. *The Moral Challenges of Health Care Management.* Chicago: Health Administration Press.

Hofmann, P. B. 1995. "Performing an Ethics Audit." *Healthcare Executive* 10 (6): 47.

Nash, L. 1989. "Ethics Without a Sermon: Ethics and Practice." In *Managing the Moral Corporation.* Boston: Harvard Business Review.

Nelson, W. A. 2000. "Evaluating Your Ethics Committee." *Healthcare Executive* 15 (1): 48–49.

Paine, L. S. 1994. "Managing for Organizational Integrity." *Harvard Business Review* 72 (2): 106–17.

Perry, D. L. 1993. "Keys to Creating an Effective Ethics Program." *Healthcare Executive* 8 (2): 26.

Petry, E. 1998. "Appointing an Ethics Officer." *Healthcare Executive* 13 (6): 35.

Trevino, L. K., K. D. Butterfield, and D. L. McCabe. 1998. "The Ethical Context in Organizations: Influences on Employee Attitudes and Behaviors." *Business Ethics Quarterly* 8 (3): 447–76.

Worthley, J. A. 1999. *Organizational Ethics in the Compliance Context.* Chicago: Health Administration Press.

CHAPTER 7

Quality and Value Enhancement

CASE IN POINT: As an executive responsible for introducing new programs, Scott Wright has been assigned the task of instituting a more vigorous program of clinical quality measurement and enhancement. His organization is doing well according to usual measurements of quality, but the board and the medical staff leadership are aware of the fact that this will not be sufficient in the years ahead.

Scott has been asked to prepare a proposal, including funding requirements, for initiating such a program. While the medical staff leadership is supportive of such an initiative, questions exist as to whether such a program would be supported by the medical staff—who tend to view the world of value and quality for the patient as medical prerogatives—as a whole.

QUESTION: How should Scott proceed to establish an enhanced program of clinical measurement? Who would be on the planning team?

INTRODUCTION

Value is an elusive term and managing value raises the specter of chaos. Value is defined as a working equation involving appropriateness of care, quality of outcomes and service, and cost. One hypothesis is that ultimately purchasers and providers will recognize that the value of healthcare services provided is critical because value, properly managed, directly addresses the volatile issue of containing healthcare costs. But to achieve success in managing value, providers must initiate new strategies and transform organizational and clinical priorities and practices. As the contest between society's infinite demand for healthcare services and the finite resources intensifies, the need to truly subscribe to the management of value will become ever more important. Those providing care will learn to appreciate that long-term success will depend on much more than mere cost cutting. This chapter addresses these critical issues.

BEGINNING THE JOURNEY

The overriding characteristic of the successfully transforming organization becomes evident when the organization makes a conscious decision to adopt a long-range strategy for creating and managing the value of the services it renders. As organizations embark on such a journey, conventional management and clinical practices are tested and, ultimately, dramatically changed. Such transformed organizations will achieve a higher level of maturity and a patient-centered consciousness that bodes well for their future.

But the journey is perilous and there are many hazards along the trail. The absence of consensus about healthcare delivery is a severe handicap. The decade ahead may well be recorded as the decade of further confusion. Policy strategists may know where the journey should end, but not the means of getting there. Purchasers of care, when confronted with the immense complexities of the structures, tend to opt for shorter-range solutions that are affordable and understandable but guarantee incremental approaches. Providers, harassed from all sides, are torn by the clash of traditional cultures within medicine and the new need to respond to market forces over which they have no control. Some become paralyzed while others make grand and disastrous sweeps into new ventures.

Dr. William Kissick (1994) referred to the contest between infinite needs and finite resources. With such high expectations of healthcare, the demand is infinite in scope. The resources, however, are finite and this latter reality is becoming increasingly evident to all.

THE CONFLICT BETWEEN SHORT-TERM AND LONG-TERM SOLUTIONS

Within the organization intent on transformation, the battle between working for the short term and preparing for the future is raging. Leaders may appreciate that continuing excessive consumption of medical resources places the institution at a disadvantage. They are torn because the short-term accumulation of financial capital through maintaining the status quo helps fund the effort to build that larger system needed to effectively compete for a larger market share. Certainly, advocating a reduction in the use of ancillary services—by educating physicians and other healthcare professionals that some tests need not be done (appropriateness of care), thereby reducing revenue—seems to fly in the face of conventional logic.

Imagine for a minute an end-of-the-budget-year conversation between the CEO and the chief radiologist in which the radiologist reports that the ordering of diagnostic films has dropped 15 percent because of changes in the practice patterns of the medical staff. In a setting of managed care contracting and risk, such a reduction might be praised, as it improved the bottom line because fewer resources were consumed. But if the organization depended on the revenue from ancillary services to cross-subsidize the development of a badly needed primary care network, would congratulations be in order? And in that capitated managed care organization, would the CEO be pleased to learn that a new diabetes-screening program had increased the costs of preventive care by 15 percent? We would hope so, but are we certain? Noteworthy in this conversation is the lack of any reference to value. This only hints at the magnitude of the change process underway.

The tradeoff in these oversimplified examples relates to the ability of the organization to balance short-range gains against long-range needs. The test of the transforming organization is whether it (1) recognizes the need for change; (2) has the courage and intent to promote change; and (3) harbors the staying power to make such change a part of a new operating culture.

A FLAWED HYPOTHESIS

Conventional wisdom would suggest that one of the following conditions might dominate the healthcare field within five years:

- The healthcare marketplace will attain optimal price efficiencies and purchasers of care will make purchase decisions based on clearly demonstrated value. The playing field will be level *except* for value ("Doing good will win out").
- The healthcare marketplace will depreciate and discount value as an essential element in purchasing healthcare. It will be the lowest price that counts because the customer will not be able to differentiate value ("We know what's best for them").
- Society will be unable to afford quality care because of the disintegration of the community infrastructure. Other societal issues will be more important and, of necessity, healthcare of an acceptable quality will be the affordable commodity of choice (The "doomsday" approach).

All three concepts are flawed because all are single-dimension concepts. It is not price/cost versus quality or service perceptions versus appropriateness of care. Nor is it the customer perception alone that matters. All of the issues are interdependent. To understand value requires a thorough understanding of these interrelationships.

HEALTHCARE REFORM

Although there has been criticism of former President Clinton's approach to healthcare reform, one positive outcome was to remind us of reform's complexities. The outcome also served to suggest that, at least for the time being, an incremental approach to change was the best way because it allows time for experimentation. Multiple approaches to reform are under study. In 1992, Paul Starr advocated a combined approach where global budgeting and managed competition might serve as the answer. Global budgeting would place limitations on the rate of increase in expenditures for healthcare and would stimulate those tough discussions about rationing of technology and services. Managed competition would fine tune the process by using the principles of price and quality competition to drive a consolidation of a cottage industry into a system of major players, each with a critical mass sufficient to meet community and citizen needs.

Global budgeting might pick up some of the working features of the Canadian health system, while managed competition played on the virtues of freedom of some choice. The Canadian health system also might bring into play the marketplace forces as a means to control the cost of care and to determine resource consumption. Other global approaches are equally worthy of study.

FOCUSING ON THE CHANGE PROCESS

An interesting question is whether the healthcare delivery system has the capability to change when faced with the need for massive reform. Predicting an organizational response to a change of this magnitude would appear to be difficult were it not for the fact that most organizations in almost any field have clearly demonstrated capacity to change. The problem perhaps unique to healthcare is that the services provided are so comprehensive and compelling that healthcare almost defies definition and thus cannot be treated as a commodity or single service. The answer, in part, lies in the definition and understanding of the pursuit of *value* as a main driver applicable to both economic and societal issues.

It is easy to reflect on the virtues of promoting value in delivering care but it is also apparent that to date it is the stick rather than the carrot that drives the delivery engine. The stick represents the fear of losing something—a segment of the market or a diminishing of clinical autonomy, for example. The carrot—being rewarded for doing right for the customer and maintaining a focus on quality and service—is there, but less tangible and visible in the rhetoric of the healthcare arena. The basic question is whether the deliverers of healthcare can pull their respective acts together rapidly enough to exert real leadership, or whether the prevailing attitudes of changing only as a protective measure versus catastrophe will prevail.

So is there room for value? Value (to the customer) is important to other industries. Based on what we should be learning as healthcare professionals, we need to get ahead of the learning curve. This would require us to (1) understand our customers; (2) deliver services that meet their needs; and (3) adjust, restructure, or otherwise alter our attitudes and competencies to be able to continuously improve our ability to deliver.

Unfortunately, people seem to respond better to threats than to soft approaches. The wave of mergers and consolidations taking the nation by storm are not necessarily actions focused on delivering a better product or service. Rather, it is a response to the perception that we must be larger or we will not be able to compete.

MANAGING VALUE

What does this all have to do with managing value? The roots of change in the delivery of healthcare lie in the understanding of the need for change; understanding the reasons to change; and the courage for leaders to give the message that, regardless of the end result of any national referendum, changes must be made for the right reasons. The incentives for change are growing but the disincentives are still well-entrenched.

Value Equation

To manage for value improvement, an early step must be to define *value*. We will use the concept of the *value equation* as the conceptual definition. The basic point is to relate, in a qualitative or, at best, a semi-quantitative way, the appropriateness of the intervention (doing the right things), the quality of the outcomes and service achieved, and the utilization of resources (defined by either charges and/or costs). Thus, the equation gives us a conceptual framework that emphasizes that value cannot be discussed without considering both the outcomes and the costs. The quality of appropriateness, outcomes, and service can be addressed independently of the costs—that is, defined and measured without consideration of costs. But value cannot. It is this combination of quality (defined by measured specifications) and costs that makes the concept of value different from the concept of quality per se.

The following value equation does not provide a standardized numerical definition of the value achieved. It is, however, possible to measure or estimate, with variable difficulty and accuracy, some or all of the items in the equation and make a rational judgment as to whether certain changes have increased or decreased the resultant value provided. It is useful in providing a conceptual framework for value improvement management, and to remind us that tradeoffs often exist between the outputs we achieve and the inputs used. The appropriateness component is designated as having a multiplier, rather than additive, effect on the rest of the equation (because if the intervention was inappropriate, the value achieved was nil).

$$\text{VALUE} = \text{Appropriateness} \times \frac{\text{Quality of Outcomes} + \text{Service}}{\text{Costs}}$$

Defining Quality

Given the tremendous emphasis on cost reduction in healthcare delivery, organizations tend to constantly cut costs in an effort to become more competitive. Although there is ample waste in healthcare and, thus, great opportunities for cost reduction, it must be remembered that cost reduction per se will only increase value if the appropriateness and quality of outcomes/service are not adversely affected. Thus, downsizing the staff of a hospital ward by laying off nurses is not necessarily value enhancement, unless one determines that the quality of care is not reduced. Or if it is reduced, is the degree of reduction trivial compared to the cost savings? This is where difficult tradeoffs must be addressed, and subjective personal or organizational values may be of vital importance.

This raises the issue of a definition of *quality* (as in quality of outcomes/service). Suffice it to say that if quality is to be a useful concept in healthcare delivery, it must be defined by measurement. Quality in healthcare is more complicated than the oft-quoted quality management definition of "meeting or exceeding the expectations of the customer." Certainly the service component can and should be defined by the customer. Such characteristics as bedside manner, compassion, empathy, communication skills, kindness, availability, and the "user-friendliness" of the system are best defined by the customer. But in the clinical content area, a quality definition is more complicated. Our definition is the degree to which we meet professionally established and explicitly defined measurable specifications, based on the best evidence and judgment available, and with appropriate consideration of the patient's needs, desires, goals, and values. Any definition of quality is somewhat subjective.

One personal definition of what constitutes quality—what level of measured performance we call quality—may differ from another. Having the world agree upon that level is not important. Rather, getting a given work unit (whether three people or a whole organization) to agree upon it, and then using that definition to improve the degree of quality achieved, is important.

Variable Outcomes

Depending upon the topic, and the interest, one might measure a variety of different outcomes or service indicators in the numerator of the value equation. These might include outcomes defined by selected clinical/physiologic parameters, patient satisfaction, functional status (health-related quality of life), or service quality performance (e.g., waiting times). One of the challenges of the near future is to prioritize different types of outcomes. The outcomes management (or outcomes research) movement that was given impetus by Paul Ellwood's

"Shattuck Lecture" (1988) has shifted the emphasis of outcomes measurement to more patient-centered elements. Given the confluence of care variation and the cost crisis, we are now in the midst of a reassessment of our ultimate goals and motivations in healthcare. What should be the most important outcome of cardiac bypass surgery: a 30-day mortality rate of less than 1 percent or a gain score of 30 points in health-related quality of life at six months? Patient satisfaction, with both clinical and service outcomes and health-related quality of life and functional outcomes, has gained new attention and application.

Because outcomes may be influenced by many factors, not all under the control of the traditional healthcare system, and certainly not of clinicians alone, we must be careful to define and measure those for which there is a definable accountability. Another concern is that outcome measurement will be used, not for purposes of continuous process improvement, but rather for marketing. Because of difficulties such as uniform standardization and definition of terms, case-mix severity of illness adjustments, and accuracy of coding, the greatest use of the value equation is not in comparing ourselves to others, but rather in promoting our own continuous improvement.

Appropriateness of Care

The most difficult piece of the value equation to measure is appropriateness of care. *Appropriateness* refers to whether a specific intervention should have been performed. Although the issue of appropriateness often provokes defensiveness—and there are very real issues related to what the standard should be—questions about the appropriateness of care arise from 15 to 50 percent of the time (Chassin et al. 1987; Asch 1995; Berwick 1994).

Any definition of value that omits some attention to appropriateness of care would be incomplete. Some examples of how to assess this element include measuring:

- The rate of compliance with *agreed-upon indications* for an intervention

- The relative incidence of one treatment versus another alternative (e.g., C-section versus vaginal delivery; lumpectomy versus mastectomy, etc.)
- The rates of abnormality (the pickup) for certain procedures (e.g., the rate of normal appendices in primary appendectomy, the rate of significant findings for surveillance colonoscopy, the positive yield in patients referred for biopsy of nonpalpable lesions detected by screening mammography, etc.)
- The rate of readmission to an acute-care hospital within a certain timeframe after discharge (looking for inappropriate early discharges)

USING TQM/CQI

Given all the buzzwords and acronyms, there is sometimes confusion about how value improvement relates to quality improvement, how that relates to outcomes research, or how that relates to reengineering or guidelines. Figure 7.1 offers an overview of most of these movements. They are all overlapping and interrelated. The main point, however, is that lasting improvements, new and better designs, better outcomes, elimination of waste, or better meeting customer needs are all goals related to improving the value of the care rendered. The method we must use is that of modern quality management. It gives us the philosophy, approach, tools, and techniques that are the means to our end of value improvement.

The philosophy and approach to management—generally known as quality management or total quality management (TQM) or continuous quality improvement (CQI)—refers to many elements. The most important of these elements is customer orientation, which has been proven time and again. The other element of a successful TQM/CQI initiative is to apply the scientific method, not only to the diagnosis and treatment of the various conditions and needs of patients, but also to the healthcare system itself. Application of the scientific method requires healthcare providers to be data driven and to rely on the collection and proper interpretation of measured outputs to better

Figure 7.1. Identifying Value Pathways

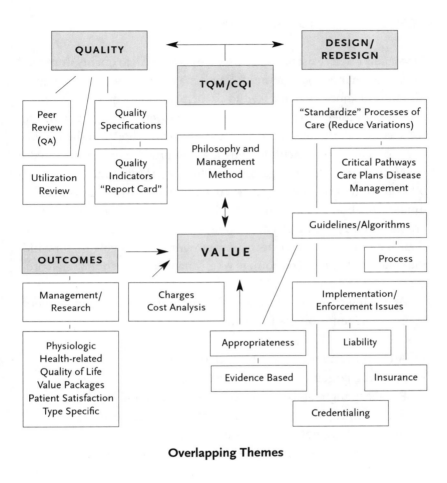

Overlapping Themes

understand our processes and outcomes of care. This in turn means using statistics and having a proper understanding of variation. Other aspects of TQM/CQI include the use of cross-functional teams, when appropriate; proper empowerment of workers; an emphasis on process and system analysis; and an appreciation of customer-supplier relationships.

ACHIEVING PHYSICIAN BUY-IN

Physicians often resist parts of this buy-in approach to quality improvement and change management. Some may even experience a degree of "cultural shock" when asked to participate as co-equals on a cross-functional project team. Few physicians, however, disagree with the basic concept and the emphasis on scientific method and the importance of data. It is difficult to deny that the practice of modern medicine has become a team game; therefore, working with a variety of other team members in a constructive manner, learning how to coordinate, collaborate, and integrate with each other more effectively, is crucial to everyone involved. Although physicians often bristle when their patients are called external customers, they quickly understand the concept of internal customers when analyzing cross-functional processes.

Achieving successful physician buy-in of the quality management approach depends on the following:

- Attracting and hiring key physician leaders
- Avoiding jargon as much as possible
- Emphasizing real data analyzed scientifically and involving the doctors in exploring variations in practice (measuring for improvement, not for inspection or censure)
- Emphasizing the service levels and outcomes achieved for patients

Berwick (1991) has emphasized building on the underlying similarity between clinical practice to improve the health of individuals and between quality management to improve the processes of work. Once some real, measurable improvements have been accomplished—especially if they are relevant to the goals of the organization—progress will quicken. As always, finding or making time for working on improvement is one of the major challenges.

THE VIRTUE OF ANXIETY

The incentives for change are most often effectively operational if the proper level of anxiety is in place. Edgar Schien's (1993) comments about *disconfirmation* as it relates to the learning organization are very useful. Organizations must perceive that their way of doing things is no longer working and create motivation to change. They must understand that if they do not learn to change, they may have to deal with negative or threatening consequences. This creates anxiety. It is only when this sufficient level of anxiety occurs that lasting change can take place.

Organizational structures are being radically modified because of anxiety about competing against high-cost structures. Without this anxiety, it is likely that change would have been minimal. Physician practice patterns based on fee for service and an ability to cost shift did not provide adequate incentives for real practice changes. In spite of the pioneering studies showing marked variations in resource utilization and practice patterns, change did not really begin to take place until these cost-related anxieties surfaced. Once it became clear that great uncertainty existed as to the most optimal and cost-effective way to do things in medical care—that there was no scientifically proven right way to deal with the myriad of common medical problems—it was inevitable that those picking up the tab would ask what value they were getting for their money. If those organizations that were most expensive could not demonstrate enhanced outcomes, patients would look elsewhere.

This anxiety and the resultant changes are important because they provide a means to an end. Significant organized change in the healthcare system will only take place when the environmental conditions are such that failure to change will result in very bad things happening. This should not be interpreted as diminishing the actions and technical excellence achieved by physician scientists at both the bedside and in the laboratory. Nor should this be interpreted as impugning the notable goals of so many to meet societal needs. The healthcare industry has assumed many burdens of society, yet its course has been wavering in the face of the need to adapt to competition.

Some interesting events have occurred. Some years ago, in Seattle, the Blue Shield organization announced that it was going to provide a list of its preferred providers. The dataset was available to demonstrate profiles of services rendered by those providers (they were efficient providers as defined by the magnitude of their charges). If a provider was not on the preferred list, the implication was that the provider was inefficient. That an insurance carrier might possibly use claim information as an indicator of efficiency created a profound effect on the professional community. Physicians began to wonder about the dataset. They were taking care of sicker patients—were the insurers aware of this? Did they even care? If the insurance carrier possessed data that the providers did not (because he/she/the group possessed only their own data), how were they to know how and what to change?

Networking primary care physicians suddenly became the game. If the world was moving toward capitation, primary care physicians were critical to survival. (The fact that physicians in all specialties, because of a general oversupply of physicians, were at risk from impending changes in the system was not considered as important.) It created a rush in which even those organizations that had prided themselves on their quality of care as evidenced by the credentials of their medical staffs started playing the numbers games. In this rush to acquire practices through the growing variety of legal entities, little consideration was given to the quality and past performance of those acquired.

Despite self-interest, most providers would agree that the system is not producing as well as it should. It is difficult to feel good about the improvement in the survival rate for patients undergoing heart and liver transplants if these marvelous accomplishments are viewed in the broader context of our difficulties in reducing infant mortality rates or improving access to healthcare for the underserved. We accommodate to these differences in outcomes because we are unwilling to assume responsibilities for both ends of the spectrum.

THE DILEMMA OF MANAGING VALUE

To manage value and promote the virtues of change, the old system must experience even more turmoil. Old cultural habits will have to be tested and even put away. New expectations and competencies will need to be carefully nourished. The leader's role is to forcefully convey the message that regardless of any future national referendum, change must be initiated or the survival of the organization is in jeopardy. This will require courage because it challenges the status quo. The new cornerstone of leadership, in fact, is courage: assumption of leadership roles in healthcare these days is not a preferred occupation for the faint of heart.

Success in developing and maintaining value depends on the:

- *Commitment* of leaders to focus on doing what is truly best for those served, even if this means absorbing short-term reductions of revenue
- *Willingness* of the organization to allocate resources to achieve that change
- *Recognition* that the process involves true teaming by physicians, administrators, and trustees to produce fundamental change
- *Acceptance* that such change will affect organizational culture

Much is at stake. There will be no quick fixes. Successful restructuring of health services delivery will depend on the organization's ability to understand all aspects of managing value. Structures will move from static organizational units to fully integrated refocused services. Value management will ultimately be graded and evaluated by the community and patients served, suggesting highly visible benchmarks by which organizations are measured.

The magnitude of changes ahead will make the current environmental concerns pale by comparison, because understanding, accepting, and implementing broad-based concepts of value conflict with the history, precedents, and politics of medical care delivery.

WHY QUALITY/VALUE INITIATIVES FAIL

Most quality initiatives fail or stagnate. Why might this happen, especially in healthcare? One reason is the lack of true commitment and constancy of purpose. Many leaders still do not understand the difference between endorsement (i.e., cheerleading) and being actively involved and leading by example (i.e., "walking the talk"). Another reason is the lack of resource support. It takes education, training, and time to work on value improvement. It also takes information and measurement systems, and increasing application of statistics. Look at an organization's budget. How much support is given to training and education to support improvement activities? Are they trying to develop measurement systems but cannot afford a statistician? What about job expectations? How explicit are they? How is feedback given? How do members at all levels understand their expected contribution to value improvement? Do leaders ask for periodic, regular progress reports on value improvement from all levels of the organization? If not, why?

Yet another reason quality initiatives fail is because they are not seen as relevant to the organization's strategic goals. If the quality/value improvement effort is not viewed as crucial and directly related to the bottom line, it will not be sustained, especially in this day of price-based competition. Too often organizations focus excessively on internal processes, indicators of involvement, the number of projects, or the training hours provided, but do not focus on the effect of those activities on desirable business results. When the primary focus of quality reporting is measuring participation in activities, it sends a confusing message to everyone that quality/value improvement is an activity separate from the "real" work of the group (of course it is difficult to document the business rewards of higher value). How many health-care organizations, when faced with another short-term, bottom-line crisis, respond with rededicated efforts at improving the value of their delivery system? Not many. Although providing higher value saves costs—costs and quality are usually directly and inversely related—it is rarely relied upon as a response to short-term financial crises. Once it is proven beyond anyone's doubt that higher quality/value is a good business strategy, not just an ideal that might appeal to some purchasers down the road, everyone will be working harder to make it a goal.

Another potential source of failure is the lack of adequate customer-needs assessment. Some organizations improve their capacities to provide services that are no longer very relevant to their customers' desires. This preoccupation with internal processes, which underemphasizes external customer needs, has been referred to as the inside-out (rather than outside-in) approach to quality management. Great products and services are great only if customers want them.

Involving Front-line Workers

Another common failure in healthcare is not effectively involving perhaps the most important customers of all—the front-line workers (referred to as those who have "blood on their shoes"). The receptionists, office assistants, nurses, technicians, orderlies, secretaries, housekeepers, maintenance workers, and, most important of all, the front-line physicians and allied health professionals must be involved and engaged in the value improvement process, or little will happen. A trickle-down approach—the hope that top leadership, then middle management, and then supervisors will be trained and enlisted into the value improvement strategy, and this will finally involve everyone—often fails. The human element is what ultimately determines success or failure of the whole effort. As one prominent quality guru and author put it, "You get things done through individuals and small groups of individuals. In structuring the organization it's important to start from the point of view of the human spirit, and from the bottom up. That's where the real work gets done—or undone" (Creech 1994). Empowerment is part of the quality management paradigm, but is often ignored or misunderstood. In its best sense, it represents an energizing feeling that comes with greater knowledge, greater skill, and greater control, which makes you feel as if you are in charge of your own work. Your job belongs to you. You have pride in what you do.

As Alfie Kohn argues convincingly in his book *Punished by Rewards* (1993), the conditions of the workplace are much more decisive in motivating people to be creative, take risks, and be more effective over the long term than are extrinsic motivators such as bonuses or other rewards. The latter are often actually counterproductive, as they shift attention from the job itself to the reward, thus making the job a means to an end, not the end in itself. The conditions that seem most important in nurturing creative work and continued learning—both crucial for value improvement—include the opportunity to learn new skills, do meaningful work, apply competence, and have some control and input into the way one's work is done. These conditions provide the milieu in which value improvement can take hold and must be cultivated when managing for value improvement. Leaders who talk about value but do not engage and coach the front-line people who deal with patients every day are unlikely to be successful.

OBSTACLES TO MANAGING FOR VALUE

Any attempt to transform an organization to provide the maximum possible value in healthcare involves meeting and overcoming many challenges and obstacles. Not the least of these is the incredible turmoil, uncertainty, and rate of change in many medical markets. This environment prompts the need for change, yet leads to varying degrees of insecurity and fear; such fear makes it difficult to focus on a long-term plan, rather than a short-term, bottom-line approach. Senge (1990) is one of many who emphasize the necessity for a certain amount of tension before any constructive change can take place; however, that fear can be extreme, paralyzing constructive effort.

Managed care, especially with provider-at-risk arrangements, brings with it many potential conflicts and tensions, including:

- The conflict between the almost unlimited expectations and desires of patients and the concept of limited resources where physicians must deal with opportunity costs and tradeoffs and tough choices about what is affordable and appropriate care
- The change from the traditional fee-for-service system to prepaid care, with its drastically different incentives
- The ethical conflict between the physician role as advocate for each individual patient and the need to also consider the care of a population of patients, a community's needs, or even a health plan's viability and profits
- The tension between a tradition of doing anything that might possibly help with one of doing only that for which there is evidence of effectiveness

- The tension between the traditional role of the physician as the largely autonomous and unquestioned "captain of the ship" and the increasingly collaborative team approach to medical care that emphasizes designing and redesigning care via pathways and guidelines to reduce unnecessary variations in the way healthcare is provided
- The tension between so-called generalists and specialists, physicians and nonphysicians, and their respective roles and optimal relationships in a healthcare delivery system
- The need for physicians to actually redefine their jobs and become doctors to the system of care in addition to their patients, to work *on* their work as well as *do* their work—quite different from the traditional physician near-total preoccupation with seeing patients and largely deferring the problems of the structures and processes of care to others

Physician Autonomy

The most important obstacles are those relating to physician autonomy, the efforts to reduce unwanted variations in care processes, and the necessity of having physicians—as well as other providers and administrative leaders—lead the effort to redesign clinical care. The traditions, education, and experience of physicians have created a culture that emphasizes independence and individualism, natural leadership, autonomy of decision making, a suspicion of any outside influence on the sanctity of the physician-patient relationship, and a natural resistance to any talk of standardization (branded as "cookbook medicine"). Most modern American physicians grew up in a system that rarely questioned their judgment or decisions, especially those relating to the utilization of resources.

In part, no doubt, to this nonquestioning culture, it has been difficult for physicians as a whole to take the lead in what is clearly in their own best interest—the promotion of the highest possible value of the care they provide. In such a pursuit of increased value, physicians must transform themselves and be more willing to:

- Become accountable for their work
- Work, using the scientific method, on the processes, systems, and appropriateness of such work
- Learn how to apply the tools and techniques and philosophy of quality management
- Lead and educate (and be educated by) cross-functional teams of providers
- Control and participate more in the care of patients
- Be less a decision maker and more of an enabler (when appropriate)
- Continue to teach, but also to learn more about systems thinking, the psychology of motivation, and how people gain knowledge

Other Barriers

Other barriers, defensive postures, or real and justified concerns can make things even more difficult. One such concern is that of time: "Where will I find the time to work on my work?" Another barrier is the lack of payment incentives. In our society, money defines the worth of practically everything, including, apparently, time spent on improving the results of professional efforts. Although it is part of conventional wisdom that monetary incentives will motivate doctors to work on value, the type of creativity and risk taking necessary for major breakthroughs in healthcare are probably decreased, not promoted, by such rewards. A third barrier is the fear that any attempt to reduce variations or adopt guidelines will lead to cookbook medicine or loss of autonomy, not to mention fears related to payment mechanisms and liability associated with the implementation of guidelines or protocols. Some also fear that measurement for improvement might be used for judgment and surveillance, as in the various report card indicators being developed.

THE IMPORTANCE OF USABLE DATA

Collecting actual data, even of initially marginal quality, is a powerful method of achieving physician involvement in value improvement work. Once doctors see actual measurements relating to their work, they become interested in learning more. "Hook them with data" becomes the rallying cry. One example is using ongoing data collection about the processes and outcomes of care to transform a non–evidence based guideline into an evidence-based one. Teaching and using a quality management approach is more successful to the degree that one can minimize jargon and discuss service and science. Appealing to a physician's science background and emphasizing the scientific method (a key component of TQM/CQI) is helpful. Education by physician leaders can usually defuse the concerns and misunderstandings about variation, redesign of care processes, or cookbook medicine. Paring down other committee obligations or using regular meetings can often free up some time, and recognition and celebration (and sometimes resultant publications) can reinforce interest. Clearly, attracting and training key physician leaders is crucial, and sometimes decisive.

CONSTANCY OF LEADERSHIP

Value as an equation does not fully describe the levels of sophistication necessary for an organization and its leaders to produce value, much less manage it. Leadership constancy is an essential element. Healthcare organizations in turmoil have a difficult time getting a fix on value. There are a number of distractions in the way. The necessary preoccupation with immediate survival in a price-competitive era is only one of the obstacles. Another is the long-standing tendency for hospital and group practice boards to "shoot the messenger" if things are not going well. This results in executive turnover, the infusion of new teams of executives, and the assumption that the turnaround group will make a quick difference.

We often think of leadership in the singular, believing a single leader makes the difference. This is not so—organizations in transformation must identify leaders of every discipline. The organization then has a distinct advantage, whereas an absence of leadership constancy can harm the organization.

On the other hand, much can be said for new talent. Organizations go through life cycles and there comes a time to seek out new ideas and competencies. Boards, equally susceptible to aging, need to remember that disassembling of old cultures to build new ones takes time. To build a working cohesive management team takes at least three to five years and consumes high levels of energy. This internally focused energy may have little to do with the value equation.

Distractions to the organization during times of change may detract from value management.

- New leaders need to build personal credibility and this can shuffle priorities away from the mission and toward organizational structure. (Is anyone watching out for quality of care?)
- The need for the positive bottom line may short circuit activities that focus on the patient and patient-centered values.
- Community health issues become less visible because the focus is internal.
- The competitive climate also takes its toll. Whether the acquisition of a group practice includes quality physicians becomes less important than does its location and what it might represent in the way of improving market share.

ACHIEVING A SHARED VISION

A shared organizational vision geared to maximizing value is crucial to success and difficult to achieve. A shared vision is the answer to Senge's (1990) question: "What do we want to create?" Instead of building incrementally on the present, a vision of the future begins with where we want to go, and then asks what we need to do to get there. With most organizational visions, there is a gap between what is said and what is done.

Although easy to wax eloquent about, it is difficult to create acceptance and enthusiasm for, and execution of, a shared vision. Such visions are not often shared if imposed from above, rather than being the result of participation from everyone in the organization. We also know there is no such thing as a static, unchanging shared vision. The engagement and involvement of everyone, the joy and pride in work that leads to creativity and continued learning, are promoted by successful execution of such a unifying vision.

The way a system looks, functions, behaves, spends its resources—the way its every day work is carried out—is the vision. How might an organization, dedicated to providing the best value in healthcare, look in three to ten years? Any effective vision includes TQM/CQI as the means (the driver) of accomplishing the end (the mission). An organization with a "driving" vision is customer oriented in a way that very few are today and places great importance on the proper empowerment, training, education, and continued learning, growth, and participation of its internal customers. Such an organization believes that if workers at all levels feel ownership and accountability for their work, feel excited and fulfilled by their job, then it is virtually ensured they will take excellent care of each other and their external customers. The focus on value will, through its continuous assessment and measurement of patient needs and outcomes, help the organization strive to delight patients with constantly improving quality of service and outcomes, based on a habit of experimentation, risk taking, and trial-and-learn improvement cycles.

This increased emphasis on the needs and perceptions of external customers—especially patients—is relatively new in medicine. In the past, healthcare was largely designed for the providers' convenience. Putting the patient at the center of the health delivery system is a major departure from tradition, a difference not yet appreciated by many physicians. In the future organization, traditional paternalism will be replaced by increased patient participation in decision making, with a much greater emphasis on shared decisions that carefully consider the patient's unique priorities and personal values prior to choosing options and defining the value of a given outcome. There will be greatly increased emphasis on truly informed consent, effective communication, fair presentation of what is known and what is not, and on a kind of partnership between providers and their patients. (This does not mean that many patients do not prefer the paternalism model of care—we must be flexible enough to adjust.) Using electronic forms of information, education, communication, and decision support to an optimal degree, organizations will be able to maximize value by continually striving for the optimal balance between self-care and provider care, high tech and high touch, between generalists and specialists, and between physicians and allied health professionals.

As technology changes, this ability to "right size" (sometimes called economies of scope) will be a continuous, never-ending task that involves streamlining many functions via redesign and reengineering processes. It will involve more decentralization, as facilitated by increasingly sophisticated information and computerized decision support systems, allowing both patients and front-line workers to do more problem solving at the point of origin. And the future organization, by virtue of this combination of information and data analysis, partnering, continual assessment of outcomes achieved, and emphasis on evidence-based (i.e., scientific) decision making, will gain the participation of, and acceptance by, its customers when making tough choices to maximize the value of care. Because of its emphasis on striving for maximal value, and its ability to engage its patients in the same mission, the organization will effectively reduce futile or marginally beneficial care. By its willingness and increased habit of putting a value on the health outcomes achieved, the organization—together with its customers—will be able to make better choices and to decide when the cost of a given health service is not worth its benefit (i.e., the value achieved does not justify the investment of resources).

If we are unable or unwilling to use the model of value assessment and enhancement outlined here to reach agreement with our customers on some limits in the use of resources, then there will be no alternative to capital budget freezes, centralized and bureaucratic controls, and legal warfare over allocation of resources.

AGONY OF CHANGE

Long-standing contracts are being broken. Permanence of employment is suddenly an outdated concept. Implementation of strategies to pursue value contributes to a certain level of anxiety. The value equation requires application of change as the constant. This means that healthcare organizations will encounter downsizing, reengineering, right sizing, or whatever the current term is to describe drastic changes. All have one thing in common—agony, and its counterpoint opportunity.

Delay compounds the problem. Executives find themselves entering a state of "suspended animation." Decision-making processes become frozen. Cycles turn into trends that can no longer be ignored. Questions are raised about leadership competency. Underlying this turmoil, however, is the inherent faith of the patient concerning the quality of healthcare and the competency of the providers. Success and years of breakthroughs have created a sense of confidence in the system that is reassuring, but also worrisome—worrisome because in the absence of clearly defined markers, one does not know when value is being affected.

The airline business is very complex. It continually goes through massive change (some airlines are in their third round of restructuring). However, a long-standing faith exists among most passengers that the airline, in spite of cutbacks, will not shortcut the maintenance of the engines. Some, however, might ponder and then appreciate the fact that the pilot is also aboard and that quite probably the engines have really been maintained up to the old standards.

So it is with healthcare. Technological excellence and intense media coverage of breakthroughs have created an enviable image of healthcare among those who have access to the system. The widespread belief is that quality will not suffer because the system will not let that happen. The cardiac surgeon, however, unlike the airline pilot, does not come with you on the trip, suggesting that a patient's confidence may not have the same justification as the airline customer's. But the confidence remains.

The fundamental turnaround question that must be posed is this: "At what point in the process of becoming efficient does the process implode and cut into the quality of care?" Sufficient excesses still remain in the system; therefore, this effect on quality will not, or at least need not, take place for the foreseeable future. The fundamental problem is that in the absence of an organized approach to the measurement of value, that threshold could be violated.

The decision to embark on a value expedition depends on gathering a number of resources and, even more fundamentally, a change in mental attitude. This attitude change is critical and contains four components:

1. A decision to do it
2. The dedication of resources to make it happen
3. A determination that results must be measurable to mean anything
4. The conviction that the promotion of value is the core element of the delivery of healthcare and that the marketplace issues will ultimately be balanced against what is best for the patient

This breakthrough in attitude typically begins in a leader's head. The leader may be at any level of the organization, not necessarily at the top. A transformation takes place that is difficult to explain, and the movement begins from passive acceptance of the need for change toward an active belief that change will matter in the most positive sense. A missionary zeal about the change process begins to develop. Old practices are examined in a new light and informal teams develop and function. These rebel teams are typically encouraged by leaders who recognize the importance of testing old ways and are willing to take chances associated with testing the existing structure.

However, other leaders, while endorsing change, still have to be convinced. They hold back and watch and some discomfort arises in unpredictable forms. Senior leaders can be caught in a difficult dilemma—as they sponsor the movement toward change, they must temper the movement so that it does not move so fast that the proponents of change burn up their credibility and flame out. Leaders, as at no other time, must be sponsors, timing artists, and caretakers of the new, still-fragile change. They become tenders and are often criticized because at times they are perceived as impeding progress. Brian Joiner (1994) covered it neatly when he noted that managers come together and ultimately figure out the importance of believing in people and treating each other with dignity, trust, and respect. This becomes a given and the new role of managers is to focus not on motivating people, "but on removing the demotivators, the things that get in the way of doing higher-quality work with higher and higher productivity."

This basic point represents a significant change in the belief structures of those responsible for managing people. The new arena provides the space for true change to take place and sets the stage for the transformation from an organization that pieces its progress together through a variety of approaches to one with a solid sense of direction. The challenge facing these organizations is how to carry it off. Change involves risk. Personalities come into play. The organization may be charging ahead, but totally out of synchronization.

DETERMINING THE WINNERS

Finally, will financial or value performance most determine future winners? Is the pursuit of value a winning strategy? Will there be decisive winners? Or is cost reduction the end game? In Rochester, New York, Eastman Kodak and other employers initiated change from the top. Governing boards and enlightened hospital executives followed suit. Rochester became a model to be emulated as the responsible corporate model for change. Change was not based on creating individual financial incentives for the providers, but rather on a strong corporate desire to leverage change through intervention, based on the conviction that things could be done better. In southern California, a traditional leader in change, the roots of managed competition took hold in a variety of forms. Those in sleepier parts of the nation watched the changes with great interest. If change could be practiced in California, others could learn what worked and what did not.

Bigger has become better—market share is the magic phrase. Also prevalent is the hope that after the price shake out, employers will place the value of services higher on the decision-making tree. The assumption is that all things being equal, patients, employers, and other consumers of healthcare services are competent enough to make the right decision about providers based on proven value.

Who will be the winners? To date there is little evidence that it will be those who invest in value; however, this assumes that traditional purchasers of care are either naive or greedy. The hope is that those organizations investing in quality/value will indeed be winners, although not defined in today's terms of market share and size. Tomorrow's winners may be those who risk by being different. An important point is that no other attractive option exists. Value must be pursued as the only viable means of reducing costs (to remain competitive) while preserving quality and mission. When all of the healthcare providers have reached that nebulous wall where costs have been reduced through the competitive route, hopefully a number will have realized the important elements of the "what" they produce—enough to make a difference in the marketplace.

Who will be the winners in the long run? The winners will be those who:

- Recognize that the ultimate consumer is the patient and the collective wisdom of patients will bear on those market forces. Value will be appreciated, if provable.
- Understand that not all opportunities are lost if not exercised in the first round. Careless ventures created in the passion of the moment may not provide the long-term sustenance necessary for implementation of the value equation.
- Exercise organizational flexibility in response to market forces (but always with the mission and value in mind).
- Invest heavily in information systems to provide the measurements and data needed to define and promote value.
- Promote a management philosophy that values decision-making input from the front-line employees.

CONCLUSION

Many, but not all, of the components and requirements of managing for value have been identified, as well as some of the barriers to accomplishing this transformation. A conceptual framework for orienting healthcare around the goal of maximizing value has been outlined. The crucial interrelationships between outcome measurement, redesign of delivery systems, quality management, and evidence-based practices have been duly noted. The argument has been made that it is essential that healthcare providers and their customers together must develop an approach to making difficult choices about how to use finite resources.

However, the question facing executives in healthcare remains perplexing: What if value is never perceived or appreciated by the ultimate customer? What if the influence of the plaintiff's bar in our society makes it impossible to ever make difficult choices, or deny any interventions, even those without proven benefit? Or what if, due to our failure to agree upon standardized, reliable measures of quality, purchasers give up and look at nothing but price? What if providers have been so successful at marketing their services as high quality that data to the contrary have no effect? What if that good bedside manner turns out to be the only gold standard used by patients to select their system of preference?

Thus, the dilemma of managing value is the lurking concern that, in the final analysis, the game will be decided exclusively by price, and those preaching value will be looked upon as rationalizing their inability to compete only on price. To head off this situation, healthcare providers at all levels will have to devote substantial energy toward building programs that create definable value and are capable of demonstrating it in terms understood and accepted and that permit valid cross-provider comparisons.

In the last analysis, why should an organization manage for value? By improving the quality of outcomes and service, you enhance your reputation for quality and thus promote market share. By reducing the costs of poor quality, rework, waste, and inappropriate use of resources, you improve the bottom line and are better able to compete on price. Finally, managing for value promotes a conceptual model for making difficult choices.

DISCUSSION

1. Provide an example of what is meant by inappropriate care.
2. What key strategy could be used to persuade physicians to embrace a program of value enhancement?

3. What role should lay healthcare executives play in the process of value enhancement?
4. Create a short outline of the barriers encountered in any value enhancement program.

NOTE

This chapter was adapted from A. Ross and L. F. Fenster, M.D. 1995. "The Dilemma of Managing Value." *Frontiers of Health Services Management* 12 (2): 3–32.

REFERENCES

Asch, D. A. 1995. "Basic Lessons in Resource Allocations: Sharing, Setting Limits and Being Fair." *The Pharos* 58 (2): 33–34.

Berwick, D. M. 1991. "Controlling Variations in Health Care: A Consultation from Walter Shewhart." *Medical Care* 29 (12): 1212–25.

Berwick, D. M. 1994. "Improving the Appropriateness of Care." *Quality Connection* 3 (1): 1–6.

Chassin, M. R., J. Kosecoff, R. E. Park, C. M. Winslow, K. L. Kahn, N. J. Merrick, J. Keesey, A. Fink, D. H. Solomon, and R. H. Brook. 1987. "Does Inappropriate Use Explain Geographic Variations in the Use of Health Care Services? A Study of Three Procedures." *Journal of the American Medical Association* 258 (18): 2533–37.

Creech, B. 1994. *The Five Pillars of TQM*. New York: Truman Tally Books.

Ellwood, P. 1988. "Shattuck Lecture." *New England Journal of Medicine* 318 (23): 1549–56.

Joiner, B. L. 1994. *Fourth Generation Management: The New Business Consciousness*. New York: McGraw-Hill, Inc.

Kissick, W. L. 1994. *Medicine's Dilemmas: Infinite Needs Versus Finite Resources*. New Haven, CT: Yale University Press.

Kohn, A. 1993. *Punished by Rewards*. New York: Houghton Mifflin Co.

Senge, P. M. 1990. *The Fifth Discipline: The Art and Practice of the Learning Organization*. New York: Currency/Doubleday.

Shein, E. H. 1993. "How Can Organizations Learn Faster? The Challenge of Entering the Green Room." *Sloan Management Review* (Winter): 88–89.

Starr, P. 1992. *The Logic of Health Care Reform.* Knoxville, TN: The Grand Rounds Press.

CHAPTER 8

Public Health and Community Involvement

CASE IN POINT: Brownsville, historically, has had a strong manufacturing base. Over the past 15 years, that base has been eroded by significant price competition from around the world. Several of Brownsville's companies went through significant downsizing in the late 1980s and early 1990s and many people in relatively high-paid positions, and who stayed in Brownsville, are now still unemployed or underemployed. The contrast with the high-tech industries that came to Brownsville in the past 15 years is sharp. People employed in these companies are paid very well. In addition, many immigrants who are willing to work in low-paying jobs with little or no benefits (in particular, no health insurance) have recently come to Brownsville as well.

As in other communities in America, the social problems of alcoholism, teenage pregnancy, AIDS, and drug use have been and continue to be serious issues in Brownsville. In response, a variety of separate state and local government agencies, as well as private agencies, have come to Brownsville to assist with these medical and social problems.

Rachel Sanders is CEO of Brownsville Hospital, where these problems are particularly apparent in the ER. As the economy has turned down, the ER activity has increased, with the severity of the community's problems reflected in the ER statistics.

Many people coming to the ER require assistance beyond medical care. The hospital social workers attempt to find housing, food, and other services. They have to deal with many people to arrange the needed services. Some individuals do not quite qualify for services at one agency, and the social worker has to try another. Dan Johnson, the head of social services at the hospital, had told Rachel a few days ago, "Given the hurdles, I wonder how some individuals are ever able to connect with services on their own."

Rachel thought about what she had heard about community care networks—networks where the community hospital, as the single largest provider of healthcare, uses its connections to other agencies providing social services to bring community services together. Although the mission of Brownsville Hospital is to provide services to all, regardless of their ability to pay, the cost of unreimbursed care in the ER and the cost of the hospital social workers' time was becoming a serious problem. In the same conversation, Dan told her he needed to hire two more social workers to handle the workload. Rachel wondered what she and the staff of Brownsville Hospital could do to provide leadership for better organizing and integrating the services. What problems might they face? What vision of community-wide links would the hospital board, the heads of state, and the local and private agencies support? Would other leaders in the community be interested in forming such an organization to better serve the community's needs?

QUESTION: What skills and knowledge of public health and community involvement will help Rachel answer her questions?

INTRODUCTION

The local community is a large part of the market for hospitals, medical groups, and locally based managed care organizations. Being perceived as serving the community is an important interest for each of these organizations. Hospitals, large medical groups, and managed care organizations all have a significant market presence. They are looked to for leadership on health-related issues. Providing that leadership through involvement with community and public health issues is an effective way of serving the community and developing a stronger market presence. It also engages the community's leadership in meeting the needs of their community—needs that otherwise might fall to the hospital as in the case of Brownsville.

This chapter relates public health and community involvement to the organization's mission and vision and outlines the unique core competence of a healthcare organization in public health and community involvement. It also presents the American Hospital Association's community care network (CCN) vision as a framework for private and public health providers to work together in serving the community. The four elements of the CCN vision are:

1. Community health focus
2. Community accountability
3. Seamless continuum of care
4. Management within fixed resources

This chapter also presents examples of what other healthcare organizations have done, and are doing, in each of these four areas.

A healthcare organization that is an effective contributor to the community's efforts to develop a CCN will have developed a significant competence in public health and community involvement. The challenge is to bring the leaders of hospitals, physician groups, and managed care organizations—and public health agencies—together with business, payer, and political leaders to identify ways that available resources can better serve the community's needs. This chapter outlines ways that others are meeting this challenge.

RELATION TO MISSION AND VISION

The mission of the organization is a fundamental statement of why the organization exists. How does the mission statement relate to public

health and community involvement? Not-for-profit hospitals have a requirement, as part of their tax exempt (501 c-3) status, to provide care
for people who cannot afford to pay. Different hospitals can have widely
divergent views on what this requirement means, as illustrated by the
hospital "dumping" scandal in the 1990s (when some not-for-profit
hospitals were refusing patients without insurance, regardless of the
patient's immediate care needs, and were "dumping" these patients by
directing them to other hospitals). In addition to having a mission
statement, what actions do hospitals or other healthcare organizations
take to carry out their missions?

The vision of the organization is what the organization's governance and leadership see the organization becoming in the future. The
vision reflects the leadership and governance view of the organization's
environment, the competitive strengths of the organization, the customers of the organization, and how the organization will grow and
develop to better serve its customers in the future. Patients are a major customer segment, arguably the most important, but how is the
broader community viewed? Is it also a customer? As illustrated in this
chapter's "Case in Point," the public health issues have both medical
and social dimensions. State, local, and private organizations in the
community are engaged in addressing these problems. The organization's relationship with these agencies can be a significant competitive
strength. Does the organization's vision include working with these
agencies to better serve the broader community?

UNIQUE CORE COMPETENCE OF A HEALTHCARE ORGANIZATION

Hospitals, large medical groups, and local managed care organizations
are looked to for leadership on issues affecting health in the community. The leadership and governance of these organizations:

- Are in a position to see the medical costs of social issues
- Have access to community leaders who are concerned about
  social and health issues in the community

- Have staff resources and knowledge to show the connection between the social issues and medical costs
- Have the position in the community to encourage services to work together in ways that benefit the community

Healthcare organizations that use their position, knowledge, and access to community leaders to support the development of a CCN will have developed a core competence in public health and community involvement.

The American Hospital Association (1993) published its vision of how private and public sector providers could come together to form CCNS. That vision has four dimensions:

1. *Community health focus:* improving the health status of the community
2. *Community accountability:* providing information to the community on what is being done to address the identified community problems
3. *Seamless continuum of care:* linking the services of separate providers to provide care that is jointly planned and coordinated so patients have consistent access regardless of how they enter the network
4. *Management within fixed resources:* moving to fixed payment arrangements (budgets and capitation are examples) that provide incentives to avoid duplication and to manage capacity as well as utilization of services

Although the expectation in 1993 that capitated care would soon become the dominant form of payment to healthcare providers has not taken place, the framework continues to be a helpful way of looking at the challenges and opportunities posed by public health and community involvement.

In *Health Network Innovations,* Bogue and Hall (1997) present 20 examples of community cooperation to better serve the social and medical needs of their communities. These 20 case study examples were taken from 25 awardees and 24 finalists in a national competition that drew a total of 283 applicants for support funding. When selecting awardees and other finalists, major consideration was given to successful prior experience in developing services to meet the needs of their community, as evidence of their future efforts at making progress toward the CCN vision (Bogue and Hall 1997). As a sample, these 20 cases represent the best examples of moving to a CCN vision. Each community is different, but the actions they took to identify, measure, and address their public health issues are instructive and provide illustrative examples for this section.

COMMUNITY HEALTH FOCUS

A community health focus is a two-part effort: (1) measuring the incidence of public health issues that affect health in your community; and (2) then acting to see that services are provided to address those issues.

Measuring the problem(s) is one of the first steps in building a community consensus for action. One might expect that a common first step would be to see what information that measures the size of the problem has already been collected. However, the perspective of someone who has seen the collection and use of health data—in public and private positions—is quite different. Jan Malcolm (2000), who is currently the commissioner of the Minnesota Department of Health, observed: "I have been struck by how rarely healthcare delivery systems tap into public health databases and planning processes, and vice versa. Each sector does its own thing and largely ignores the data of the other. They give 'lip service' to each other's capacities, but rarely make that a basis for their own strategic planning."

Sources of Data

Some CCNs do use baseline data that have been collected by other organizations: the state or local department of health and the local United Way may be sources of useful information. In cases where those data are lacking, CCNs can generate baseline data using survey instruments that have been developed by the Centers for Disease Control and the American Hospital Association.

As will be discussed later in this chapter, a common theme for CCNs is an emphasis on community involvement—from identifying and prioritizing the problems to be addressed to shared participation in the ongoing governance of the CCN itself. It is not surprising, then, that a primary source of information on needs in the community can be gained simply by asking the people to be served by the CCN. The asking takes a variety of forms, including community forums, focus groups, and surveys. The surveys can be conducted by people in the community, such as a teen center at the local high school. Others have contracted with survey research and consulting firms to gather this information.

Services

The specific services provided, sponsored, or coordinated by the CCN will depend on the needs identified in the community. In thinking about the kinds of services a CCN can provide, it is useful to look at the types of services provided by the 20 case studies in *Health Network Innovations* (Bogue and Hall 1997). There are three broad themes that focus on the care provided: care for children (prenatal to early childhood); care for teenagers; and other early diagnosis, prevention, and chronic care services. The following points are examples of the types of services provided.

Prenatal to early childhood

- Providing outreach workers to concentrate on women at high risk of giving birth to low-birthweight babies
- Working with the media to reach high-risk women with information on how to get prenatal care
- Well-child exams
- Immunizations

- Caring for vulnerable children (assisting with health, education, and social services)
- Family enhancement and parenting services

Teenagers

- Supporting school-based health clinics
- Developing and implementing effective programs to reduce teen pregnancies, alcohol and drug use, and risk-taking behaviors
- Increasing access to affordable healthcare

Other early diagnosis and intervention programs

- HIV/AIDS
- Diabetes detection, education, and monitoring
- Birth control
- Gynecological health
- Smoking cessation
- Glaucoma and blood pressure screening
- Health maintenance and foot care services for the elderly
- Low-cost/no-cost sliding scale prescriptions
- Indigent care clinics

Although the above examples are not intended to be comprehensive, they do indicate the types of services that CCNs have provided to address needs in their communities.

COMMUNITY ACCOUNTABILITY

Community accountability is reporting to the community on what has been accomplished. Publishing annual reports is one way to demonstrate accountability to the community. Most of the 20 case examples used a broadly based, inclusive governance structure as a means of involving community leaders and gaining their support. The involvement of these leaders gives them direct knowledge of the organization's accomplishments.

There are two parts to the support required. The first is internal, building initial board-level and physician-leadership support for the organization's initiative to identify and help address community needs. The second is external, assisting other community leaders to assist in bringing together the community's resources to identify and address public health issues. The external effort, as it identifies and quantifies specific issues such as teen pregnancy or the special learning challenges faced by poor children, provides the specifics that can capture the interest and build active support of the organization's initiatives as part of a CCN.

Values and mission statements are important because they frame the expectation that the organization is concerned about the community it serves. Hospital boards can commit their hospital to collaborate with other community healthcare and human services providers. That commitment is a significant step in moving the hospital and the community to form a CCN.

Values and mission statements are a necessary first step in the right direction, but many hospitals and health systems already have stated values and missions to serve their community and the poor. The question is: "What distinguishes those that become part of active, vibrant, productive networks from those who have the words but show little action?" The case studies presented in *Health Network Innovations* (Bogue and Hall 1997) are an important reference. Each case describes an organization that assisted its community to establish necessary services. For example, rather than simply decide as a hospital board to support a "public health good" (e.g., influenza shots for all people over age 65), an organization worked with leadership groups—healthcare providers, human services agencies, and public health, political, and ethnic groups—in its community to identify specific needs. Each leadership group focused on what it could do with a "bias toward action," identifying and measuring the incidence of problems, then prioritizing the problems to address.

A principle in sales is that people "buy on problems they see" (i.e., they "buy" actions and services that will address those problems). The healthcare organizations that are part of successful community organizations have, at least implicitly, recognized this principle. They have actively sought to include the community leaders concerned with the community's healthcare needs. Consider the following examples from Bogue and Hall (1997).

- *A hospital-led community health system in New York.* The initial community organization included the hospital and many community organizations with the support of local elected officials. The community was 70 percent Latino in the 1990 census, and the leaders of the Latino community were key partners in establishing the community health system.
- *A joint effort led by two community hospitals in Massachusetts.* Broad-based community coalitions organized to identify issues, develop explicit action plans, and monitor progress.
- *A healthcare partnership in Georgia.* Hospital CEOs, school superintendents, physicians, business leaders, city/county commissioners, a United Way president, and a director of public health formed a partnership to improve the health status of the community. Early efforts concentrated on a health education program for children in grades K-6 and a workplace wellness program.
- *A mayor's health services advisory committee in Virginia.* Problems were addressed by task forces with broad representation from the hospitals, public schools, health department, local medical society, research foundation, community health center, indigent care clinic, local clergy association, department of social services, and local citizens.
- *A wellness partnership in rural northern California.* The hospital, department of public health, and community leaders worked together to build on the experience of a successful wellness center and develop similar services in other communities.
- *A county health commission in rural Iowa.* Two members of the County Memorial Hospital board, representatives from a mental health organization, citizens on the public health advisory board, a county-based primary care physician, emergency medical services, and the chemical dependency center worked

together to provide a continuum of care for a rural population of 12,000.

In some of the case studies, the leaders of healthcare organizations have taken the lead in bringing interested community leaders together. In others, political leaders have seen the need and taken the initiative. In each of the cases, however, healthcare leadership has been actively involved in the CCN. These organizations have consistently built community support for their initiatives by:

- Carefully structuring a steering committee with balanced representation of the components
- Identifying common interests in the community based on ethnic groupings, geography, income levels, and social concerns, and organizing around those common interests
- Identifying community healthcare issues based on group-sponsored community assessments
- Identifying priorities as a group
- Creating a shared identity so that being a part of the group enhances each individual's identity
- Using the group members with access to the community's leadership to build support for the group's initiatives

A representative body is a powerful force. It includes leaders of the community and has access to other leaders. Such groups make good use of their strength by finding ways to support the needs they identify.

There is a broadening awareness that the health system cannot do it all—a partnership is needed with public and private health agencies, the schools, and local government. Jan Malcolm (2000) observed: "I would hope that all healthcare delivery systems would see community health as part of their mission. The more we learn about the broader influences of community conditions on the health status of individuals and populations, the more critical it is to build better connections between the worlds of clinical medicine, public health, social services, and community development."

SEAMLESS CONTINUUM OF CARE

The idea of a seamless continuum of care is to see that all of a patient's needs are cared for, regardless of where they enter the network, in a seamless, interrelated way. The network takes responsibility for the links between the patients and needed services.

Several ccns have been able to use their position in the community to sponsor the financing and development of a community healthcare center. These healthcare centers have helped address all four dimensions of the ccn vision—a healthcare focus, accountability, a seamless continuum of care, and managing within fixed resources—as they colocate services and reduce costs through shared support services.

ccns have also served as the vehicle for dialog between the community providers and the community served. That dialog has led to both formal and informal referral relationships—both within and beyond the services provided by the member organizations—as well as reductions in the duplication of services.

ccns faced with the challenges of serving rural areas have sponsored mobile health units that serve as mobile community healthcare centers to bring care to people in remote parts of the county and to people who likely would not receive services otherwise. The mobile unit also provides a link between people who are identified as needing added services and the other providers in the network (Bogue and Hall 1997).

MANAGEMENT WITHIN FIXED RESOURCES

The following paragraphs outline ways that hospitals and ccns are paying for public health and community improvement.

Capitated Medicaid

There is one significant way in which the aha's 1993 vision for ccns has not been fully realized. In 1993, many leaders in healthcare were convinced that some form of the Clinton plan for national health insurance would be passed by Congress and implemented. The future of healthcare delivery was to be capitated reimbursement, paying networks of healthcare providers to care for populations of patients. The Clinton plan did not pass, and there is still the issue of caring for some 43 million Americans who are uninsured.

Historically, Medicaid patients have found it difficult to find physicians and other providers interested in caring for them. Medicaid patients have used hospital emergency rooms as a source of primary care. The cost of this care has been high, with little or no continuity of care.

Capitated care for Medicaid patients is, however, growing. States are transferring their Medicaid patients to providers willing to care for these patients on a capitated basis. Although the Medicaid programs set the capitated reimbursement rates at less than the full usual cost of caring for these patients, providers who do manage the care for these patients find they can do so profitably. Organizations with a capitated responsibility for providing care to Medicaid patients change how care is delivered to these patients. They establish systems that enable, and incentives that encourage, patients to use primary care physicians, nurse practitioners, and physician assistants for primary care. These systems promote continuity of care as a way of both providing better care and managing the cost of that care. Developing an organizational competence in providing managed care for Medicaid patients is one effective way of managing within fixed resources.

Managed Care and Community Partnerships

A second organizational competence is to build on the recognition that managed care has led to substantial changes for healthcare delivery and for public health over the past 10 to 15 years.

From the perspective of public health and community involvement, managed care has brought both negative and positive changes. On the negative side, managed care has restricted payment for services to network providers. Few public health clinics have been able to qualify for network participation, and third-party payments have dropped (Levi 2000). Obtaining third-party reimbursement for the community services provided by a CCN is a significant challenge.

On the positive side, managed care has brought a public health, population-based focus to the healthcare system. Collaborations between healthcare organizations, public agencies, payers, and employers can be established to provide education and sponsor health risk assessment and early detection efforts that address the entire community (Koplan and Harris 2000). The incentives for collaboration are there. The costs to the health plans of treating heart disease, cancer, and diabetes, to name three examples, are costs that payers and—ultimately—employers and patients must pay. The public health perspective of risk factors and the implications of these risk factors—diet, smoking, and the value of early detection—are a basis for healthcare providers, public health agencies, payers, and employers to work together on joint community efforts.

Private and Public Grant Funding

There are two big hurdles in obtaining grant funds—identifying sources of grant funds and obtaining approval for a specific project or program. Typical sources of funding include support from local foundations and city, county, and state governments. Community leaders who are involved in the governance of the CCN can be particularly helpful both in identifying funding sources and in building political support for the funding.

GOOD INTENTIONS ARE NOT ENOUGH

Why is it that "public health and community improvement" appear near the top of many organizations' "*should* do" lists, but near the bottom of most organizations' "*did* do" lists?

Hospitals & Health Networks (HHN) presented the results of its 1999 leadership survey in its November 1999 issue. The survey included responses of 16 executives chosen to represent three groups of healthcare executives: managed care, physicians and group practices, and hospitals and health systems. The 1999 survey was a follow-up to a survey of 700 executives in 1998, and the results of the two years were similar.

The summary conclusion of the article is that improving community health is "important, but ..." Healthcare executives see improving community health as "the right thing to do." The "but" reflects questions of "What difference can we make?" and "How can we justify the added effort?" (Hudson 1999). These questions are particularly difficult to answer in metropolitan areas where the community served can be difficult to identify, where the potential payoff from the public health effort is measured in years rather than the annual cycle of insurance plan and provider selection, and where declining reimbursement has severely limited the dollars available for discretionary investment.

Most organizations are working hard to survive. Declining reimbursement has led to competition between organizations for patients. The competition for patients has led to less cooperation between community organizations to meet the community needs.

The challenge is to bring the leaders of hospitals, physician groups, and managed care organizations—and public health agencies—together with business, payer, and political leaders to identify ways that available resources can better serve the community's needs. The following two examples will serve as a summary for this section.

Examples

One example is a diabetes program in San Diego, California. The San Diego Health and Human Services Agency joined with more than 20 hospitals, physician groups, health plans, insurers, voluntary organizations, and educational institutions to form Community Health Improvement Partners (CHIP). CHIP targets public health priorities that, in addition to diabetes, include access to care, school health, needs assessment, immunizations, and mental health (Koplan and Harris 2000). Diabetes is one of the costliest diseases in a health plan. Public health efforts focus on early recognition of the disease and prevention of its potentially serious outcomes including renal disease, retinopathy, heart disease, and amputation. National clinical trials have identified the critical importance of careful control of blood sugar levels in preventing these outcomes. Public health efforts, and efforts by the healthcare system to carefully manage these patients, are both required to produce good outcomes and to care for these patients with minimum cost. The success of the CHIP program is reported in the article

"From the Board Room to the Community Room, a Collaboration that Is Working" (CHIP 1998).

A second example is the Lehigh Valley Hospital and Health Network (LVH) in eastern Pennsylvania. LVH provides a full continuum of services, from network-owned/affiliated primary care practices and ambulatory care sites to substantial tertiary care services (1,200 annual open-heart surgeries, a Level I trauma program with burn center, and a Level III neonatal intensive care unit). LVH has supported an extensive series of collaborations with other members of the community, using income from operations and the Dorothy Rider Pool Trust (a supporting organization with a long-standing commitment to the concepts of community health, and with a conscious policy of engaging community members). LVH's community improvement efforts reflect two related ideas: (1) measurable enhancement of the status of health (MESH), and (2) an emphasis on collaboration, community ownership, and assistance for the development of organizations that will provide continuous support for community health improvement.

The implementation of the MESH program in 1997 was the transition point to a greater focus on performance measurement. It began with a baseline assessment of the community's health needs, and that assessment is repeated as a way of evaluating progress. Three examples illustrate their focus on community ownership.

- ALERT partnership. This partnership is a 160-member community coalition of representatives from education, prevention, law enforcement, healthcare, business, and others in Lehigh and Northampton counties. ALERT seeks to prevent the illegal use and abuse of alcohol, tobacco, and other drugs through a unified community effort. The hospital provides space, payroll services, and technical assistance, while the organization's leadership is responsible for staff and other operating expenses.
- AIDS activity office. A team of clinicians, nurses, case managers, and others provide clinical care for people infected with or affected by AIDS. They continually assess available services and work with LVH and the community to identify and fill gaps. This office is administered as part of the Department of Community

Health and Health Studies and has been successful in obtaining increased federal funding to support the patient population growth.

- *School health unit.* A nurse and pediatrician from LVH work with school nurses and teachers to address problems encountered by children of low-income families that limit students' ability and readiness to learn. The core support for the present program is provided by LVH, but any growth will require external funding.

CONCLUSION

Lehigh Valley Hospital's interest in involving the community is best summarized by Young, Laskowski, and Sussman (2000): "By recognizing that communities themselves have strengths, we in healthcare can avoid a mentality of 'curing the community patient.'" A healthcare organization's competence, in public health and community involvement, is in its ability to assist and be part of the community's efforts to develop a CCN.

DISCUSSION

1. What unique core competence can a healthcare organization bring to a community to assist in meeting community health needs?
2. Identify two sources of data on community health needs and discuss the importance of each.
3. Why is it important to involve a community in "owning" a CCN?
4. Identify CCN actions that a healthcare organization should support to build a sense of community ownership. Why are these actions important?

REFERENCES

American Hospital Association. 1993. *Transforming Health Care Delivery: Toward Community Care Networks.* Chicago: AHA.

Bogue, R. and C. H. Hall, Jr. (editors). 1997. *Health Network Innovations—How 20 Communities Are Improving Their Systems Through Collaboration.* Chicago: American Hospital Publishing, Inc.

Community Health Improvement Partners. 1998. "From the Board Room to the Community Room: A Collaboration that Is Working." *Journal of Quality Improvement* 24 (10): 549–65.

Hudson, T. 1999. "Leadership 1999." *Hospitals & Health Networks* 73 (11): 36–44.

Koplan, J. P. and J. R. Harris. 2000. "Not-so-strange Bedfellows: Public Health and Managed Care." *American Journal of Public Health* 90 (12): 1825.

Levi, J. 2000. "Managed Care and Public Health." *American Journal of Public Health* 90 (12): 1823–24.

Malcolm, J. 2000. *Personal communication.* June.

Young, M. J., R. J. Laskowski, and E. J. Sussman. 2000. MESH: *Measurable Enhancement of the Status of Health.* Allentown, PA: Lehigh Valley Hospital and Health Network.

CHAPTER 9

Health Policy and Law

CASE IN POINT: John Mitchell was executive vice president and coo of Midwest Medical Center (MMC) in 1992. MMC was a large multispecialty medical group with over 250 physicians and 19 office locations throughout the city. The central office that provided service for most of the specialists was located in Delville Park, an older suburb of Midwest City. The initial building had been built in 1975 on a city landfill site. A major addition, constructed on supports, had met the center's space needs in the early 1980s.

In 1988, again running short of space, MMC spent several months planning a 100,000-square-foot addition. Talks with a major national bank as late as the end of 1988 indicated that financing would not be a problem. However, in April of 1989, the bank officials denied the loan because the building site had been "red circled" as an old landfill. Other banks cited the same findings and no one would provide mortgage financing.

Several alternatives, including moving to a new site, were explored. However, development on the existing site, if some reasonable way could be found to address the interests and concerns of the several parties involved, finally proved to be the best alternative.

The analysis of the different alternatives had taken 18 months of concerted effort by John, his staff, a developer, lawyers who specialized in real estate and environmental issues, and a lobbyist. The effort involved understanding and addressing the issues of the several parties involved:

1. The medical foundation that owned the building had to transfer ownership to the MMC.
2. The state Environmental Protection Agency (EPA) had to be satisfied that the construction program and remediation plan would reduce the groundwater risk of the landfill site.
3. Delville Park's city council had to agree to its role in developing the site and the adjoining areas. This role would include condemning and acquiring privately held parcels of land, developing a city parking ramp to support the construction, relocating streets, and approving tax-exempt financing in return for significant development in the center of Delville Park and an increased stream of tax revenues and payments by MMC in lieu of taxes.
4. The state representative had to propose and get approval by the state legislature for a tax increment subdistrict bill to extend the life of the district to recapture the 30-year cost of the remediation program.
5. The developer had to agree to develop and pay taxes on the portion of the site that would not be needed for MMC purposes for 30 or more years.
6. A hospital merger partner had to be satisfied that the remaining environmental issues presented little or no risk.
7. MMC's board had to agree that the final proposal was a "good deal" for the center.

Now, in February of 1992, the final papers formalizing the agreements have all been signed. In the process of identifying issues and reaching an agreement, many elements had been identified and addressed. No one had foreseen the many hurdles and the complexity of the total agreement at the beginning of the process. John speculated on how the experience of reaching an agreement for the development compared to the process of getting healthcare legislation proposed and passed to become law.

QUESTION: How is healthcare legislation proposed and passed to become law?

INTRODUCTION

This chapter presents the issues of health policy and law: how health policy is decided; the process by which it does, or does not, become law; and the opportunities for healthcare organizations and their associations to affect what becomes law. This chapter focuses on legislation at the national level, which is likely to have the most significant effect on healthcare. The possible passage of national health insurance—such as the Clinton plan proposed in 1992–93 and the Health Insurance Portability and Accountability Act (HIPAA) passed in 1996—will be explored as examples of such national legislation.

The efforts to pass and to block the Clinton plan are instructive because they identify strategies that were effective and those that were not. They provide insights into the strategies that will be required to pass or block legislation affecting healthcare in the future. An organization that understands and is able to employ these strategies, as appropriate, will have developed an organizational competence in health policy and law.

This chapter draws extensively on information in the book *The System* by Haynes Johnson and David S. Broder (1997), which offers an up-close look at American politics through the lens of the Clintons' failed national health reform effort of 1993–94. The authors present a reporter's view of the legislative effort, based on extensive interviews. They address the initial policy concerns and the actions (and reactions) that were taken to push or to block passage of the legislation. *The System* is highly regarded for its thoroughness and accuracy.

IDENTIFYING THE NEED FOR HEALTH POLICY LEGISLATION

A legislator's personal experience, the experience of individual constituents, and data that show the problems experienced by broad groups of constituents all demonstrate the need for health policy legislation. Legislators are continually challenged to distinguish between the trees of individual experience and the forest of a general health policy issue, but personal experience is a powerful motivator.

In 1991, Harris Wofford achieved an upset victory in Pennsylvania, running for—and winning—the U.S. Senate seat vacated by the death of John Heinz. His victory allowed him to become an early driver of interest in national health insurance at the beginning of the Clinton presidency. Healthcare was a significant issue in his campaign. He had personal and professional experience with healthcare issues. His wife had a chronic medical problem and it was a continuing concern, as he changed jobs, that she would be denied coverage. As Pennsylvania's labor secretary, he also knew that healthcare was of particular concern for the voters in Pennsylvania: "Increasingly, every labor dispute, every strike, turned in whole or in part on the issue of healthcare. Increasingly, companies were trying to reduce costs, limit choices, cut benefits. Unions were fighting them" (Johnson and Broder 1997).

In the early stages of Wofford's campaign, a physician and potential contributor gave Wofford a copy of the U.S. Constitution. "Take this Constitution, Senator," the doctor said, "and tell people that the Constitution says if you're charged with a crime, you have a right to a lawyer. Every American, if they're sick, should have the right to a doctor." That became Wofford's television spot: "If criminals have a right to a lawyer, I think working Americans should have the right to a doctor." In the words of Johnson and Broder (1997), "Wofford's victory attracted national attention and convinced Democrats they had found a powerful issue to use against President George Bush in the upcoming 1992 campaign."

By 1993, data for the country as a whole were showing healthcare to be a national concern. The possible loss of adequate health insurance coverage had become a white-collar, middle-class issue, as highlighted by the following statistics (Johnson and Broder 1997):

- Healthcare costs were consuming $1 of every $7 of goods and services and rising rapidly.
- At a time when real household median income increased by $1,500, healthcare costs increased by $1,400, virtually wiping out the economic gain.
- 37 million people (15 percent) had no coverage at all, and an added 30 percent (72 million people) had no prescription coverage.
- The restructuring of the American economy in the early 1990s led to the loss of hundreds of thousands of high-paying jobs— including the first significant loss of white-collar jobs since the Depression.
- Businesses were having difficulty covering the costs of health insurance.
- In 1992, 1,200,000 American families had lost insurance; a million of those families earned between $25,000 and $50,000 per year.
- Many who became seriously ill found their coverage inadequate.

RELATIONSHIP BETWEEN HEALTH POLICY AND THE LAWS THAT AFFECT HEALTHCARE

Health policy identifies the public interest as it answers the question: "What should be done to promote the health and welfare of the public?" Laws affecting healthcare result from the conclusions by a majority of legislators that a law or government regulation is necessary to ensure that the public interest is served. Moving from proposed public policy to law is a matter of votes.

Marshaling arguments and addressing the concerns of those opposed to pass legislation can take a considerable amount of time. America's political leaders have recognized the need for universal health coverage since the early 1900s (Johnson and Broder 1997). In the 1912 presidential campaign, both Theodore Roosevelt and Woodrow Wilson pledged to improve the nation's health. In 1935, Franklin D. Roosevelt included medical benefits in his Social Security bill, but the opposition of doctors forced him to remove the benefits. Harry S. Truman made healthcare a major issue in his 1948 campaign, but a "national education" campaign by the American Medical Association after his election stopped that effort as well. In 1960, John F. Kennedy made Medicare a significant part of his presidential campaign, but had too narrow an election victory and too little political support to pass legislation. He renewed the effort in his 1962 mid-term campaign. In 1965, Lyndon B. Johnson saw the passage of Medicare and Medicaid as part of his "Great Society" legislation. Medicare provided universal coverage for seniors with benefit limits; Medicaid provided care for welfare recipients and children and provided long-term care for the indigent elderly and the disabled. That legislation was made possible with the biggest Democratic majorities in Congress since the early 1930s (Johnson and Broder 1997). Richard M. Nixon introduced the Health Maintenance Organization (HMO) legislation in 1971 to support the expansion of HMOs as a way of providing broader coverage to more people at less cost. A companion measure requiring employers to provide a minimum level of benefits to all employees was dropped when opposed by the AMA and the insurance industry. In 1988, Medicare Catastrophic Coverage was passed with strong bipartisan support to address a gap in Medicare coverage. However, strong opposition by seniors to paying supplemental premiums for other seniors who had not already purchased "MediGap" insurance coverage led to the repeal of the Catastrophic Coverage legislation (Johnson and Broder 1997).

Despite the support by many American presidents since 1912 and the substantial efforts of the Clinton Administration in 1993–94, the votes to pass national health insurance have been lacking.

WHO DECIDES HEALTH POLICY?

Health policy is envisioned by a political sponsor who sees the value and opportunity for possible legislation. The political leader may be a legislator or leader of the executive branch. Healthcare policy is decided in the process of attracting enough votes to pass.

Role of the Executive

The leader of the executive branch—a president, governor, or mayor—
is critically important in outlining the principles for major change.
They have the public platform to call attention to both the issue and
the principles they consider important. As an example, the principles
of the Clinton plan (from September of 1992) are summarized in the
following points (Johnson and Broder 1997):

- All workers and their families would receive health insurance
  through their jobs, with employers paying most of the premiums. The economic costs to small business would be cushioned
  by direct subsidies and a slow phase-in.
- Every American would be covered; those outside the workforce
  would have their premiums paid by the government.
- Networks of hospitals, physicians, and other medical professionals would be organized in every community to compete in
  this expanded marketplace, charging flat fees for a standard pack-
  age of benefits for everyone who signed up. The government
  would set the top fee; market forces might undercut it.
- States would organize health insurance purchasing cooperatives
  (later called alliances) through which small firms, the self-
  employed, and other individuals could buy policies at better rates
  than they would otherwise get. The alliances would put competitive pressure on the healthcare networks to improve quality and
  reduce costs.
- To ensure that the anticipated savings were realized, the federal
  government would set an overall national health budget, and
  both insurance premiums and providers' fees would have to stay
  under that ceiling.

President Clinton went beyond the outlining of principles when on
January 5, 1993, he announced the formation of a National Health Insurance Task Force, headed by Hillary Rodham Clinton. This task force
approach kept control of the process, but tied President Clinton to the
success of the specific proposal. It limited his options and the ability

of the political process to make tradeoffs. How these limitations affected the final outcome is open to conjecture. It was, however, a departure from the usual political process that uses tradeoffs to pass legislation.

The Political Process ("The System")

The process of developing legislation that attracts enough votes to pass typically follows a set of specific steps, as summarized here by Johnson and Broder (1997).

- Political appointees—many with extensive backgrounds in health policy—hook up with career officials in the Department of Health and Human Services (HHS) to assemble options.
- Think-tank authors, academics, congressional staffers, and the staffs of the many interest groups with a stake in health policy produce memos and position papers.
- Drafts of proposed legislation are shown to other departments.
- The Office of Management and Budget double checks the financial assumptions.
- Members of the president's staff are shown the ideas and asked for their reactions to the political feasibility.
- Key players on Capitol Hill and interested parties are brought in to discuss both the policy and the politics of the proposed legislation.
- By the time the president acts, the policy has been scrutinized by a wide spectrum of people and the coalition of support is in place.

Johnson and Broder (1997) suggest that if Clinton had assigned the job of developing national health legislation to the HHS, this process would have been followed. Opportunities would have existed to gather input, make political tradeoffs, and build a coalition of support before President Clinton had to commit himself to a course of action.

In contrast, three people, with their tight control over the process, made the final decisions on the Clinton plan: President Clinton, Hillary Rodham Clinton, and Ira Magaziner (Johnson and Broder 1997). Ira Magaziner, a senior advisor to President Clinton for policy development, worked with Hillary Rodham Clinton and led the process that developed the plan.

Examples of Legislative Success

Two legislative victories illustrate the successful application of following the steps outlined above: (1) The Tax Reform Act of 1986 that gained bipartisan support in Ronald Reagan's presidency; and (2) HIPAA (the Kassebaum-Kennedy bill) in 1996, a follow-up to the failed Clinton health plan.

The Tax Reform Act began with Ronald Reagan's statement of the principle: "Eliminate special interest loopholes and you can have lower tax rates for everybody." The Treasury Department professional staff drafted their view of the best policy, which was then turned over to political leadership to develop legislation with sufficient bipartisan support (votes) to pass. Ronald Reagan was free to sign the resulting legislation or veto it (Johnson and Broder 1997).

The Kassebaum-Kennedy bill addressed two concerns with the broadest agreement in the Clinton health plan debate: (1) no one could be denied insurance because of a preexisting medical condition, and (2) health insurance coverage could not be denied because a person changed jobs or lost a job. Republican Senator Nancy Kassebaum and Democratic Senator Ted Kennedy cosponsored the bill and introduced the legislation in August of 1995. Again, opposition by the Health Insurance Association of America (HIAA) and other political interests had to be addressed. The bipartisan leadership developed a compromise bill that passed with "no dissenting voices in the Senate and only two in the House" (Johnson and Broder 1997). President Clinton signed the bill into law on August 21, 1996.

Had the development of national healthcare legislation followed the normal legislative process ("The System" as outlined above), Clinton would have been in control of two very important points: the content of the health policy proposal that was sent to the HHS (the set of principles first outlined in late September 1992) and the approval or veto of the legislation produced by the system.

THE HEALTHCARE ORGANIZATION'S RESPONSIBILITY

Healthcare organizations have distinctive knowledge that no other element in society has access to. Those organizations that use their knowledge to develop sound health policy, and to support the passage of legislation to implement that policy, have a significant competence in health policy and law.

Physicians and other professional caregivers possess knowledge of how to best care for patients. The work of John Wennberg, M.D., as published in the *Dartmouth Atlas of Health Care* (1997), shows wide variations in the actual care provided, and the costs of that care, to achieve the same outcomes. Physicians and others have demonstrated, however, that given appropriate incentives, they can work together to identify and adopt "best practices," that produce high-quality outcomes at least cost.

The leaders of the organization, working with the clinical care professionals and with specialists in other areas such as finance, have the knowledge and ability to identify alternative ways of addressing the health policy concerns, and to estimate the costs of alternative ways of implementing health policy. With that knowledge, they can determine how to best address the health policy concerns at least cost.

Organizations that use this knowledge to support health policy in the public's interest develop a distinctive competency. Leaders of these organizations are sought out and listened to when health policy issues are considered. Political stripe is not important—both Republican Senator Dave Durenberger and Democrat Hillary Rodham Clinton sought the views of Mayo Clinic and other leading healthcare organizations. Providing information that contributes to the development of health policy in the public's interest, over time, is important. It develops a cooperative, supportive relationship with legislators and their staffs and gives the organization significant say in affecting the development of effective, workable legislation.

CONTRIBUTING TO THE DEVELOPMENT OF HEALTH POLICY

Health policy asks the question: "Should the status quo change, and if so, how?" The strength of the status quo is shown in Machiavelli's (1952) famous quotation:

> There is nothing more difficult to carry out, nor more doubtful of success, nor dangerous to handle, than to initiate a new order of things. For the reformer has enemies in all those who profit by the old order, and only lukewarm defenders in all those who would profit by the new order ....

Major policy change typically takes an inordinate amount of time. The question is: "Why?" Major policy change requires time to marshal the arguments and to demonstrate that continuation of the existing system does not work. Winston Churchill once observed that, "Americans will always do the right thing ... after they've exhausted all the alternatives." Persistence and adaptability are key. If one approach does not work, try another. Few big ideas that make a difference pass the first time they are proposed.

The development of health policy is a fluid, formative process. "The System" is a system of political give and take. John Mitchell's experience in this chapter's "Case in Point" is a small example of the steps needed to build a coalition of votes to affect a political decision. When a policy is being considered, ideas and information become the basis for arguments that support the proposed policy or indicate policy change is necessary.

Alternatively, some people stand back and wait to see what happens: "If something happens that I don't like, then I will get involved." This attitude, however, is a risky one. Once a new policy is formalized with legislation, it becomes the "status quo" and gains significant strength. Changing the new law requires starting from the beginning, with only an idea. The effort of marshaling the arguments, gaining the attention of the political process, and building a coalition of support behind proposed legislation has to be done all over again. The actions of those who opposed the Clinton plan show that sophisticated participants do not wait to see what happens. They use their energies to effect the political result they want to see in proposed legislation.

ROLE OF ASSOCIATIONS IN CONTRIBUTING TO HEALTHCARE POLICY

Associations are key to developing consensus and building political support for, or opposition to, proposed legislation. They have access to their members and can develop information across an entire industry, information that can lead to a consensus understanding of what should be done. Some associations have carved out a niche as a recognized source for information. The Medical Group Management Association, as an example, is the source for information on the revenues and costs of medical group practice.

Associations hire lobbyists to monitor legislation that will potentially affect their members. As shown in the defeat of the Clinton plan, associations exercise considerable power in mobilizing political support for, or opposition to, proposed legislation. The HIAA and the National Federation of Independent Businessmen led the effort to defeat the Clinton plan with sophisticated campaigns. Particularly effective were the efforts of the HIAA members—270 mostly small and medium health insurers that, combined, covered a third of all Americans.

In response to the Clinton plan, the HIAA hired A. Willis Gradison—a respected, moderate conservative Republican who had served nine terms in the House and was influential on the Ways and Means Committee, the Health Subcommittee, and the Budget Committee—as its new president. Gradison appointed Charles N. (Chip) Kahn III, who had been Republican health policy counsel on Ways and Means, as executive vice president. The HIAA then met with Ira Magaziner and objected to three elements of the Clinton plan:

1. The need for insurance companies to be certified by the health alliances to continue to sell health insurance and potentially limit the market access of these insurance companies
2. Health insurance "premium caps" as a cost control
3. Pure community rating, which would take away their ability to selectively insure only the best (least expensive) risks

HIAA eventually became convinced there would be no negotiation on those points.

In early 1993, HIAA retained two consultants who had successfully defeated an employer mandate proposal in California in November 1992, and two Washington pollsters, Democrat Bill Hamilton and Republican Bill McInturff, to monitor public opinion. Outside lobbyists Republican Nicholas E. Calio (former top congressional liaison for the Bush White House) and Democrat Lawrence F. O'Brien III were hired to handle the congressional liaison task. HIAA also began a $3.5 million advertising campaign based on Hamilton and McInturff's focus group findings that the public distrusted government and responded to phrases such as: "They choose, you lose," and "There's got to be a better way." The findings also revealed that the public trusted their own agents but distrusted the industry, prompting the association to form a coalition of allied groups, the Coalition for Health Insurance Choices.

Based on the focus group findings and Gradison's conclusion that, "This issue will be settled at kitchen tables all across America," HIAA decided to mount a major television campaign and developed the "Harry and Louise" ads. In these ads, an announcer says, "The government may force us to pick from a few healthcare plans designed by government bureaucrats," to which Louise replies, "Having choices we don't like is like having no choice at all." Harry responds with, "They choose," and Louise concludes "We lose."

With these efforts, HIAA raised and spent $50 million—$30 million more than its normal budget of $20 million. The association's grassroots campaign produced more than 450,000 contacts with Congress, or "almost a thousand to every member of the House and Senate" (Johnson and Broder 1997). Finally, HIAA created field organizations in six states with senators and/or representatives in crucial positions and relied on hired field agents and member company employees, managers, and agents. These organizations were particularly effective because they identified people who had close, personal relationships with Congress and then used these people to contact members of Congress.

In efforts to support or block legislation, the challenge is to be more effective than the opposition. The HIAA's extensive efforts—and obvious results—prove that associations can be a powerful force in preserving the status quo and protecting the perceived interests of their members. The challenge for associations—just as for individual organizations—is to find ways to address the problems that concern the public. To retain and build political influence, they must show that what they represent is in the public's interest. In November of 2000, HIAA, the American Hospital Association, and Families USA—a consumer lobbying group that had supported passage of the Clinton plan—announced a jointly developed plan to cover the uninsured.

GRASS-ROOTS INVOLVEMENT AND LEGISLATIVE RELATIONSHIPS

In the Clinton health plan battle, the deciding factor was votes, not dollars. The money was a wash, but the votes made the difference (Johnson and Broder 1997). Grass-roots involvement equals votes. Personal contact with legislators is crucial. The person making the contact may only be a friend of someone who grew up in the same neighborhood, but it gives that person special access. Personal stories abound in healthcare (i.e., what this issue means to me, my family, or my coworkers), and those personal connections focus the legislator on the problem and the implications of proposed solutions.

Legislators are often approached by people who have a problem and want assistance in addressing the problem. Developing close working relationships with legislators is imperative in gaining their support on issues. The key is in securing the relationship before there is an acute need. Helping them get elected and helping them understand healthcare through your organization is the best way to ensure a beneficial relationship.

Inviting legislators to your facility is an effective way to educate them about healthcare. Encourage them to meet with the organization's administrative and clinical leadership and to discuss issues being raised by their constituents. Such a conversation is an opportunity to show concern for addressing the issues, to outline what your organization is doing to address those issues, and to outline the obstacles that must be overcome.

Meetings with legislators also offer an opportunity to provide information on healthcare issues on a prospective basis. Many important topics help promote an understanding of the healthcare system. One is the idea that better care can be provided at less cost—which is, still, for many people, a counterintuitive idea. Providing examples will help legislators understand what can be done. The early work of Brent James, M.D., at Intermountain Healthcare found that surgeons who did operations in less time had less blood loss, better outcomes, and lower total cost of care. The surgery department in the school of medicine at Michigan State University recently reported similar findings (Taylor 2000).

The question of financing system incentives is another important topic. What are the differences between the single payer and the managed care models? What incentives does each provide for the organization to better manage care? Because the incentives provided by fee-for-service payments versus capitation or global fees are different, how care is reimbursed is important.

Legislators who take the time to understand these healthcare-related issues deserve support. Providing a legislator with information on healthcare issues to respond to the concerns of constituents is an important way of helping them serve their constituents and retain/build voter support. Legislators need financial support and votes to be reelected.

ROLE OF LOBBYISTS

Lobbyists are individuals who are known by the legislators and have cultivated their relationships with the legislators to gain access to effectively present their clients' interests. Industry associations are a good place to start to locate a lobbyist. The leaders of those associations can use their contacts to identify the lobbyists who are particularly knowledgeable and effective on specific issues.

In instances where the organization and individuals have not developed a personal connection with the legislators as outlined above, lobbyists provide a valuable connection and ensure that the organization's concerns are heard.

Lobbyists also offer valuable assistance when reaching agreement requires negotiation, as in the "Case in Point" example of Midwest Medical Center, the city council, and the state EPA. The lobbyist serves as a facilitator and tests ideas in the process of developing an agreement that meets the interests of all parties.

VALUES, MISSION, AND HEALTH POLICY

Values take on a deeper meaning in deciding how to address issues of health policy.

Some organizations value taking care of all patients without regard for ability to pay. Other organizations value taking care of patients who can pay best. The organization's values and mission determine how the organization will best serve its own interests and those of its patients. Competency and experience come from the problems an organization faces and the care it has provided to its patients.

Advocating for the organization when it may not be in the interests of patients—is this ever the best thing to do? Although it may be difficult to determine the action that is in the best interest of patients, patients choose their healthcare based on trust in their physician and the organization. That trust is a core asset of the organization. To build and retain that trust over time, the organization must continue to ask—and act on—the question: "What is in the best interest of our patients?"

CONCLUSION

Healthcare is subject to substantial government regulation. Healthcare organizations have the knowledge and personal interest to make significant, positive contributions to the development of health policy.

Understanding the issues as seen by legislators—and regulators—is the first step. Identifying their perspective is an opportunity to search for the common ground. Once identified, the challenge is to help reach the common ground as efficiently as possible.

Healthcare organizations have, or must develop, an organizational competence in health policy and law. The basis for the organization's competence is in its distinctive knowledge of healthcare. Proactive involvement in the development of health policy—using that knowledge—is the way to become a respected source that governmental agencies and legislators will look to when developing health policy issues. This chapter has shown strategies used to pass or block legislation affecting healthcare. An organization that also understands and is able to employ these strategies, as appropriate, will have developed an organizational competence in health policy and law.

DISCUSSION

1. How is the need for legislation identified?
2. Who has to agree to the proposed legislation?
3. How are the interests of those who must agree identified?
4. What changes are made in the process of getting agreement on the proposed legislation?
5. What challenges do organizations and associations both face as they work to influence health policy?

REFERENCES

Johnson, H. and D. S. Broder. 1996. *The System: The American Way of Politics at the Breaking Point.* Boston: Little, Brown and Co.

Machiavelli, N. 1952. *The Prince.* New York: Mentor/New American Library.

Taylor, M. 2000. "One by One" in "Risk Management Rewards." *Modern Healthcare* 30 (45): 40, 42–43.

Wennberg, J. and Dartmouth Medical School Center for the Evaluative Clinical Sciences. 1997. *Dartmouth Atlas of Health Care.* Chicago: American Hospital Publishing, Inc.

CHAPTER 10

Alternative, Complementary, and Integrative Medicine

CASE IN POINT: George Daniels, M.D., is the president of Smithtown Medical Clinic. Smithtown, a suburb of a major metropolitan area, houses the state university and medical school. The clinic was founded in 1951 and is recognized as the leading private, multispecialty physician group in the area.

George has had a long-standing interest in the development of medical practice. Looking back at the founders of Smithtown Clinic, he is impressed at how these physicians have been on the forefront of advances in medical practice over the years. They had often been the first to add new specialists to their community practice. In some areas, such as ophthalmology, the clinic has more fellowship-trained specialists, in more specialties, than the university. The clinic also has a strong primary care base and prides itself on providing comprehensive care for its patients. It provides 60 percent of the admissions to Smithtown Community Hospital.

George had read, with interest, the results of the research published in 1993 by Eisenberg and his colleagues that indicated that 34 percent of adults used unconventional therapy in the year surveyed, but only 30 percent of those had talked with their physician about that care. Their research estimated 427,000 visits nationally, more than the estimated total of 385,000 visits to all primary care physicians in that year. Unconventional therapy—defined in the research report as "medical interventions not taught widely at U.S. medical schools or generally available at U.S. hospitals"—included acupuncture, chiropractic, and massage therapy. The idea of bringing some of these practitioners into the clinic just did not make sense to him, but many patients were clearly finding value in these services, even paying out of pocket for them.

Terry Waters has been the president and CEO of Smithtown Community Hospital for the past five years. He is proud of the breadth of services and the continuum of care offered by the hospital and its medical staff. Smithtown Medical Clinic represents over half the medical staff and is highly regarded in the area, but the other members of the medical staff are highly qualified and competent physicians as well. The hospital staff bylaws require physicians to be board eligible or board certified to be granted privileges to practice; to retain those privileges, they must be board certified within five years of joining the hospital staff.

George and Terry meet weekly to discuss general topics of interest. Both had noticed the growth of healthcare-related services in their community: more chiropractors had moved into the area; two acupuncturists opened offices following Medicare's approval of acupuncture as a reimbursed service in 1996; a large megavitamin and herbal therapy store had opened; and others were offering relaxation consultations, massage therapy, and hypnosis.

When Eisenberg and his colleagues published a follow-up report, "Trends in Alternative Medicine Use in the United States, 1990–1997" (Eisenberg et al. 1998), Terry and George were impressed by the key findings. Visits to all primary care physicians had remained the same from 1990 to 1997, while visits to alternative medicine providers had increased from 427 million to 629 million. Total out-of-pocket expenditures for alternative therapies were estimated at $27 billion—comparable to total out-of-pocket expenditures for all U.S. physician services in 1997 and more than double the total out-of-pocket expenditures for all U.S. hospitalizations in 1997.

As George and Terry talked about the report, they realized they should be looking for ways to incorporate these unconventional, or "alternative," therapies. George knew some physicians in the clinic referred patients to alternative providers for care, but he doubted it was widespread—likely most patients were self-referring for care. In some cases, patients were at risk for complications because of uncoordinated care including drug interactions between herbal therapy and prescription medicines. George and Terry had heard stories that indicated some alternative providers were better than others—some were credentialed in some way, while others provided services without any such regulation.

Terry and George knew that a strong cultural bias against alternative medicine existed in the clinic and in the hospital. They began to frame several questions: Should the clinic and the hospital provide alternative medical care in the community? What relationship should they try to develop with the existing services? Should they develop competing services? Should they develop referral relationships? What should they do to educate the boards of both organizations about the possible value—for their organizations and the community—of a closer relationship with providers of alternative medicine? If they were to decide to develop such relationships, how should they begin?

QUESTION: What knowledge of alternative, complementary, and integrative medicine will assist George and Terry to answer their questions?

INTRODUCTION

This chapter presents research findings on the prevalence and use of alternative and complementary medicine, the factors that attract patients to alternative and complementary medicine, and the attraction for both patients and physicians of *integrative* medicine—the joint use of alternative, complementary, and conventional medicine in ways that benefit patients.

The National Center for Complementary and Alternative Medicine (NCCAM) defines complementary and alternative medicine as "those treatments and healthcare practices not taught widely in medical schools, not generally used in hospitals, and not usually reimbursed by insurance companies" (2000). *Alternative medicine* refers, historically, to all nonconventional therapies (several of the articles referred to in this chapter use "alternative medicine" in this way). More recently, alternative medicine refers to therapies that are used alone, as a substitute for more conventional medicine. *Complementary medicine* refers to therapies that are used in conjunction with conventional medicine (NCCAM 2000; and Milton and Benjamin 1999). As the value of a particular alternative medicine technique is identified and accepted by conventional medicine, that technique will come to be identified as a complementary therapy. *Integrative medicine* is most broadly defined as the synthesis of alternative, complementary, and conventional medical care (Milton and Benjamin 1999).

The term *alternative medicine* refers to the broader historic meaning in many of the references cited in this chapter. The context will provide a guide as to whether the reference is to the broad case of alternative therapies or the more limited reference to substitute therapies. The terms *complementary* and *integrative* medicine will have the above definitions as these terms are used in this chapter. The general category of complementary and alternative therapies is also referred to as CAM.

Healthcare organizations that bring together the capabilities of alternative, complementary, and conventional medicine to improve the health and sense of well-being of their patients will have developed an organizational competence in alternative, complementary, and integrative medicine.

ALTERNATIVE AND COMPLEMENTARY MEDICINE— SIGNIFICANT THERAPIES

The original work by Eisenberg et al. (1993; 1998) provides a framework for understanding what is included in CAM. The 1993 research is based on 16 groupings of interventions that were identified in pilot research as "representative of unconventional therapies used commonly in the United States." The 1998 research continued to measure the prevalence and use of these therapies, as shown in Table 10.1.

The totals for these 16 therapies show significant increases in use in 1997 versus 1990 (the 1993 research). The percentage of people surveyed who used at least one of these therapies increased from 33.8 percent to 42.1 percent. The percentage of people using one or more of these therapies who saw an alternative medicine practitioner increased from 36.3 percent to 46.3 percent. The mean number of visits per user decreased from 19.2 to 16.3, but the total visits per thousand increased from 2,373 to 3,176. Total visits to alternative medicine practitioners increased from an estimated 427 million in 1990 to an estimated 629 million in 1997.

WHY PATIENTS USE COMPLEMENTARY AND ALTERNATIVE MEDICINE

The growth of CAM on an individual-pay basis shows that individuals are finding value in these therapies. The research by Eisenberg et al. (1993; 1998) estimated that the total dollars paid annually by individuals for this care is significant. Total out-of-pocket payments for visits to alternative medicine providers in 1997 were estimated at $12.2 billion. Total out-of-pocket expenditures related to alternative therapies were estimated at $27 billion. The primary reason people gave for using these therapies was their perception that these therapies work.

The fourteen most common problems for which patients sought alternative treatment in 1997 are listed in Table 10.2.

The percentage of people who saw a medical doctor for a condition who also used an alternative therapy increased from 19.9 percent in 1990 to 31.8 percent in 1997. Data reported but not included in Table 10.2 show that an average of 13.7 percent who saw a medical doctor for a condition in 1997 also saw an alternative provider, an increase from 8.3 percent in 1990.

In terms of who uses alternative medicine, Eisenberg et al. (1998) found in 1997 that rates of use varied from 32 percent to 54 percent in

Table 10.1. Comparison of Prevalence and Frequency of Use of Alternative Therapies Among Adult Respondents, 1997 vs. 1990*

Type of Therapy	Used in Past 12 Mo. (%)		Saw a Practitioner in Past 12 Mo. (%)		Mean No. of Visits per User in Past 12 Mo.		No. of Visits per 1,000 Population		Estimated Total No. of Visits in 1997 (in Thousands)†	Total Visits (%)‡§
	1997	1990	1997	1990	1997	1990	1997	1990		
Relaxation techniques	16.3¶	13.1	15.3	9.0	20.9	18.6	521.2	219.3	103,203	16.4
Herbal medicine	12.1**	2.5	15.1	10.2	2.9	8.1	53.0	20.7	10,491	1.7
Massage	11.1**	6.9	61.6#	41.4	8.4	14.8	574.4	422.8	113,723	18.1
Chiropractic	11.0	10.1	89.9**	71.1	9.8	12.6	969.1¶	904.8	191,886	30.5
Spiritual healing by others ‖	7.0#	4.2	—	9.2	—	14.2	—	54.9	—	—
Megavitamins	5.5**	2.4	23.7	11.8	8.6	12.6	112.1	35.7	22,196	3.5
Self-help group	4.8**	2.3	44.4	38.3	18.9	20.5	402.8	180.6	79,754	12.7
Imagery	4.5	4.2	23.1	15.1	11.0	14.2	114.3	90.1	22,640	3.6
Commercial diet	4.4	3.9	43.2	24.0	7.3	20.7	139.8	193.8	27,474	4.4
Folk remedies	4.2**	.2	6.2	.0	1.0	—	2.6	—	516	.1
Lifestyle diet	4.0	3.6	8.0	12.5	2.8	8.1	9.0	36.5	1,774	.3
Energy healing	3.8**	1.3	26.3	32.2	20.2#	8.3	201.9¶	34.7	39,972	6.4
Homeopathy	3.4**	.7	16.5	31.7	1.6	6.1	9.0	13.5	1,777	.3
Hypnosis	1.2	.9	62.7	51.8	2.8	2.6	21.1	12.1	4,171	.7
Biofeedback	1.0	1.0	54.3	20.8	3.6	6.4	19.5	13.3	3,871	.6
Acupuncture	1.0¶	.4	87.6	91.3	3.1	38.4	27.2	140.2	5,377	.9
≥1 of 16 alternative therapies	42.1**	33.8	46.3#	36.3	16.3	19.2	3,176.0	2,373.0	62,8825	—
Standard error	1.2	1.4	1.9	2.5	1.8	4.5	378.7	599.7	74,997	—
Self-prayer ‖	35.1**	25.2	—	—	—	—	—	—	—	—

* Percentages are of those who used that type of therapy. Dashes indicate data not applicable.

† Estimate based on 1997 population estimate of 198 million.

‡ Percentage of total visits of the 16 therapies (i.e., excluding self-prayer).

§ Because of rounding, percentages do not total 100.

‖ Respondents who received spiritual healing by others were not asked for details of visits in 1997, nor were those who used self-prayer in either year.

¶ p ≤ .05; # p ≤ .01; ** p ≤ .001.

Source: Eisenberg et al. 1998.

Table 10.2. Use of Alternative Therapies for the Most Frequently Reported Principal Medical Conditions, 1997

Condition	Percentage Reporting Condition	Used Alternative Therapy for Condition in Past 12 Mo. (%)	Saw Medical Doctor and Used Alternative Therapy for Condition in Past 12 Mo. (%)	Therapies Most Commonly Used in 1997
Back problems	24.0	47.6	58.8	Chiropractic, massage
Allergies	20.7	16.6	28.0	Herbal, relaxation
Fatigue	16.7	27.0	51.6	Relaxation, massage
Arthritis	16.6	26.7	38.5	Relaxation, chiropractic
Headaches	12.9	32.2	42.0	Relaxation, chiropractic
Neck problems	12.1	57.0	66.6	Chiropractic, massage
High blood pressure	10.9	11.7	11.9	Megavitamins, relaxation
Sprains or strains	10.8	23.6	29.4	Chiropractic, relaxation
Insomnia	9.3	26.4	48.4	Relaxation, herbal
Lung problems	8.7	13.2	17.9	Relaxation, spiritual healing
Skin problems	8.6	6.7	6.8	Imagery, energy healing
Digestive problems	8.2	27.3	34.1	Relaxation, herbal
Depression	5.6	40.9	40.9	Relaxation, spiritual healing
Anxiety	5.5	42.7	42.7	Relaxation, spiritual healing
Weighted average*	—	28.2	31.8	Relaxation, spiritual healing

* Weighted averages are calculated based on all 37 conditions studied in 1997 and all 24 conditions studied in 1990 (i.e., condition is a unit of analysis).

Adapted from: Eisenberg, et al. 1998.

the wide range of sociodemographic groups surveyed. Use was more common among women (48.9 percent) than men (37.8 percent), and less common among African Americans (33.1 percent) than other racial groups (44.5 percent). People aged 35 to 49 reported use rates of 50.1 percent versus lower rates for those older (39.1 percent) and younger (41.8 percent). Use was higher in those with some college education (50.0 percent) than those without (36.4 percent), and greater for people with incomes above $50,000 (48.1 percent) than for those with lower incomes (42.6 percent). Use was more common in the West (50.1 percent) than elsewhere in the United States (42.1 percent).

In addition to perceived value, what factors are behind this use of CAM? Some conclude that it provides a more optimistic view of an individual's condition and focuses on self-help to connect with a healing, healthy nature and "vitalist life supporting forces" (Kaptchuk and Eisenberg 1998). It affirms patients' experiences as a significant source of data about their condition. Spirituality and healing are closely related, and individuals can positively affect their healing.

A national survey by Stanford researcher John Astin (1998) tested three theories proposed to explain the use of alternative medicine.

1. *Dissatisfaction:* patients are dissatisfied with conventional treatment because it has been ineffective, has produced adverse effects, or is seen as impersonal, too technologically oriented, and/or too costly.
2. *Need for personal control:* patients seek alternative providers and therapies because they see them as less authoritarian and more empowering, offering them more personal autonomy and control over their healthcare decisions.
3. *Philosophical congruence:* alternative therapies are attractive because they are more compatible with patients' values, world views, spiritual/religious philosophies, or beliefs regarding the nature and meaning of health and illness.

In response to these three theories, Astin's survey (1998) found the following:

1. *Dissatisfaction:* not a significant factor. Of those reporting that they were highly satisfied with their "conventional practitioners" (54 percent of those surveyed), 39 percent were also users of alternative medicine. Of those reporting that they were highly dissatisfied (9 percent of those surveyed), 40 percent were users of alternative medicine.
2. *Need for personal control:* not a significant predictor of use.
3. *Philosophical congruence:* having a holistic philosophy of health (the health of the body, mind, and spirit are related, and should be taken into account) was predictive of alternative therapy use. Of those with this philosophy, 46 percent were users of alternative therapies as compared to 33 percent of those who did not have this philosophy.

The survey also found that those with poorer health status were also higher users of alternative medicine.

Only 4.4 percent of the respondents relied primarily on alternative medicine, which is similar to the 3 percent found in an earlier survey (Eisenberg et al. 1993). For this group, significant factors were (1) distrust of conventional physicians and hospitals; (2) desire for control over health matters; (3) dissatisfaction with conventional practitioners; and (4) belief in the importance and value of one's inner life and experiences.

LEGITIMIZATION OF ALTERNATIVE THERAPIES

In 1972, the Food and Drug Administration followed the recommendations of its advisory committee and labeled acupuncture devices as investigational. In 1996, the FDA removed the investigational label (Freshley and Carlson 2000).

Today, at least 30 medical schools in the United States now include some content on alternative therapies in their curricula (Milton and Benjamin 1999). The NCCAM has seen its annual budget increase from $2 million in 1993 to $68.7 million in 2000 and is funding research to evaluate the efficacy of alternative medicine therapies in the areas of:

- Addictions
- Aging and women's health
- Arthritis
- Cardiovascular diseases
- Cardiovascular disease and minority aging
- Craniofacial disorders
- Neurological disorders
- Pediatrics

Institutions funded for this work include conventional academic institutions such as Columbia University, the University of Arizona, the University of Maryland, and University of Michigan, as well as unconventional ones such as the College of Maharishi Vedic Medicine. In October of 2000, Harvard Medical School and Stanford School of Medicine, among others, cosponsored a conference on "Complementary and Alternative Medicine: Practical Applications and Evaluations." Conference content included models and therapies, coverage by insurers and managed care companies, legal liability and financial aspects, outcome measurement strategies, and prototypes of clinics and managed care plans offering CAM (McGrady 2000).

PHYSICIAN INTEREST

Physicians may have a greater belief in the efficacy of complementary and alternative therapies than is indicated by either their own practice of these therapies or their referrals to these therapies. A survey of physician attitudes found the following percentages of physicians believed in the efficacy of the particular therapy, used it in their practice, and referred patients for the therapy (Berman et al. 1995).

Therapy	Belief in Efficacy	Own Practice	Refer Patients
Acupuncture	49	14	26
Chiropractic	49	27	56
Homeopathy	27	5	6

| Herbal Medicine | 23 | 7 | 5 |
| Massage | 58 | 35 | 35 |

In late 1996 and early 1997, the *Journal of the American Medical Association (JAMA)* mailed a survey to a stratified sample of 500 practicing physicians, asking them to rank 73 topics—CAM among them—in the order that *JAMA* should emphasize them in future issues. In sharp contrast, the group of medical experts on whom *JAMA* typically relies ranked CAM 68 out of 73, whereas the practicing physicians ranked the topic 7 out of 73 (Lundberg, Paul, and Fritz 1998).

The top four reasons cited by physicians for practice of, referrals for, or interest in CAM, in order of frequency, are:

1. Patient's lack of response to conventional treatment
2. Patient's request or preference
3. Belief in efficacy
4. Fewer adverse effects

Conditions for which physicians use CAM or refer for CAM include psychological problems, pain, back problems, musculoskeletal disorders, chronic illnesses, anxiety, headaches, smoking cessation, and weight problems (Astin et al. 1998).

NEED FOR INTEGRATED CARE

Integrated care is the synthesis of alternative, complementary, and conventional medicine. Part of the value of integrated care is helping patients avoid a combination of CAM that poses risks for their health. In their book, *Complementary & Alternative Therapies,* Milton and Benjamin (1999) note that herbal preparations, for example, can interact with prescription medications. Although herbs are the basis for many prescription drugs, they do not require a prescription. "For example, St. John's Wort, an herb commonly used for depression, is thought to work in a fashion similar to widely used prescription antidepressants, so people should not take both simultaneously. Ginger is recommended for nausea and other gastrointestinal upsets, but it can increase bleeding risk in people who are taking warfarin or aspirin. Some herbs, such as black cohosh, work in a manner similar to estrogen and should not be used during pregnancy" (Milton and Benjamin 1999). Eisenberg et al. (1998) estimate that 15 million adults are at risk for potential adverse drug interactions involving prescription drugs and herbs or high-dose multivitamin supplements, although the exact extent of these interactions has not been documented.

A second potential value of integrated care is helping patients sort through the choices. Thanks to computers and the Internet, patients have access to extensive information about diseases and treatments. The conflicting advice can be confusing and contradictory, seeming like a "tower of Babel" of opinions (Materson 2000).

INTEGRATED CARE—A UNIQUE CORE COMPETENCE

Physicians know conventional medicine and can learn how to provide complementary medicine themselves or how to refer appropriately to providers of complementary medicine (Materson 2000). Hospitals and insurers can develop health centers where patients can receive valuable therapies (Nadel 2000; Silberman 2000). The biggest challenge may be in bridging the communication gap between patients and physicians on the subject of CAM. National surveys reported in 1993 and 1998 that fewer than 40 percent of patients discussed alternative medicine use with their physician. Eisenberg (1997) concludes that the status quo, described as "don't ask and don't tell," needs to be abandoned. However, an April 2000 survey by *Consumer Reports* indicates that communication may be improving. The survey found that 60 percent of those members surveyed who used alternative medicine informed their doctor of that use. Those who did inform their doctor reported that most doctors (55 percent) were thought to approve of the use and an additional 40 percent were at least neutral (*Consumer Reports* 2000).

Physicians have a unique core competence in knowing both conventional medicine and the patient. Physicians are in a position to provide a high value-added service for their patients. The choice is to assist patients in identifying complementary therapies that will benefit the patient, or to leave them to try alternatives on their own, which patients have shown they are willing and able to do. The question is whether there is any real alternative for conventional healthcare providers. Assisting the patient helps the patient obtain the best care available and provides a continuum of care. It maintains the relationship and is a rewarding way to practice, providing the services directly or by referral. When patients need the competencies of conventional medicine, the relationship is there.

EFFECTIVE WAYS OF INTRODUCING COMPLEMENTARY MEDICINE

Hospital service lines such as heart treatment, cancer treatment, women's services, and pain management have proven to be effective avenues for introducing complementary medicine into a healthcare organization (McGrady 2000). A heart program may offer the Dr. Dean Ornish program for individuals willing to make the significant lifestyle changes that program requires. Cardiac rehab programs already include the value of healthy nutrition and exercise. Complementary approaches to cancer treatment include both treatment modalities and palliative care. In women's services, plant estrogens are proving to be a source of choice for postmenopausal women. Acupuncture is safe and effective for pain management (Abuaisha, Costanzi, and Boulton 1998).

McGrady (2000) notes several structural options to begin integration of complementary medicine, in addition to incorporation as part of the hospital's service lines:

- Establish a complementary medicine mall comprised of independent practitioners located in space managed by the hospital.
- Establish a hospital-based or hospital-owned complementary medicine center, either freestanding, within the hospital, or as part of a wellness center.
- Establish an informal relationship with a network of complementary medicine providers who can serve as feeder and referral sources and eventually become part of the hospital managed care integrated delivery system.

One way to develop a financially successful complementary medicine program is to take a "retail" approach to the incorporation of complementary medicine (Nadel 2000). Best structured with its own employees and compensation and benefit structure, billing and collections should also be operated from a retail perspective. Hospitals and health systems that have learned these points through the experience of acquiring physician practices will recognize the value of this advice.

Legal and credentialing issues must be considered as well. One recommended source for understanding the regulatory issues is *Complementary and Alternative Medicine: Legal Boundaries and Regulatory Perspectives* by Michael Cohen (1998). Credentialing is a particular challenge given the lack of a single, overarching credentialing source for alternative medicine providers. Several specialties have their own form of credentialing, or an organization may choose to implement its own credentialing program (Milton and Benjamin 1999). A useful model is the set of requirements developed by Elizabeth Brown, M.D., as national medical director for Blue Cross Blue Shield Association (Brown 1998):

- Sufficient work experience
- Proof of malpractice insurance
- Sufficient office hours (availability)
- Adequate service facility
- Participation in quality improvement
- Compliance with NCQA credentialing standards

One of the keys to getting started is to learn who is providing the services now and to begin to build a relationship with them.

KEYS TO SUCCESS—QUESTIONS TO ASK

Several lists exist to assess readiness for developing a complementary medicine program (Milton and Benjamin 1999).

- Mission or key strategy focused on wellness or health maintenance

- Support of top management
- Physician and nurse champions who are respected for their clinical skills
- Support in the community for integrated healthcare
- A community member interested in serving on the planning committee
- Availability of competent, qualified, and successful CAM providers in the community who are interested in a working relationship

The advice is to start small and, as noted above, approach complementary medicine with a retail expectation of self-sufficient (for payers, offsetting cost savings) performance.

Milton and Benjamin's *Complementary & Alternative Therapies—An Implementation Guide to Integrative Health Care* (1999) is an excellent, step-by-step guide to implementing a program that brings together conventional medicine and complementary medicine.

CONCLUSION

Complementary and alternative medicine is a significant part of healthcare today. Conventional healthcare providers have an important opportunity to bring conventional medicine and complementary medicine together in ways that benefit patients. Alternative medicine deserves attention as the results of ongoing evaluations are known. Healthcare organizations that bring together the capabilities of alternative, complementary, and conventional medicine to improve the health and sense of well-being of the patients they serve will have developed an organizational competence in alternative, complementary, and integrative medicine.

DISCUSSION

1. Why do most patients choose to use complementary and alternative medicine, and why do they continue to do so?
2. Why should "conventional" healthcare organizations be interested in complementary and alternative medicine?

3. Identify two structural ways of bringing together conventional and complementary medicine and discuss the merits of each.

4. Identify six keys to success with complementary medicine and briefly outline the importance of each.

REFERENCES

Abuaisha, B. B., J. B. Costanzi, and A. J. Boulton. 1998. "Acupuncture for the Treatment of Chronic Painful Peripheral Diabetic Neuropathy: A Long Term Study." *Diabetic Research in Clinical Practice* 39 (2): 115–21.

Astin, J. A. 1998. "Why Patients Use Alternative Medicine—Results of a National Study." *Journal of the American Medical Association* 279 (19): 1548–53.

Astin, J. A., A. Marie, K. R. Pelletier, E. Hansen, and W. L. Haskell. 1998. "A Review of the Incorporation of Complementary and Alternative Medicine by Mainstream Physicians." *Archives of Internal Medicine* 158 (21): 2303–10.

Berman, B. M., B. K. Singh, L. Lao, B. B. Singh, K. S. Ferentz, and S. M. Hartnoll. 1995. "Physicians' Attitudes Toward Complementary or Alternative Medicine: A Regional Survey." *Journal of the American Board of Family Practice* 8 (5): 361–66.

Brown, E. 1998. "Complementary and Alternative Medicine: The Daunting Challenge." *The Physician Executive* 29 (6): 16–21.

Cohen, M. 1998. *Complementary and Alternative Medicine: Legal Boundaries and Regulatory Perspectives.* Baltimore: Johns Hopkins University Press.

Consumer Reports. 2000. "The Mainstreaming of Alternative Medicine." *Consumer Reports* 65 (5): 17–25.

Eisenberg, D. M. 1997. "Advising Patients Who Seek Alternative Medical Therapies." *Annals of Internal Medicine* 127 (1): 61–69.

Eisenberg, D. M., R. C. Davis, S. L. Ettner, S. Appel, S. Wilkey, M. V. Rompay, and R. C. Kessler. 1998. "Trends in Alternative Medicine Use in the United States, 1990–1997." *Journal of the American Medical Association* 280 (18): 1569–75.

Eisenberg, D. M., R. C. Kessler, C. Foster, E. F. Norlock, D. R. Calkins, and T. L. Delbanco. 1993. "Unconventional Medicine in the United States— Prevalence, Costs, and Patterns of Use." *The New England Journal of Medicine* 328 (4): 246–52.

Freshley, C. and L. K. Carlson. 2000. "Complementary and Alternative Medicine: An Opportunity for Reform." *Frontiers of Health Services Management* 17 (2): 7.

Kaptchuk, T. J. and D. M. Eisenberg. 1998. "The Persuasive Appeal of Alternative Medicine." *Annals of Internal Medicine* 129 (12): 1061–70.

Lundberg, G. D., M. C. Paul, and H. Fritz. 1998. "A Comparison of the Opinions of Experts and Readers as to what Topics a General Medical Journal (JAMA) Should Address." *Journal of the American Medical Association* 280 (3): 288–90.

Materson, R. S. 2000. "We Are a Nation of Lonely Molecules." *Frontiers of Health Services Management* 17 (2): 37–42.

McGrady, E. S. 2000. "Complementary Medicine: Viable Models." *Frontiers of Health Services Management* 17 (2): 20–21.

Milton, D. and S. Benjamin. 1999. *Complementary & Alternative Therapies— An Implementation Guide to Integrative Health Care.* Chicago: AHA Press, Health Forum Co.

Nadel, M. A. 2000. "Observations from a Bottom-line-oriented True Believer." *Frontiers of Health Services Management* 17 (2): 31–35.

National Center for Complementary and Alternative Medicine. 2000 "Major Domains of Complementary and Alternative Medicine." [Online article.] www.nccam.nih.gov/nccam/fcp/classify

Silberman, A. L. 2000. "Alternatives that Work—An Insurer's Path to Integrated Health Care." *Frontiers of Health Services Management* 17 (2): 43–50.

Part III: Personal Leadership Competencies

PART III FOCUSES ON several practices applicable to executives in the process of building their leadership capabilities. The chapters do not represent an entire inventory of personal leadership competencies; instead, they focus on competencies of particular value during volatile times.

This section focuses on decision making, risk taking, team building and evaluation, managing conflict, professional mentoring, and career management. These personal competencies also are useful as touchstones in planning a life-long continuing education program. As you explore these topics, it might be useful to rate yourself on a scale of one to ten as to whether they represent strengths or weaknesses.

CHAPTER 11

Decision Making

CASE IN POINT: Sam Smith is the CEO of Western Medical Center, a 300-bed hospital with a 70-year history in an urban community. Positioned next door is a large multispeciality clinic of some 225 physicians who admit their patients to several community hospitals, with the majority of their admissions to Western.

The net margins from operations have been declining now for several years. This year—for the first time in a decade—estimates suggest that Western Medical Center will end the year with a loss of about a million dollars.

Dr. Rebecca Jones, the president of the group practice, The Reber Clinic, has arranged a confidential meeting with her COO Ted Keyes and Sam Smith. Dr. Jones and Ted Keyes are concerned that the instability of the hospital's finances may lead to an erosion of support for the group by the hospital. Physician income is also becoming unstable. One of Dr. Jones's long-range goals was to see to a merger of interests between the group and the medical center. With these current uncertainties looming, a competitive hospital across town might succeed in its efforts to attract members of the group to their site in a new office building. This would be destructive to The Reber Clinic. She asks whether Western Medical Center would consider a merger with the group practice, explaining that a merger would offer opportunities to improve the hospital's market share as well as produce efficiencies for both organizations.

Sam agrees that this is a distinct possibility. The hospital would be interested in discussing a merger. Dr. Jones accepts this as a commitment to proceed. Twenty-four hours later, because Dr. Jones has dispatched a memorandum to all of the group physicians, the news of the possible merger hits the street and Sam's telephone starts ringing off the hook. A board member calls to suggest that something as important as a merger should have been discussed first by the board. Several physicians who have been regular admitters to the hospital but who are not part of the group practice call to express their anger at the prospect of a merger. They state emphatically that if the merger talks proceed they will move all their patients to a competing hospital. Sam's coo drops by to report that the hospital is buzzing about the news and asks how the management team should respond to questions.

Sam has created a communications firestorm. His instincts about the advantages of merging were probably correct, but he may have lost the game because he was careless in underestimating the effect the news of a possible merger would have on an unprepared audience. Now that the news is out, he realizes not only that he should have assessed the situation more carefully but also that he should have planned the orchestration of the decision-making and communication processes. In this case, Sam will lose some credibility in the eyes of members of the board, members of the group practice medical staff, unaffiliated members of the medical staff, and his management team. As a seasoned executive, he should have known that the higher the risk of the decision and the more people affected, the greater the need to prepare not only the members of the organization (in advance), but also those external constituent groups, for acceptance of the plan.

QUESTION: What should Sam do to repair the situation?

INTRODUCTION

Healthcare executives are expected to make sound decisions based on facts and figures as well as past experiences. Members of the medical staff, employees, and constituency groups expect executives to provide both leadership and stability. Under normal conditions this is accomplished through predictable and consistent decision-making processes. Most healthcare executives are secure in carrying out decisions when they have the time to consider all sides of an issue. However, this cautious weighing, while contributing to stability and measured progress toward a goal, can also lead to excessive bureaucracy. This tactical strategy also does not work well when the times are unsettled. This chapter addresses several of the assumptions associated with creative decision making.

INTUITION AND INFORMATION: FINDING THE RIGHT MIX

In a field now characterized by volatility and rapid change, healthcare executives need to make decisions quickly. The stakes are higher and the timeline for decision making is shorter, so the ability to assess situations quickly and accurately and to employ a range of management skills depending on the circumstances becomes essential. At times, in spite of careful preparation, the wrong conclusion is applied because of a lack of awareness of the critical nature of timing. The external environment may shift so rapidly that the rationale for making the decision is left behind in the dust.

Executives who work in larger organizations may have the advantage of employing the skills of the team to the problem or challenge at hand, but too many opinions can cloud issues and lead the indecisive leader down a path of procrastination. In smaller organizations, however, where the absence of collegial interchange means that the executive receives little input or assistance, decision making can become a very lonely and risky affair.

Leaders in all organizations face the same dilemma of knowing when to intervene and to make a decision based on instinct and an acute sense of timing, instead of letting the process flow through the normal decision-making processes. Knowing how to make a decision well—employing the right combination of intuition and information—is one of the essential core competencies of the successful executive.

CREDIBILITY AND INNOVATION IN DECISION MAKING

If irrefutable facts suggest a particular outcome, but the leader makes a decision that seems contrary to logic, the leader's judgment is obviously subject to scrutiny. Others in the organization will determine whether or not to support the decision based on their perception of the leader's track record. Leaders therefore must constantly work to enhance their credibility by summoning all possible intellectual, organizational, and creative skills to the task. If an alternate path is chosen, leaders should explain the intent behind the choice so staff members will know that there are good reasons for countering the anticipated process. Wise leaders protect their credibility by being straightforward even when making controversial decisions. Although it is risky to overrule logic in favor of instinct, occasionally such decisions bring about the best results. The trick is to identify those occasions.

The leader's credibility is also enhanced through a continual process of fine tuning style to meet current organizational needs. Modifying one's style to address a particular problem might short circuit customary decision-making processes, but this does not necessarily convey a bad message to the organization. As long as the executive guards against exploiting the power of his or her position, a thoughtful change in style might even help to point out ineffective organizational processes, thus contributing to the potential for future innovations.

Imagine a hospital CEO whose associate for professional services is unable to correct or even confront a behavior problem in one of the hospital managers who has been abrupt and rude to employees. The CEO usually practices a hands-off management style, preferring to delegate authority rather than get involved in issues that should be handled by members of the management team. However, after all normal approaches (counseling and suggesting approaches to the problem) are exhausted without success, the leader elects to confront the manager directly. Before doing so, the CEO discusses the situation with the associate to make sure they agree on the importance of the intended action. The two collaborate and make a joint decision that it is in the best interests of the organization for the leader to intervene.

The process of bypassing the hierarchical structure in the organization creates some interesting dynamics in an already complex interpersonal relationship. The potential benefit of taking direct action is well worth the risk, however, if the intended outcome (in this case, changing the manager's behavior) is achieved. The CEO is in a position to use the authority of the leadership role to influence the manager's behavior. However, the leader must also avoid any misapplication or misuse of power when addressing the problem. The key to doing this successfully is to maintain credibility and to instill confidence by communicating with both staff members and by clearly defining the roles that both should take. Failure to set up the confrontation on a collaborative basis would have raised the risk that the leader's intervention, while solving the immediate problem, would undermine the trust between the two senior executives.

Being able to deviate from normal procedures to achieve specific objectives is an occasional but very important part of the leader's role. Because the executive in the case above recognized the importance of intervening straightforwardly and deliberately in what normally would have been a matter between two subordinates, it was possible to effectively resolve the ongoing issue. Not intervening might have contributed indirectly to diminished team performance. The leader's awareness that it was time to look beyond the normal channels and to step in to resolve the problem exemplifies the intuitive, even mysterious, aspect of leadership that is so unique to each individual and so difficult to describe.

ORGANIZATIONAL BUREAUCRACY

Most healthcare executives accept bureaucracy as necessary and inevitable. After all, an effective bureaucracy grapples with ambiguity and uncertainty by establishing control systems that allow it to operate with a wider base of power than is generally granted to most individuals. There is security in knowing that the bureaucracy will counter divided responsibility and attack paternalism through group decision making. Therefore, we think of bureaucracy as basically good if it is driven by benevolent motives. By creating interdependent rather than subservient relationships, benevolent bureaucracies acknowledge and promote the idea that the future depends on the performance of all parts and all members of the system. Bureaucratic systems also work to measure and improve quality. Organizational systems driven by the development of data comparing historical performance with current events are inevitably concerned with issues of quality and performance improvement. The movement toward continuous quality improvement that is sweeping the healthcare field is just one example of the way bureaucratic practices can provide systematic approaches to problem solving (Ross 1986).

Tyranny

It is tyranny—the excess of bureaucracy—that should concern us. Tyranny reduces work commitment and destroys individual and professional value systems by taking power out of individuals' hands and depriving them of motivation. The unexpected termination of a staff member by a health services CEO might serve to demonstrate executive power, but it also conveys values that will ultimately destroy team building and effectiveness. Another pervasive and less visible form of tyranny occurs when the executive withholds needed information as a means of testing the employee's ability to arrive at a proper management decision (for example, when the CEO knows that an affected third party has useful data but does not share that knowledge with his or her colleagues).

Excessiveness

Excessive bureaucracy threatens organizational ethics and values. It is natural for organizational values to differ, but organizations that focus exclusively on the bottom line, without regard to any other goals, may end up in a state of ethical conflict. In nonprofit health services organizations, where making a profit is not the goal, any "profit" serves only as a means to the end goal of achieving the mission. Similarly, executives of successful for-profit organizations are quite aware that too much focus on the bottom line (and the use of organizational tyranny to improve it) will ultimately be destructive. If the organization has only one goal (that is, turning a profit), the CEO can justify virtually any decision that earns money for the organization. No other ethical underpinnings exist on which to base individual or organizational behavior.

Accountability

Overdeveloped bureaucracies shield individual managers from personal accountability since responsibility for tough decisions is shared. Although sharing responsibility is an essential part of managing, without a system of personal accountability, responsibility can too easily get shifted around without resolution when things go wrong. For example, an operating room supervisor with no sense of personal accountability could easily avoid a conflict between surgeons and anesthesiologists by dismissing the conflict as an interprofessional problem rather than recognizing it as a scheduling conflict created by the operating room system itself. More than once in the world of business bureaucracy, capable and trusting managers have been maneuvered into serving as scapegoats for one another's decisions. In these situations, a manager may "behave like Attila the Hun, but if [the manager] contributes substantially to organizational effectiveness, all is forgiven" (Scott and Hart 1979).

Conformity

Organizational bureaucracy tends to breed conformity, which contributes to corporate culture but may inhibit individual growth. If asked to comment on how things really work in a large healthcare system, middle managers (such as chief radiology technologists, supervisors of the medical records department, or operating room or nursing unit managers) would often give responses such as:

- "Key issues always seem to require group input. Why doesn't someone simply make a decision?"
- "There are days when I think that the reward system depends more on my social accountability than on what I really accomplish. My social behavior in group meetings is important. My superior's jokes are more important than my own."
- "If I really want to confront someone because I believe they're wrong, the team doesn't like it. Everyone around here avoids head-on confrontation. We go around smiling even when we're hurting."

By fostering widespread conformity and dependence, zealous bureaucrats can easily reinforce their own power base, taking advantage of the willingness of staff members to work as a team. They know that an atmosphere of conformity discourages individuals from rocking the boat or acting on their own ideas.

Delegation

All CEOS must unbundle and delegate responsibilities so their time can be spent on strategic issues. But CEOS who practice tyrannical bureaucracy have other motives for delegation and unbundling: to keep their options open, minimize personal risk, and distance themselves from error. Unscrupulous CEOS might even send inadequate instructions to their staff and then back away to watch what happens. They are willing to send the whole organization off in the wrong direction so they can step in at the last minute and play the hero by saving the organization from disaster.

Such situations are extreme, but the point is that when bureaucracy is out of control, unsupported by an ethical basis for operation, there is inherent potential for misuse of the leadership role. The leader's responsibility is to employ the best that organizational bureaucracy has to offer—a structure for making and supporting important decisions—without using it to stifle individuals' innovations or avoid personal accountability. Leaders who want to encourage innovation and creative decision making, in themselves and their staff, will build teams that can function effectively in the organizational structure without compromising individual autonomy.

PRINCIPLES OF DECISION MAKING IN BUREAUCRATIC ORGANIZATIONS

Working within the organizational bureaucracy, leaders should base their decision-making strategies on three basic principles:

1. Believe in process, even though they know that the usual procedures do not work to resolve every critical situation. Decision-making processes must be functional, derived to address daily issues and occurrences. The leader who believes in process will also be better equipped for situations that call for unconventional approaches.

2. Look for the "wild card" when making decisions on key issues. The wild card is the instinct for the right time to act (or not to act) in spite of data that indicate the contrary. The ability to recognize and trust this instinct is one of the unique characteristics of real leaders. Willingness to consider and act on unconventional approaches often stimulates organizational innovation. Leaders who believe in the action they are taking are able to rally the organization by encouraging them to stretch a little further. As a result, management staff and others see that they possess more potential than they had imagined. For example, a leader who has had to reduce expenses and downsize the organization, but who then finds an opportunity to take on a needed community service, sends the message that the organization has begun to heal.

3. Realize that sometimes the usual approaches to decision making have to be challenged, even if straying from the norm seems like a risky proposition. The opportunity to set aside convention will test the strength and flexibility of management teams. It might

ruffle a few feathers in the process, but it will usually lead to improved decision making in the future, as well as to the successful outcome of the situation at hand.

Organizations Stagnate in the Absence of Creative Decision Making

Although the organizational structure should always be designed to support efficient and effective decision-making processes, it should also allow the leader to take full responsibility for making the best decision in the most timely fashion. Developing an environment of trust within a team and providing team members room to grow is part of that responsibility. Good teams usually make good decisions. The leader who believes in the team's ability will enable the group to make decisions without encouraging "group think," where team members agree with the leader in spite of their better sense. Confident leaders who have faith in the contributions the team can make will create an open atmosphere that permits discussion and debate.

LEADERSHIP GOALS FOR ARTFUL DECISION MAKERS

Finding the right balance between conventional and unconventional approaches to decision making, between individual and bureaucratic control, and between withholding and exerting personal authority is a never-ending process. Most leaders have tried numerous decision-making strategies with varying degrees of success. Although different approaches work for different people, the most successful decision makers work with several principles in mind.

First, building teams is the best way to discourage turf guarding and to ensure that decisions are accepted throughout the organization. Organizations that pride themselves on team building eliminate any reason for divisional managers to build protective walls around their responsibilities or to discourage communication between teams. Allowing divisional directors to drive the decision-making process can be unhealthy, even destructive, if it leads to an overly competitive environment. The very nature of team building is such that it recognizes group more than individual effort. Thus, in a mature and fully functional team, peer pressure should make it difficult for a single individual to impede the group's progress by holding back vital information or otherwise operating in a dysfunctional fashion.

Second, allowing staff members to make mistakes is the best way for them to learn and build confidence in their own decision-making abilities. If you do not allow a certain amount of error, employees will become overly cautious, unable to take even well-considered risks for fear of committing the slightest error. Executives need to make it clear that they are willing to take the heat for mistakes made by less-experienced staff. They should see to it that staff members are never in a position of being unprotected in organizational confrontations. Backing up staff decision making does not give the leader license to demand a reciprocal relationship. CEOS who encourage their staff to be loyal to them rather than the organization (by taking the "I'll protect you, but you had better protect me" attitude) undermine the foundation of the relationship. In addition, CEOS who tell employees that mistakes are okay but then use the mistakes to justify dismissals or transfers are guilty of entrapment. Professional executives must be sensitive when applying the tools of their trade to ensure a benevolent, well-managed bureaucracy.

Third, to create order out of chaos, healthcare leaders sometimes have to function autocratically. Effective leaders realize this. They know what is best for their organizations, and they are able to assume different roles to meet shifting organizational needs. Ineffective leaders also shift roles, but they are more likely to use a tyrannical style that is arbitrary, capricious, and confusing to employees.

Fourth, the way a leader is perceived is very influential in determining the extent to which decisions are accepted and supported by staff. Be conscious of the image you project. In any organization, employees pick up clues about their CEO and about how the CEO perceives them. Well-intentioned executives should be conscious of this vigilance and of how they are perceived by members of the board, the medical staff, fellow executives, employees, and the community. Some CEOS might be surprised at what they discover.

In thinking about the image you project, it might be helpful to consider questions such as:

- How accessible am I?
- Do I contribute to the preservation of the organizational culture, or do I try to develop a personal cult?
- Am I arrogant or friendly in communications with fellow professionals, particularly those I do not know?
- Do employees fear me or trust me?
- Have I stood up for the right of the individual who has been intentionally or accidentally wronged by the system?

Your answers to such questions reveal a lot about your image and probably about your credibility with staff.

RESPONSIBILITY: THE BUCK STOPS HERE

Since the early 1990s, it has become more obvious that organizational commitment will not flourish in a workplace dominated by traditional models of control. Managers who want to do well need to rethink their relationships with their workers. A bureaucracy must be monitored to ensure that it remains benevolent and works to secure moral and ethical values. Controlling a bureaucracy requires an executive who can create and maintain management approaches—including skilled decision making—that are sensitive to the environment but also maximize the commitment and involvement of employees, managers, boards, and physicians.

In a complex healthcare system, the ultimate decision-making responsibility falls to the leader. Executives must oversee many organizational functions to ensure that patients receive appropriate care. If senior executives stop short of taking full responsibility, things go wrong and people are hurt. For example, a CEO who is unwilling to confront a situation involving an impaired physician jeopardizes both the patient and the organization. Making the right decision for the organization can sometimes mean facing conflicts between dedication to individuals and the greater responsibility to the organization.

CONCLUSION

Much of leadership is the art of knowing when to conform to normal decision-making processes and when to exert additional personal and organizational energy. Leaders who understand the importance of this art try to cultivate the intuitive side of managing, learning to trust their instincts as well as the technical competencies involved in making decisions. They know that the best decisions result from a combination of intense study, but also include the factor of intuition.

DISCUSSION

1. What kind of a decision maker are you? How do you make decisions?
2. Identify several leadership styles and give your opinion as to their advantages and disadvantages.
3. What personality traits are identified with a risk taker?
4. What leadership traits will be most in demand in the future?

REFERENCES

Ross, A. 1986. "Healthcare Executives: Are We Benevolent Bureaucrats?" *Healthcare Executive* 1 (6): 40–43.

Scott, W. G. and D. K. Hart. 1979. *Organizational America*. Boston: Houghton Mifflin Co.

CHAPTER 12

Risk Taking

CASE IN POINT: Several years ago, increasing market share was viewed as the critical point in strengthening health systems. Harbor Island Medical Center's planning director, Fred Hazard, in concert with Jim Buckles, the CEO, and other members of top management, had laid out a comprehensive strategic plan to surround the area with groups of physicians. These groups would refer patients to Harbor Island and, most importantly, provide service access points to HMO members. Harbor Island had been eyeing a particular group practice located in a key area in the suburbs with the intent of acquiring the group.

As negotiations proceeded, it was discovered that Harbor Island's main competitor, Pleasant Hills Hospital, was also courting the same group practice. Counting on the importance of a market share and that access point for HMO patients, Harbor Island's negotiating team raised the ante significantly and outbid its competitor by a good amount. In addition, Harbor Island indicated to the group that it was not necessarily important for patients requiring specialty care to be referred to them. This was welcome news to the physicians, who did not want to lose contact with their patients who might elect to stay downtown with

Harbor Island's specialists. Pleasant Hills, to the contrary, would have insisted on sending referrals to them.

As the contract documents were being signed, the CEO acknowledged to himself that things had moved very fast. There had not been time, for example, to do any benchmarking with other out-of-area systems to learn what was working and what was not. It was also disconcerting to realize the competitor had bid so much lower and had backed out of the negotiations early. The process of due diligence also had been minimized so as to not jeopardize the deal.

Jim Buckles, the CEO, had considerable credibility with his board. However, because of the timing issue, commitments were made before fully informing the board as a whole, although the board's executive committee had been involved.

At the first full board meeting following the acquisition of the group, several members asked some tough questions and others quietly expressed the opinion that Harbor Island had been "taken." Seven months later, reports reached Jim Buckles that physician productivity had fallen 10 percent since the buyout. (All physicians in the group had been placed on a straight salary based on their specialty.)

QUESTION: Clearly the CEO had taken a risk in moving the acquisition process forward so rapidly. What could he have done to reduce the risk?

INTRODUCTION

By virtue of their positions, executives are in the risk management business. The challenge for executives is to learn how to take those risks while being well-informed about the downside consequences of failure. The process of deciding on risks is complicated and involves a number of contemporary factors. This chapter identifies several risk factors and suggests approaches to measuring them.

RISKS IN DECISION MAKING

Five environmental factors increase the degree of risk in decision making:

1. *Volatility of the marketplace.* The shift in the healthcare system from a position of status quo to one marked by intense competition required changes in decision-making processes. During this shift, mergers between insurance carriers and providers occurred with great speed. If an organization did not move to secure a market share or enhance services to beat the competition, the game would be lost. This volatility required speedier decisions and raised the risk ante.

2. *Payment systems.* The extensive discounting by insurance carriers, government, and others placed considerable strains on healthcare delivery systems. To survive and remain competitive, executives engaged in ruthless cost reductions. Such reductions required extra effort by decision makers and consumed much time and energy, weakening the ability of management to respond to other challenges.

3. *Speed of communications.* Access to multiple means of gathering data, Internet capacity, and sophisticated software programs provided powerful tools for decision making, but the technology also contributed to an overload of information that discouraged its use. Frequently, the fully engaged executive failed to take advantage of this capacity partially because learning how to fully utilize that technology took too much time and effort.

4. *Medical technology.* Keeping up with a competitor required an investment in new high-priced machines or new programs requiring heavy front-end investments. Some of these decisions were clearly driven by marketplace competition. Solid fact finding in making purchase decisions was often minimal as physicians and executives felt pressured to have the newest and best, regardless, to a degree, of the economics involved.

5. *Downsizing of managerial capacity.* In the midst of this turmoil, the need to cut costs forced a reduction of the management structure. While some cuts were clearly required, some organizations lost the ability to deal with management problems. As internal operational problems increased, the fire-fighting aspect of management took attention away from other issues, including rational responses to environmental factors.

Elements Associated with Good Decision Making

Several key elements contribute to the making of good decisions and are germane to the conduct of the decision makers. The first is balance. Successful decision makers strike a balance in their decision-making processes. They know their weaknesses and can apply a perspective that demonstrates a grasp of the whole rather than a narrow focus.

The second element involves the decision maker's sense of direction. Decisions are made with reference to a larger plan. This reference point allows the executive to set a direction toward a strategic plan, to provide a testing ground for decisions. Does the decision contribute to the overall goal or is it inconsistent with the plan? Beer and Nohria (2000) report that 70 percent of all major change initiatives fail. Why? Because many managers become so immersed in countless initiatives that they lose sight of the visions or goals.

Flexibility is the third element. Although flexibility may seem inconsistent with establishing a sense of direction, it is actually complementary and necessary to achieve the goal. Decision makers must continually react to changing circumstances. The volatility in the healthcare system demands responsive attention. Clearly, when obstacles arise, the route may have to be redefined to achieve the desired result.

The fourth element is vision (Ulschak and SnowAntle 1995). A decision maker must have vision to confront the intangibles and make an educated guess on the outcomes of decisions. Peering over the horizon provides an early-warning system. While the visioning may be flawed, it nevertheless acquaints the decision maker with options and opportunities.

Weighing the Risk Involved

Because decisions must frequently be made under time constraints and pressure, it is necessary to develop a rational process for making a successful decision under pressure. As General George S. Patton, Jr., put it: "The time to take counsel of your fears is before you make an important battle decision. That's the time to listen to every fear you can imagine! When you have collected all the facts and fears and made your decision, turn off all your fears and go ahead!"

Having a well-developed assessment process when faced with a difficult decision can help to increase the chance of success.

1. *Relate the risk to the strategic plan.* As mentioned earlier, the relationship of the project to the strategic plan helps to verify that the overall direction is sound. If the project does not relate to a goal or plan, the decision maker might want to spend a little extra time identifying why. Failing to relate the project to the plan may confuse others, draw off resources needed elsewhere, or result in a loss of confidence in the decision-making process or the decision maker.

2. *Identify barriers and incentives.* The ability to identify barriers and incentives is critical. Decision makers and their teams must be in touch with the political and organizational environment to determine the concerns and people that will help or hinder the cause. Doing so provides the means of mapping and developing the tactical approaches, including the identification of key players. Both barriers and incentives must be addressed, as the incentive aspect is often overlooked in the haste to move a project forward.

3. *Determine the capacity to act.* Launching a program without having determined that sufficient resources are in place to ensure successful implementation raises the risk of failure considerably. Resources refer to organizational competency and human and financial capital. Organizational competency is that factor which permits organizational change and needs

to be in place well ahead of project implementation. A frequent cause of failure is the inability of leaders to understand potential cultural conflicts within the organization or between partner organizations. Too frequently, leaders attempt to manage change without specific information about the individuals involved in the process.

4. *Establish measurements for success or failure.* At the beginning of the project, decision makers must record and articulate the hard data that can determine success or failure of the project. Failing to gather and report the necessary data can lead to procrastination and make it immensely difficult to determine success or failure and bring closure to the process. Guideposts should be in place during the implementation phase to allow mid-course changes as needed. Continually monitoring progress is very important.

5. *Create an inventory of warning signals.* Warning signals are points along the way that can predict success or failure. An example of a warning sign would be a project to improve accounts receivable where commitments concerning improvement are not met according to the timeline. Failure to delve into the reasons why the commitments were not met clearly increases the risk of failure. There is a considerable propensity for those managing the program or project to justify missed marks. This is understandable but, nevertheless, inquiry into the validity of the justification is warranted.

6. *Nurture a culture of analyzing failures.* Although the literature has much to say about failure analysis, most references refer to manufacturing issues. The methodology, however, is similar in healthcare delivery. The process is not focused on finding the "bad apples," but rather on a rational exploration with involved participants of what went wrong and why (Boyle 1988). The identification and establishment of means to measure results are also critical to the process to counter purely subjective assessments. Concepts associated with clinical review of cases can be applied to administrative and management problems. Much can be learned from monitoring clinical review processes. A formal

program of failure analysis needs to be part of the accepted culture of the organization, as contrasted with sporadic use that can appear threatening.

Sustaining or Abandoning the Effort

Along the projected path for implementation of a project, decisions may have to be made to modify a course of action, add energy to the process, or admit failure. Team leaders can easily become vested in the effort since success is typically rewarded more than failure (Atchison 1999). This is why it is so necessary to establish measurement sign points. The process needs to be highly visible. An action to sustain or abandon a project requires thoughtful preparation. Plans should be in place to ensure that communications with project managers, decision makers, and other stakeholders are continuous and that a concept of full disclosure is evident (Scott-Morgan 1994). A process of continuous communications can sometimes create problems if those who do not support the project use the information they receive to undermine it. Executives need to monitor the use of information to provide adequate balance and commitment to a course of action.

Celebrating Success

When projects are successfully implemented, leaders should make sure that the accomplishments are recognized with celebrations. Such celebrations should be thoughtfully designed to recognize individual effort as well as team accomplishments. A celebration should be sincere and reserved for recognizable accomplishments—overuse (i.e., celebrating events that are clearly not success stories) minimizes the effectiveness of the approach. When a failure takes place (if there are no failures, one can be fairly certain that risk taking is not rewarded) executives must take great care to avoid practices that focus on fixing blame. For example, it may be appropriate to celebrate a failed project where the participants—after monitoring the implementation process and addressing the decision points—had sufficient courage to terminate the effort.

When failures occur (or even successes) some members of the staff can feel wounded. Some may view success in a project involving more than one section of the organization as a failure, as when the diversion of resources to ensure success may negatively affect another section. The healing process begins with a culture that clearly recognizes and rewards total organizational effort. The credibility of the leaders comes into play in such recognition practices.

CONCLUSION

A key organizational competence involves the identification and cultivation of risk taking. The ability of the organization to respond to change requires individuals who not only see opportunities but who are encouraged to promote and experiment (Kouzes and Posner 1997). Innovation can be a rare commodity in formally structured organizations. Profiling and recognizing risk takers who demonstrate innovation helps create an essential mindset. Incentive and reward systems should recognize the importance of risk taking. Position descriptions and vision statements must be structured to outline the importance of innovation as a method of encouraging risk taking.

DISCUSSION

1. How should one go about creating a culture of risk taking in an organization?
2. What are the major barriers to developing a risk-taking culture?
3. Why is "visioning" so important?
4. What are the leadership core competencies that promote risk taking within an organization?

REFERENCES

Atchison, T. 1999. "Managing Change." *Frontiers of Health Services Management* 16 (1): 15.

Beer, M. and N. Nohria. 2000. "Cracking the Code of Change." *Harvard Business Review* 78 (3): 133.

Boyle, R. L. 1988. "Will You Be Singing in the Rain?" *Health Care Forum* 21 (5): 10–18.

Kouzes, J. M. and B. Z. Posner. 1996. *The Leadership Challenge: How to Keep Getting Extraordinary Things Done in Organizations.* San Francisco: Jossey-Bass.

Scott-Morgan, P. 1994. *The Unwritten Rules of the Game.* New York: McGraw-Hill, Inc.

Ulschak, F. L. and S. M. SnowAntle. 1995. *Team Architecture.* Chicago: Health Administration Press.

CHAPTER 13

Team Building and Evaluation

CASE IN POINT: John Front was the associate administrator of Star Health, a 250-bed hospital associated with a group practice of physicians. He was known as exceptionally talented but someone who had no use for teamwork. In fact, other members of the management team almost universally disliked him. He found that by being pushy he could "bulldoze" decisions through the system and no one would stop him. Under his direction, things happened and goals were met, but not without a significant cost to the staff's team spirit.

Because John's budgets were on target, the CEO tolerated his poor interpersonal skills. Colleagues learned that direct confrontation with John was painful and unproductive, so they looked for creative ways to avoid interaction. At one point, a former employee had filed a lawsuit claiming unfair treatment by John. The hospital settled out of court to resolve the lawsuit, which only added to the problem as other managers viewed the settlement as proof of wrongdoing.

Complaints increased and the CEO finally realized that he had only been seeing the tip of the iceberg. He had been shielded from nearly all of the bad news and had accepted operational results as evidence of John's competence. He had accepted the poor interpersonal behavior on the premise that tough decisions had to be made and, as he himself often said, "you can't please everyone." Finally, however, it was time to act.

QUESTION: What should the CEO have done to head off this problem?

INTRODUCTION

In any healthcare organization, a strong management team enhances creativity and innovation. Team building is the ultimate in executive orchestration requiring discipline, balance, and hard work. Building effective teams is especially difficult in the healthcare setting. Medical organizations are both hierarchical in structure and staffed with specialists, many of whom relate more closely to their specialty than to the organization as a whole. Physicians, nurses, and pharmacists, for example, tend to build relationships within the clinical environment rather than naturally becoming involved in organizational relationships. Thus the healthcare leader has a particularly difficult task and must rely heavily on the support of an effective cross-sector management team to support organizational initiatives (Ridderheim 1986). This chapter addresses a number of team-building issues.

DEFINING THE TEAM

A team must be more than a collection of individuals. A functioning team is a cohesive, interdependent, and focused group that knows where it is going. All members should participate in setting team goals. Team members are able to clearly articulate objectives that relate to the mission of the organization. The leader will want to create an environment in which the following dynamics can occur within the team:

1. *Identification with a mission.* The team and its members recognize that the overall mission of the organization is more important than personal ambition.
2. *Confidence and trust.* There is a high level of interpersonal confidence and trust, which allows team members to cross traditional organizational lines. Turf issues are minimized and team members exchange information openly and are aware of the problems and frustrations faced by their colleagues.
3. *Promote debate.* Team members possess enough self-confidence to disagree with each other and to soundly debate issues from different viewpoints. Once a decision is made, however, the team rallies and closes ranks to move programs forward.
4. *Identify with team success.* Team members identify with team success. They are willing to share the limelight and are diligent about sharing credit for successes with their colleagues. One interesting check to determine how much team members value the team is to scan memos written by leaders and team members. If the memos are sprinkled with many references to self (I) rather than with references to team activity (we), the organization may need some work on the team-building process.

TEAM STRUCTURE

The healthcare organizations that are best positioned for the future are those in which leaders stimulate organizational flexibility. For example, they should be willing to share power rather than centralize it (Ricklerheim 1986). Perhaps the first step toward improving performance or creating a functional management team is to carefully evaluate the existing management structure. Simplifying the organizational structure (with more people reporting to fewer) is in itself a process that aids team building. Executives who have more people reporting to them must learn to be more trusting of the judgment of their staff or they may flounder under the weight of detail. Many organizations are surprised at how well a simplified structure works. Traditional habits need to be challenged, and decision-making processes streamlined. Once the team functions effectively, it will be linked with other staff teams, so the leader must work to eliminate interteam barriers. Team leaders must learn more about change and renewal, and must be on alert against the development of self-serving bureaucracies that could counteract the synergism of effective team operation.

Structural Simplification

Structural simplification is associated with successful teams. The subspecialization and fragmentation of so many occupations in health services have led to the creation of very complex reporting relationships. Cross training to streamline managerial responsibilities is very useful and strengthens the organization's ability to react promptly to change. Who is to say, for example, that a highly competent laboratory manager is incapable of also managing other departments? Management practices clearly transcend departmental specialization.

SELECTING THE MANAGEMENT TEAM

The leader should begin the process of building a team by matching the strengths and weaknesses of the existing team against the needs and goals of the organization. Members of the management team should be ranked according to their abilities in four areas:

1. *Technical competence.* Are the managers competent to perform their particular specialty, and are their skills and knowledge up to date?
2. *Interpersonal skills.* Do the potential team members care about fellow employees and take the time to know and understand what it is that makes a team function (trust, professional respect, and so on)? Are members of the team recognized as team players, and how is this demonstrated? Are these team leaders fair and capable of confronting and resolving people problems?
3. *Ability to identify and solve problems.* Can teams address problems from both a tactical and a strategic angle? Are

alternatives adequately inventoried, and is the potential effect of decisions on the organization identified and a part of recommended solutions? Or do team members successfully identify a problem but then simply transfer it to another person or team?

4. *Leadership ability.* Are the team leaders really capable of leading others? Are they capable of communicating ideas and then energizing those around them in order to achieve a specific goal? Team members might be geniuses in a technical sense, but if they cannot lead and communicate ideas in the process, the organization will not be fully served.

BALANCING THE TEAM

The leader must also examine the balance of skills on the management team. If the existing team lacks competency in a particular area—for example, financial affairs—then it becomes necessary to strengthen the team by adding an individual with this skill or by providing existing members with special training. If the senior executive devotes substantial time to outside community or professional engagements, it is essential that strong operational professionals are in place to manage internal affairs.

Because it takes such a long time to build a team, change in the team's composition should be considered carefully. Teams are easy to destroy but difficult to build. Organizations that have had frequent changes in leadership learn this lesson the hard way as they try to carry on in a constant state of management flux.

When leaders new to an organization inherit existing teams, they have the challenge of matching their personal style with the existing team while simultaneously assessing and adjusting assignments. A special look at team balance is important in this situation because the incoming executive usually arrives with different strengths and weaknesses than his or her predecessor.

Because of the difficulty in building or transforming existing teams, leaders new to the organization will often disrupt the team by quickly replacing existing team members with new members from outside the organization. In times of rapid change and organizational stress, this may be the only viable alternative. Robert Waterman (1987) observes how the country's "best" companies maintain their competitive edge and advocates some change for change's sake, noting that leaders in competitive companies create change processes in order to develop an enterprising attitude. These leaders also work to treat all employees as potential sources of creative input.

Role Definition

Role definition enhances collaboration and minimizes competition between team members through the clarification of levels of power and authority. Too much definition, however, can create barriers to effective team operation by overcompartmentalizing functions. For example, the executive who specifies the job responsibilities in too much detail may diminish the staff member's sense of taking charge of his or her own destiny. Adequately rewarding team members who function as team players contributes to the process of integrating different skills and disciplines and applying them to a common cause.

Involving Physicians in Management Decision Making

Today's environment requires efficient, effective, and integrated teams drawing on multiple professional disciplines. Of particular importance is the involvement of physicians. Physicians need to be key participants in managerial decision making. Organizations need to identify and involve physicians who have the interest, instincts, and competence to help manage and lead.

Executives need to work at dispelling stereotypes and narrow attitudes held by both administrators and physicians (Waterman 1987). Some healthcare executives continue to believe that physician involvement in management is inappropriate. Perhaps some lay executives, particularly those who have had confrontations with physicians, view physician involvement as personally threatening. This is a normal reaction to a perceived threat, but it is an attitude that executives cannot afford to have.

From the physician viewpoint, although a growing number of physicians are intrigued with management processes, too much association with management is often perceived by other medical staff members as a sign of clinical disinterest (or even clinical incompetence). In addition, some physicians seem to be conditioned, beginning with their clinical schooling, to consider administrators as barriers to progress and certainly a threat their clinical autonomy (Holm 2000). These attitudes may in part account for the increased interest by physicians in pursuing management skill training as a means of taking back management from lay executives. Younger administrators and physicians seem to possess fewer of these traditional attitude problems, but there are still a considerable number in both camps who would prefer to remain separate. These attitudes are unfortunate; they will lead only to further fragmentation within the healthcare system (Medical Group Management Association 1993).

Building Administrator-physician Teams

Team building requires an organizational attitude that fosters physician involvement in decision making. The attitude must start at the top of the organization. Once this commitment is accepted as a part of the organization's culture, the implementation of these teams will flow more naturally.

In team building with physicians, healthcare executives should consider adopting a "buddy system" to link physicians and administrators on projects, to encourage involvement, and to reward cooperation that results in the integration of professional and management disciplines. When professional administrators and physicians work together, both gain respect for their different orientations and skills, and share the satisfaction of achieving a common goal.

Physician participation in management must be based on more than just an expressed interest by a physician. Leaders in the organization must evaluate physicians on their management skills, not just their clinical ability. Techniques (such as performance-based goals and objectives) used in evaluating lay executives work well in evaluating the management skills of physicians. Prospective physician leaders should also be provided with opportunities to learn about the practice of management through attendance at seminars, enrollment in short courses, or investment of their time to acquire a management degree.

Some organizations seem to be marketing programs exclusively for physicians with the subtle message that physicians should leave the lay executive behind in learning what management is really all about. Executives should monitor the organization and act to curtail this "us versus them" attitude. For joint administrator-physician teams to be effective, there must be interpersonal respect, credibility, and compatibility. As noted earlier, teams function best when members recognize that others on the team have skills that complement their own. Team balance, aided by clear definition of roles, is essential.

CULTIVATING THE TEAM

Growing organizations that are creative and innovative tend to flourish when these qualities are reinforced with management continuity and stability. Even under excellent leadership, it can take three to five years of solid work and involvement for a group of individuals to build an effective team. When management experts recommend that younger colleagues should relocate to another organization every three years to advance in their careers, this advice does a disservice to both the organization and to the individual staff members. Too much movement deprives younger professionals of the experience of a full cycle of team development.

Many important factors must be considered when cultivating teams.

Team Evaluation

Healthcare leaders must pay close attention to the processes of evaluating and rewarding colleagues and staff, as well as ensuring that those processes are functioning elsewhere in the organization.

A key to effective evaluation practices is keeping accurate and updated position descriptions. These descriptions provide points of reference against which an individual's performance can be measured fairly and objectively. In a volatile environment jobs change continually. Staff should be asked to update their position descriptions regularly, and their descriptions should be discussed with them and then officially accepted. Without up-to-date job descriptions as a basis for comparison, leaders and managers will have to redefine evaluation criteria at every performance review.

Of course, the job of keeping position descriptions current does not rest only with the CEO or supervisor. For example, an associate administrator in a skilled nursing facility who wants to be recognized for taking on new community responsibilities should make sure that those new responsibilities are reflected in an updated job description.

At higher levels in the organization it may be more difficult to provide precise, objective criteria for purposes of evaluation. The broad area of responsibility assigned to upper management usually carries broad expectations, making evaluation criteria difficult to pin down. How does one evaluate, for example, the CEO's ability to keep the organization viable and progressive? In spite of intangible responsibilities, it is important to penetrate generalities and work to define specific, objective criteria.

When evaluating senior members of the management team, the leader should supplement formal organizational criteria with criteria reflecting performance on strategic management issues.

- Does the manager personally confront problems in a timely fashion and, in the process, exercise good judgment? (Or does the executive avoid personal involvement and risk by inappropriately relying on subordinates to confront others?)
- What about the executive's competence in processing complex issues? Does the manager possess the intellectual capacity to wrestle with an entire strategy? (Or does the executive only look at the next step in the process?)
- How is the executive perceived by his or her peers in terms of leadership? Does the manager rank well among other executives with the same level of experience? Is the executive respected and

valued as a person of high integrity? (Or does the executive "just get by"?)

- Is the executive truly a team leader? Are strong members of the team successfully recruited and retained? Is there team continuity, mutual respect, and interdependence? (Or does the executive try to be surrounded by team members who will agree with the leader without providing direct and honest input in decision making?)
- What about the team members' level of self-awareness? Is the executive able to see the big picture? (Or does the executive consistently translate events only as they seem personally relevant, which might suggest a problem of an oversized ego?)
- Is the executive able to explain complex affairs to boards, management, medical staff, and employees? Are written and verbal skills average, above average, or superior? (Or is the executive dependent on colleagues to pull together the presentations and carry the weight of the dialog?)
- How does the executive's overall track record look? Has performance been consistent? (Or is there a lack of consistent performance in matters of judgment?)
- Is the executive truly keeping up with new professional developments through active participation in continuing education and involvement in professional societies? Does the executive network well externally? (Or does the executive rely on past practices as the only way to solve a problem, or follow a practice of professional isolation?)
- How effective is the executive as a teacher or mentor? Does the team member display enthusiasm in interchanges with colleagues, managers, students, and others? (Or does the executive communicate that teaching and mentoring is an extra burden, a task to be assigned to others?)
- Does the executive use a single standard for evaluating and rewarding others in the organization in order to ensure equity, and does the team member evaluate employees objectively according to actual performance? (Or does the executive follow a

double standard and display signs of favoritism in making such decisions?)

- What about the executive's personal ethics and values? Is there understanding and ongoing demonstration of ethical behavior? Does the executive operate with respect for and belief in the rights and welfare of others, regardless of their position in the organization? Is there honesty in relationships with colleagues?
- Are the executive's performance and behavior perceived as complementary to the mission of the organization? Is the individual loyal? Is the executive known for objectivity, or are biases displayed to others?

The contemporary healthcare leader who values team effort needs to spend time contemplating all of these questions (and others as well) when designing a philosophy of leadership that encourages a thorough and exacting process of evaluation of the executives (including the leader) in the organization. Care should be taken to avoid stressing the ranking of team members (one against the other) since this can develop counterproductive competition.

Timing, Procedures, and Processes

Members of the management team should be formally evaluated at least once each year. However, concurrent and continuous evaluations should supplement annual reviews. To put it simply: pluses and minuses should not be tallied for a whole year before they are ever discussed. There should be an open dialog regarding performance, and that will require constant monitoring and ongoing communication.

One technique that will assist in the evaluation process is to ask individuals to complete a self-assessment. A self-assessment should be based on criteria selected jointly with the individual's supervisor. Each party should complete the evaluation, and the two should then meet to compare and discuss ratings and rankings. This process is more interactive, allowing both individuals an opportunity to express their perceptions, rather than simply having the supervisor complete the written evaluation, schedule a meeting, and talk through the evaluation.

Another process that can be both useful and revealing, although it might be perceived as more threatening, is to have managers select individuals to complete an anonymous evaluation of their performance. The goal is to obtain honest input on performance, so managers must be willing to take the risk of learning about their own performance problems! Obviously, this process is most successful in an organization with a high level of trust among its staff.

Regardless of the approach to the actual evaluation, the criteria used to evaluate staff members should always be shared with them in advance, and copies of results of interviews and the annual performance evaluations should be provided to the individual being interviewed. Verbal and written feedback are both critical to the process.

CONCLUSION

In any valid evaluation process, three elements are crucial. The first is competency, which refers to the determination of how the individual team members perform in their areas of responsibility. Are correct decisions made? What objective factors are used in the evaluation? The second element involves interpersonal relationships, or proficiency as a team participant. Do members focus properly on organizational goals and are they capable of building esprit de corps with superiors, colleagues, and subordinates? Finally, trust and value refer to whether team members are perceived as being team oriented and trustworthy. Will they share information willingly? How are they viewed with respect to their personal and interpersonal values?

DISCUSSION

1. How should the CEO encourage differences of opinion among team members in order to avoid "group think" practices by the team?

2. Identify an approach to encourage interteam cooperation within an organization.
3. How would you encourage physicians or other clinicians to participate in managerial decision making?
4. Is the team leader's evaluation process different from that of team members, and if so, how?

NOTE

This chapter was adapted from Austin Ross's *Cornerstones of Leadership*, Health Administration Press, Chicago, 1992.

REFERENCES

Holm, C. E. 2000. *Next Generation Physician–Health System Partnerships.* Chicago: Health Administration Press.

Medical Group Management Association. 1993. *Integration Issues in Hospital/Physician Affiliations.* Denver: MGMA.

Ridderheim, D. S. 1986. "The Anatomy of Change." *Hospital & Health Services Administration* 31 (3): 7–21.

Waterman, R. H., Jr. 1987. *The Renewal Factor: How the Best Get and Keep the Competitive Edge.* New York: Bantam Books, Inc.

CHAPTER 14

Conflict and Confrontation

CASE IN POINT: Jim was an excellent vice president of professional affairs at Davenport General Medical Center, a 600-bed tertiary care medical center. His supervisors liked working with him and he excelled in every respect except one. His only weakness was that he found it very difficult to confront physicians and other clinicians about their need to conform to established practices such as prompt and accurate billing for procedures.

Jim's superior, Nancy, decided to lay it on the line and insist that Jim "toughen up." She called a meeting with Jim to confront him on the matter, and the outcome was very interesting. Jim's defense of his behavior was based on several points. The first was that he felt he was being asked to do something beyond his ability because he was friendly with the physicians and clinicians. His second point was that at no time had he ever been instructed to be tough; in fact, he was under the impression that if he lost credibility with the physicians and clinicians he had reason to worry about his future with the organization. His job was to keep everyone happy. He noted that every time one of the hospital executives made another systems pronouncement, the credibility of the entire management team was questioned by the professionals and that he had personally rebuilt bridges that had been destroyed by his management colleagues.

After the meeting, Nancy spent time reflecting on the conversation. Was it possible that she had taken it for granted that members of her management team did not understand the finer points of confronting an issue?

QUESTION: What should senior executives do to help members of the management team address issues involving conflicts and necessary confrontations?

INTRODUCTION

Although many people consciously shy away from conflict, avoiding confrontation in an organizational setting can send messages that are counterproductive and affect operational effectiveness. Much energy can be wasted by unnecessarily avoiding conflicts. It is the leader's responsibility to monitor the organization to ensure that "management by avoidance" is not the operating standard. Such avoidance may send messages throughout the organization that the executive leadership is weak and may not support program development or other organizational initiatives that demand close team interdependence. Knowing when (and when not) to confront requires considerable skill on the part of leaders and team members. This chapter discusses some key issues associated with confrontation techniques.

ALTERNATIVES TO CONFRONTATION

Because the outcome of confrontation is not usually predictable, leaders should be judicious in their use of confrontation as a management tool. Leaders must consider all the options for addressing a particular problem, including such processes as one-on-one negotiation, group processes, and "collegial pressure" (where people with influence are brought into the situation as problem solvers).

One-on-one negotiation addresses the problem by looking for solutions that result in a win for both parties while conforming to the task at hand. Such personal negotiations are clearly a first step before confrontational steps are initiated. Group processes consider the broader goal as outlined to the management group and seek consensus on a proper solution. Such processes could include the appointment of a task force or focus group to consider the broader ramifications that in turn can be focused by the leader on the prevailing problem. Collegial pressure is a political approach where respected associates are involved in helping to solve the problem. This approach typically is most effective where a reasonable level of trust exists among the parties involved. Lack of trust by one of those involved can create dysfunction.

Confrontations with Physicians or Other Clinicians

Executives who do not have enough technical or scientific expertise to address professional conflicts between technical and scientific staff should be careful about employing confrontation techniques. For example, clinical professionals may resent a lay executive's intrusion in an area viewed as clinical in scope. Physicians often are willing to debate differences of clinical opinion with each other without making an emotional investment in the process, and in most cases they are challenging each other to determine the appropriate treatment approach or other course of action to take on behalf of a patient. They all know that the ultimate resolution of the issue will be up to the physician in charge of the patient's care. Clinical differences seem to generate less conflict than would differences between a clinician and a lay executive involving management matters where the physician may elect to superimpose a clinical decision-making process on a management issue.

A useful strategy for the lay executive is to identify and involve physicians or other clinical leaders early in the process of decision making involving management affairs affecting physicians. This provides opportunities for gaining a consensus without having to resort to a confrontation approach.

Confrontations with Members of the Governing Board

Confrontations with board members are also difficult and risky affairs. Board members bring different skills, personalities, interests, and talents to the health scene. They are also responsible for the recruiting, nourishing, and, if necessary, the firing of the CEO. There are occasions when executives are sorely tested by the unevenness of this playing field. For example, how should the CEO respond to a perceived conflict of interest by a board member? It takes courage for the CEO to orchestrate resolution of such a problem; as with clinicians, peer pressure is a useful strategy. Peer pressure would include drawing the board chair or other board members into the fray. One way of anticipating and avoiding conflicts of interest is to require that a conflict-of-interest questionnaire be filed annually by all board members and management. A separate board committee can be organized to identify any possible relationships that might put the individual and the organization in either financial or ethical conflict.

By anticipating the conflict in advance and using peer pressure or other negotiation processes to resolve issues, the CEO is able to establish norms for board-directed policies and at the same time minimize unnecessary confrontation. Sometimes confrontation with a board member or the board as a whole is required. Usually such confrontation issues involve questions on ethical practices, differences of opinion on missions or goals, and fundamental differences of opinion about executive performance. Clearly care should be taken in thinking through the process and selecting the appropriate action measure.

In Defense of Disagreement

Good decision making requires nurturing a climate that allows for dissension. Opinions from team members that are contrary to the viewpoint of the majority need to be considered carefully. A decision-making process can be easily flawed if the participants consciously or unconsciously permit the development of group thinking.

Group thinking occurs when:

- The team too quickly comes to a consensus without considering the tough questions
- Others on the team intimidate team members
- Team members are selected for their propensity to agree with the team leader
- The technical composition of the team is intentionally unbalanced, leaving the expertise in only a few hands
- Decisions are predetermined by executives with higher authority and team input serves only as lip service

Proactive involvement by all team members is essential to the process of good decision making (Covey 1989). Minority opinions need to be valued. Sometimes decisions have to be made without a consensus. Making tough decisions is a part of the job for executives who must know how and when to make decisions (Wetlaufer 2000).

RISK AND TIMING

When determining whether or not to confront a particular issue, leaders should consider the level of risk inherent in the confrontation. If the confrontation is aimed at correcting personal behavior problems, it will carry more import than addressing a clearly defined organizational problem. When the parties involved in a conflict are not at an equal level in the organization's hierarchy, the lower-ranking staff member may feel at risk. It is important that the executive anticipate the effect of these differences ahead of time. The wise executive will listen carefully, gather the facts, and determine the level of confrontation needed based on the circumstances.

The executive also has to consider timing. When is the correct time to confront a situation? The right time to confront is more apparent when less-risky problem-solving practices have been tried without success, or when the problem is clearly interfering with organizational operation. When aberrant behavior undermines the value system or the ethics of the organization, rapid intercession is essential. When organizational goals are involved and there is a substantial difference of opinion, the risks are higher but the cause determines the method of confrontation. Timing may also depend on the environmental circumstances affecting the organization. Confrontation as a tool usually becomes more urgent when the organization is facing difficult times (financial or otherwise). The healthcare executive who employs confrontation as the tool of choice needs to look beyond the immediate crisis in order to anticipate the outcome. This also requires a willingness to take the risks associated with an adverse outcome to the process.

USING APPROPRIATE CHANNELS

The thoughtful leader looks for opportunities to confront an issue while recognizing that it is important to respect appropriate channels. For example, if the misbehaving member of the team is a level down in the organization, typically the leader should deal with the problem through the individual's direct supervisor.

Occasionally executives will unintentionally intimidate others on the staff. Signals are sent out to others to stay clear of that individual's agenda or suffer the consequences. This style of intimidation is subtle, but destructive, and the senior leader who observes such practices should not let these practices go unconfronted. Senior executives are not always privy to these behavioral patterns, even if the behaviors are obvious to others. They may be accused by staff of avoiding conflict when in fact they are unaware of the problem. To compensate, leaders need to create formal and informal channels for input and feedback.

Competency Issues

Individuals who create personnel or organizational problems often are highly competent and simply need some individual counseling. Others, however, need to be warned that although they are competent, their behavior cannot be tolerated. Unless their behavior improves, changes will need to be made. When required, this type of confrontation should be direct and straightforward. Leaders who are obtuse and indirect often fail to convey the seriousness of the confrontation, yet these situations must be solved before erosion of team effort occurs.

It is the leader's responsibility to intervene to remove obstacles that are inhibiting the team's ability to do its job. Staff members (assistants, managers, supervisors) are often well aware of performance problems and observe how the executive approaches the problem.

PREPARING FOR CONFRONTATION

There are several key steps in preparing for confrontation:

1. The executive must verify the facts to ensure that the problem has been diagnosed accurately and all sides have been considered. For example, has an individual's behavior pattern changed recently because of some particular organizational or personal stress, or is it a management style or personality problem?
2. When assessing the problem, the executive should remember that individuals who behave poorly might not be aware that they are doing so. Poor behavior may be related to a practice style that was acceptable when the individual was working in another organization or setting.
3. It is important to determine the conditions required for acceptable performance and to also identify who will be responsible for ensuring that changes are underway.
4. The executive, in consultation with others involved, clearly must establish a schedule for measuring improvement. Once the process begins, it must be followed through to an ultimate conclusion.

Rewarding Behavior

When performance has improved (and it usually does), it is important to communicate to the individual involved that the problem has been resolved. It is unfair to leave a sanctioned action (such as possible loss of position) hanging over an individual's head. If the problem has not been resolved within the time limit, then the predetermined course of action needs to be taken.

CONCLUSION

Competence in knowing when and how to confront situations is not an inherited trait. It is an acquired skill. Thoughtful considerations of the circumstances requiring the implementation of direct confrontation are essential. In these turbulent times, careless approaches to confrontation and conflict management can be highly hazardous to executive tenure. Courageous leaders can make the difference if they understand the appropriate use of confrontation techniques.

DISCUSSION

1. Identify specific examples of organizational problems that must be dealt with expediently.
2. If a manager is weak when confronting problems, what steps should be advised to improve performance?
3. Design an outline of the key points for a management training exercise to train team members on confrontation issues.

REFERENCES

Covey, S. 1989. *The 7 Habits of Highly Effective People.* New York: Simon & Schuster.

Wetlaufer, S. 2000. "Common Sense and Conflict." *Harvard Business Review* 78 (1): 116–17.

CHAPTER 15

Professional Mentoring

CASE IN POINT: After careful consideration, Jeff Grange, CEO, selected Susan Crosby to be the new administrative fellow. Unfortunately, the office setup for Susan was less than desirable. Her cubicle was located in medical records, several floors away from administration. From there the situation worsened. Contact between Susan and Jeff was limited to a meeting per week, which was frequently canceled by Jeff because of his very hectic schedule.

Assigned projects were limited in scope and actually represented staff work for several department heads. Project reporting was strictly to the department head involved. While some mentoring was taking place between Susan and the individual department heads, clearly the tie with her designated mentor, Jeff, was lacking. Susan felt neglected and, more importantly, felt that her mentor was failing to live up to the commitment made to her when she accepted the position. After several months, Susan decided that she had to do something to remedy the situation.

QUESTION: What should Susan do to correct the situation? How could it have been avoided in the first place?

INTRODUCTION

Homer described the original mentor as "the wise and trusted coun-
selor" whom Odysseus left in charge of his household during his trav-
els. In his book *The Mentor Connection* (1990), Michael Zey interviewed
150 executives from Fortune 500 corporations and concluded that a
positive mentoring relationship was often the single most important
factor contributing to an individual's corporate success, even more important than academic credentials. This chapter explores mentoring
relationships and offers suggestions for creating a special mentoring
relationship.

THE VALUE OF MENTORING

Mentoring is one of the cornerstones of team building. When newcomers are added to any team, the leader has several major responsibilities: to provide the new member with opportunities to learn from and
share information with seasoned professionals in the organization; to
expose the new member to the organization's values and expectations
concerning behavior and performance; and to properly utilize the skills
and competencies of the newcomer. A well-rounded mentoring program should specifically address these responsibilities.

Mentoring can serve as the best way to build continuing educational
experiences, both for young professionals and for established healthcare managers and executives. The mentor fuels the protégé's enthusiasm and provides guidance and coaching. In turn, the protégé offers
fresh insight and, with mutual trust, can serve as a valuable listening
post to the mentor.

The National Academy of Sciences (1997) summed up the role of
mentor as an advisor, teacher, role model, and friend, noting the following.

- In a broad sense, a mentor is someone who takes a special interest in helping another develop into a successful professional.
- A good mentor seeks to help a student optimize an educational experience, to assist the student's socialization into a

disciplinary culture, and to aid the student in finding suitable employment.
- A fundamental difference between a mentor and an adviser is that mentoring is more than advising: mentoring is a personal as well as a professional relationship.
- An effective mentoring relationship is characterized by mutual trust, understanding, and empathy.
- The goal of a mentoring relationship is to advance the educational and personal growth of students.
- A good mentor is a good listener.
- Everyone benefits from having multiple mentors of diverse talents, ages, and personalities.
- A successful mentor is prepared to deal with population diversities, including those peculiar to ethnicity, culture, sex, and disability.

Mentoring Categories

Mentoring falls into three broad categories: educational, career, and personal development (Dennis 1993). Academic mentoring typically focuses on competency development and skill training. Career mentoring is associated with development of an individual, broadening his or her exposure to new executive tasks and assignments. Personal development mentoring is associated with the validation of value systems, ethics, and culture enhancement. All three categories overlap and the optimal mentor relationship encompasses all three.

ESTABLISHING A PROGRAM

Clearly the mentoring relationship is beneficial for those who have just finished college degrees. As they move from campus to practice, some new graduates find that they miss the easy access to the faculty and the free exchange of thoughts and ideas with peers that were the hallmarks of their college careers. Once they move into the healthcare field, they may miss the security offered by a curriculum with more defined expectations and relationships. Flexibility is the rule in the healthcare setting, and a newcomer may have difficulty adapting to a quickened pace. Mentoring is not limited, however, to newcomers to an organization. Establishing ongoing mentorship programs between existing professionals within the organization can be of major benefit as well.

Opportunities for "reverse mentoring" also exist. Reverse mentoring occurs when a senior executive seeks out a subordinate to access specialty information. For example, a CEO who wants to improve his or her computer skills could arrange to work with the organization's CIO. Although this reverse mentoring has great potential, it is probably an underutilized tool in practice because senior executives have a tendency to conceal any lack of competencies.

A mentor helps by quietly tracking the individual's experiences on the job to ensure they include growth and learning opportunities—and, if not, to help guide the individual in seeking such opportunities. A good mentor also monitors the organization to ensure that it accommodates the individual's need to work with others who can share their knowledge and experience. Fundamentally, the mentor is responsible for overseeing—keeping in touch and gently guiding—the individual, but without creating internal conflict or a perception of special privilege.

Similarly, when an individual moves from one healthcare organization to another, a mentoring relationship can enhance the transfer of knowledge and enrich the professional experience by lending continuity to the process. If trust levels are high between the parties involved, any gaps in experience can be identified early and subsequently filled. As the individual moves on, the mentor should take the opportunity to give closure to the process by providing a thorough and candid appraisal of the individual's performance. This is not the time to overlook deficiencies. Part of the mentor's role is to give as complete an assessment as possible.

Mentoring need not be limited to those individuals who show specific signs of leadership potential, although certainly this is a good investment in future leaders. In fact, anyone can benefit from a relationship with a mentor, but not everyone will benefit in the same way. The key to making the program work for the newcomer is to find mentors who can adjust their approach to meet the needs of the individual. The ideal mentor will be grateful for the opportunity to work with the "raw material" and to help by being responsive to individual needs.

WHY MENTOR?

A successful and enriching mentoring relationship takes time, effort, and much energy. Why would healthcare managers and executives, who already have so many demands on their time and energy, agree to participate in a mentoring program?

Mentors like to teach, which is fundamental to a successful program. Management team members who enjoy sharing knowledge and ideas, and who enjoy working with others, will be energized by a mentoring relationship. Good mentors recognize the value of testing and exchanging ideas in a risk-free setting. They know that they too will learn by working with new employees who have a fresh base of knowledge.

The process of mentoring strengthens organizational leadership and continuity. It is no accident that many successful fellows and administrative residents end up with their first postfellowship position in the same organization. Mentors realize that mentoring is an opportunity to contribute to young professionals' careers and that, in the process of helping younger administrators succeed, they are helping their own careers as well. They enjoy working with an energetic new staff member, and they inspire the new member to do excellent work.

In a sense, mentoring is a form of networking; it helps the mentor keep in touch with trends in the environment and expands the newcomer's contacts in the field. Experienced administrators recognize that time spent on developing solid relationships is important throughout one's career. They also realize that even mentors need mentoring, and they build and rely on lifelong contacts with others who are willing to share their expertise. Good mentors who acknowledge this priority are an invaluable resource for incoming employees.

DEVELOPING THE MENTORING RELATIONSHIP

To make the mentoring experience work, the relationship must be developed on a solid basis of mutual trust (Lanser 2000). The mentor must be willing to take risks, to share thoughts and concepts, and to trust that the information will be kept confidential when appropriate. He or she must be willing to share examples of personal failures as well as successes. The new employee must be able to understand the investment the mentor is making and to trust that the learning process itself will not be judged.

Mentoring requires periods of uninterrupted time and cannot always be dictated by tight schedules. The good mentor is an accessible one. He or she listens carefully and avoids posturing and sermonizing. The mentor should be insightful, able to read between the lines and pick up on the individual's reactions and thoughts.

As the relationship develops, the mentor takes time to reflect on the tasks that have been assigned to the new employee. There should be an attempt to continually increase the protégé's responsibilities during the formal mentoring relationship. Regular and formal reviews of the new team member's progress, as well as the mentoring relationship itself, are essential. The reviews need to be thorough and candid. Mentoring relationships early in one's career sometimes provide the last significant opportunities for candid reviews, since evaluations tend to become more superficial and political, and therefore less personally valuable, as one's career advances.

Desired Characteristics of Mentors

Not every member of your management team who would like to participate in the mentoring program will be suited for the task. The qualities that contribute to excellence in mentoring are much the same as those contributing to excellence in teaching. Both teachers and mentors understand the virtue of the well-directed question, appreciate persistence in working out logical solutions to problems, and relish the experience of observing individual growth. There is a genuine and overriding interest in the business of "developing" people. Mentors make time to teach. It is not just an assignment, it is an avocation.

Good mentors teach by example (Iberre 2000), so they must be emotionally secure individuals who behave in a rational and consistent fashion. The mentor should have high ethical standards and values, supported by the knowledge that value systems established early in a career guide an individual's capacity to lead others to value-based decision making. Mentors serve an important role in upholding organizational standards and setting an example by their own personal and professional integrity.

Characteristics associated with good mentoring include:

- *Genuine interest in helping and building a personal relationship.*
  Mentors must be especially motivated to make the relationship
  work, and this requires an expenditure of time and energy
  beyond that which might be expected.
- *Commitment to their profession.* Outstanding mentors have a conviction that that which they do is important and that their profession matters.
- *Commitment to continuing education and career development.*
  Mentors who are recognized as outstanding will be known for
  their determination to remain at the forefront of their profession
  through continually learning.
- *Personal insight, empathy, and listening skills.* Outstanding
  mentors know their weaknesses, possess a sensitivity that
  permits them to "feel" where the protégé is on an issue,
  and convey a genuine interest and capacity for listening
  carefully.
- *Willingness to take risks in the sharing of concepts and
  information.* The mentor must trust that the student will
  honor confidences and the private, special nature of certain
  exchanges.

Protégé Responsibilities

Protégés have responsibilities to make the relationship work as well:

- Communicate clearly and negotiate with the mentor your goals
  for your time together.

- Invest time in learning about the mentor's organization and professional roles and responsibilities.
- Initiate regular meetings with your mentor and take responsibility for structuring a preliminary list of what is to be discussed.
- Monitor the relationship and take the initiative to make it meaningful, and have the courage to "back off" if it is not working.

Avoiding Pitfalls

What are the major obstacles to the development of a solid mentoring relationship? Perhaps the most inhibiting obstacle is a lack of openness on the part of the mentor. If administrators are unwilling or unable to share enough of themselves, they will not be able to invest adequately in the mentoring process. If the individual being mentored cannot penetrate the mentor's protective shell, it is unlikely that the two will be able to share and confide in each other, and the purpose of the mentoring process will be defeated.

A related obstacle occurs when mentors become preoccupied with their own careers and neglect their responsibilities to the new team member. In some cases, mentors succumb to an overdeveloped personal ego, allowing the relationship to revolve around their own base of knowledge. Obviously a one-sided relationship is unhealthy because it does not allow the mutual and free exchange of ideas and experiences. A mentor's inability to challenge the individual by asking for opinions is a further indication of a failing relationship, since it probably means that the mentor has little interest in the young professional's ideas.

Another problem occurs if a mentor is not keeping up with current management practices. Mentors need to be on top of events and practices in order to convey knowledge to the new team member. The mentor's credibility will be impaired if the less-experienced team member recognizes that the mentor's information is not current.

A protégé's sense of worth and recognition grows in almost direct proportion to the degree of access to the mentor. It is important for those being mentored to be persistent enough to establish regular and consistent interaction with the mentor. On the other hand, a mentor's insensitivity to the protégé's need to network both within and outside the organization can also create a problem if the mentor monopolizes the new member's time. New employees do not prosper if they are locked up behind the scenes with second-level project work. The mentor should ensure that networking opportunities are available so the new associate enjoys a sufficient degree of visibility and can take advantage of a wide range of experiences working with others in the organization.

Information must flow in both directions, but the mentor must be sensitive to confidentiality issues when sharing information with the newer associate. (The younger associate may not be aware of all of the political ramifications involved.) Others in the organization might welcome the opportunity to hear impressions or comments made by the mentor, but the protégé's failure to maintain confidences would undermine an otherwise successful relationship. Conversely, a mentor who uses a younger colleague as an organizational spy would ruin the relationship as well (and reveal the sad state of corporate values).

Mentoring and Teamwork: Issues in Orienting Newcomers

Mentoring provides an excellent opportunity to orient newcomers to the organization's culture, values, and expectations. Careful attention to the orientation of new staff will help the team and the organization as a whole to maintain a unified sense of purpose and direction. Because this relationship is essential to initiating and stimulating creativity among new team members, it is important to look at some of the issues that should be considered in selecting mentors and in anticipating the protégé's adjustment. Some of the most common issues that arise when new members are added to an existing team are outlined below (Ross 1992). Although they apply most specifically to less-experienced or newer team members, they are also relevant to more experienced administrators who enter a new environment.

Problems with time management

The transition from the academic world to the working one comes as a shock to some young professionals. A newcomer to an organization may experience difficulty in handling multiple projects simultaneously—a reality of the working world. As a mentor, the experienced administrator can help the protégé by letting the individual know that the time pressure problem is a common condition and by giving suggestions for scheduling each project.

Failure to be specific in assigning tasks

If the executive is not specific about priorities and the scope of the assignment, the protégé often will spend too much time and energy completing the assignment (for example, devoting several weeks to a project that only required a quick fix). The protégé will not know—and should not be expected to know—the level of involvement needed until the leader explains it in adequate detail.

Underestimation of the effect of operational demands on others

A new staff member might unconsciously make unreasonable demands on others to collect data or information, failing to realize how much effort is required to accomplish the task. This is simply a reflection of the protégé's desire to succeed and build credibility, but additional work assignments suddenly added to an already heavy workload will not be easily absorbed and will frequently be resented by staff. A mentor can help by informing the new team member of workflow patterns and demands on staff time, and by providing suggestions for how to time special requests.

Lack of awareness of organizational relationships

New staff sometimes overlook the importance of assessing the organizational culture before charging into unknown waters. In some ways, organizational charts are like road maps. Both identify major routes, but unlike organizational charts, road maps also show alternate routes to destinations. Since organizational charts only show official relationships, they sometimes mislead newcomers. Actual relationships between executives are much more important than how the relationship looks on paper. Newcomers need to spend time learning about these relationships, and leaders have a responsibility to spend enough time with them to provide this essential orientation.

Inappropriate expectation levels

Another common problem is that the new team member often underestimates the amount of time it takes to establish personal credibility. Previous experience and academic credentials do not carry much weight with new colleagues. The newcomer must earn the respect of the team. In addition, the authority and power that the newcomer has inherited by virtue of his or her new position in the organization should be applied with sensitivity, wisdom, and judgment. Applying authority thoughtfully will enhance the individual's credibility and ability to meet other people's expectations. A good mentor will help the new team member to understand the expectations of the team.

Inadequate implementation of ideas

One very important asset that newcomers bring to the organization is their unique knowledge and experience. Sometimes newcomers transfer this knowledge (about new technology, for example) without being conscious of the fact that their method of offering information threatens existing staff members. New tools learned in the classroom or in other institutions need to be used thoughtfully. On the other hand, it is unfortunate that, after a year or two, many new executives forget or ignore their previously acquired skills. The older team members' inertia and the newcomer's desire to be accepted can combine to inhibit the newcomer's ability to contribute to the change process. The mentor who values new insight but understands the rest of the staff's point of view can encourage positive, nonthreatening outlets for the new-comer's creative energy and ideas, and can give directions for the appropriate timing for introducing new information.

Isolation

Another frustration faced by protégés is that they fail to recognize that CEOS, dealing with many different issues, may not always be easily accessible for counseling, support, and direction. This creates a sense of isolation. The mentoring relationship helps alleviate this problem, in part by urging the new member to merge successfully into team processes by keeping in close contact with many others in the organization.

Failure to network

As projects and activities accelerate, some new staff members have a tendency to retreat to focus on specific projects and to get work done. This is unfortunate. It is important that individuals circulate freely within the new organization and that they develop contacts with peers in other organizations. All of these contacts should be maintained and strengthened continually. Outside exposure is vital because it provides important environmental surveillance input that allows ideas developed elsewhere to be applied internally. A good mentor will keep an eye on the protégé and try to ensure that specific project demands do not deter the individual from seeking information and input from outside the organization.

Retention of self-centered ideas

Sometimes new members of the team arrive thinking that the organization should change its ways to accommodate them and that such change should occur easily and naturally. Obviously change does not work this way. Personal sacrifice is necessary in lasting relationships, and early adjustment to the organizational climate will help the protégé to develop trusting relationships with team members. Once trust has been established, innovation will occur more rapidly through the group process, and new ideas will be more readily accepted. The mentor can help with this adjustment by talking with the protégé about the dynamics and orientation of the team, and by giving advice on how to express suggestions for change.

Suggestions for the Mentor

Here are several suggestions that may ease the mentor into a satisfying relationship:

- Make a special effort to be available to your protégé at least once a month, away from the distractions of your work.
- Share up front your specific expectations for the relationship.
- Invest time in learning about the aspirations, attributes, and preferences of your protégé.
- Periodically identify special learning opportunities for your protégé in your organization or in professional networks.
- Actively assist the student in developing his or her personal network of professional contacts.
- Honor any commitments to and confidences of your protégé.
- Periodically validate the value of the information and counsel you are providing.
- Provide honest, caring, regular, and diplomatic feedback.

Examples of Mentoring Activities

Use these approaches to initiate the process of mentoring:

- Develop a mutual professional reading list and discuss a few articles at a time, emphasizing their practical application and relevance to the professional experience.
- Exchange and discuss ideas relevant to each other's professional and academic roles, particularly upcoming, concrete challenges.
- Discuss various management or leadership styles, what works, and what does not.

- Attend professional seminars or meetings together, sharing ideas on the insights gained from those experiences.

THE MATURING MENTORING RELATIONSHIP

Being a mentor means more than just having individuals seek you out for information. Ideally, mentoring is an effort to develop a very close relationship with another individual; it involves sharing thoughts and concerns, and approaches to decision making. At times, the closeness can create a sense of mutual dependence. Seasoned mentors understand this and, as the new associate matures, will seek ways to carefully step back from the process and allow the less-experienced colleague to develop independently.

However, the solid mentoring relationship need not be severed altogether. In fact, some mentoring relationships are maintained over a period of years or throughout one's career. But care should be taken by both parties to avoid excessive dependence. Care should also be taken to ensure that the mentoring relationship does not irritate others in the organization. The healthcare leader should monitor the effect that the relationship has on others, guarding against any perception of undue favoritism, which could undermine the development of a total team effort.

SPECIAL CONCERNS: DIVERSITY

A serious problem faces minority employees. Research by John P. Fernandez (2000), president of ARMC Consultants in Philadelphia, reveals that 78 percent of those surveyed in 1995 reported they were excluded from informal work groups and unable to find sponsors and mentors. Often the impetus for creating a mentoring initiative comes from minority employees who find themselves locked out of informal mentoring and not advancing as rapidly as others. The responsibility of executives at all levels in the organization should be to level the playing field by seeking mentoring and team-building matches that address this problem.

CONCLUSION

The mentoring process is complex, but the relationship provides positive, professional growth for both parties. The best mentoring situation is one that encourages introspection, self-awareness, and a considerable amount of hard work. When mentoring works well, it is the result of a good investment of energy by both parties. Mentoring represents one of those core competencies absolutely essential to the dedicated professional.

DISCUSSION

1. Define the differences between advising and mentoring.
2. Assuming that you are a protégé, what list of topics would you like to see developed during a session with your mentor?
3. Describe several of the ethical standards associated with mentoring.
4. Identify the major barriers to good mentoring.

REFERENCES

Dennis, G. 1993. *Office of Educational Research and Improvement (OERI): Consumer Guide #7.* Washington, DC: U.S. Department of Education.

Fernandez, J. P. 2000. "Diversity." *HR Magazine* 45 (3): 42.

Iberre, H. 2000. "Making Partner—A Mentor's Guide to the Psychological Journey." *Harvard Business Review* 78 (2): 148–49.

Lanser, E. 2000. "Reaping the Benefits of Mentorship." *Healthcare Executive* 15 (3): 19–23.

National Academy of Sciences, National Academy of Engineering, Institute of Medicine. 1997. *Adviser, Teacher, Role Model, Friend: On Being a Mentor to Students in Science and Engineering.* Washington, DC: National Academy Press.

Ross, A. 1992. *Cornerstones of Leadership for Health Services Executives.* Chicago: Health Administration Press.

Zey, M. 1990. *The Mentor Connection: Strategic Alliances in Corporate Life.* New Brunswick, NJ: Transaction Publications.

CHAPTER 16

Managing Your Career

CASE IN POINT: Jessie is the clinic manager of a 40-physician group practice. The practice is a satellite, one of 18 in the health system. Jessie received her master's degree in health administration ten years ago. She is happy in her job and reasonably well compensated but she is beginning to wonder what the future holds for her.

She has attended several local meetings of the Medical Group Management Association but otherwise she has pretty much learned the business from the ground up. She recognizes that professionally she is getting outdated. What she learned in graduate school does not seem to meet the current needs of her profession. Jessie recently asked for expense reimbursement to attend a national meeting, but her request was turned down for budgetary reasons.

Jessie has reached a critical point in her career and is wondering how to jump-start the process of continuing education.

QUESTION: What are several possible reasons that Jessie feels outdated?

_____

INTRODUCTION

Professionals carry the responsibility of designing their own continuing education programs. Those who feel that it is primarily their employer's responsibility are running the very real risk of becoming outdated. Designing a personal growth program also requires a personal awareness of one's strengths and weaknesses that goes far beyond employer-based evaluations of one's competencies. The beginning point in developing a continuing education program starts with a commitment to a formal process. This chapter identifies several elements in that process and obstacles that can interfere with or disrupt continuous learning.

DEVELOPING THE PLAN

Developing a plan for continuing education involves conducting a thorough self-audit to truly understand one's strengths and weaknesses. Fortunately, professional organizations can help by offering an organized approach to this task. Comparing competencies to those of others in similar peer groups can help to highlight strengths and weaknesses.

A self-directed educational process involves four primary factors.

Professional Needs Assessment

Leaders need to maintain a constant and continuing self-assessment of their core competencies. Skill sets need to be inventoried and self-rated. Self-assessment programs, such as those developed by the American College of Healthcare Executives and the American College of Medical Group Executives, are immensely valuable. Skill sets also need to be relevant to the environment, such as the economic woes of group practices or the changing level of expectations by patients. If lacking the selected core competencies, the smart leader will ensure that others on the team possess such skills.

Understanding your leadership style or styles is an important step in the self-assessment process. It is also important to reflect on how that style relates to the changing needs of the organization. Leadership styles can be broadly grouped into the following six categories (Goleman 2000):

1. *Coercive:* demands immediate compliance
2. *Authoritative:* mobilizes people toward a vision
3. *Affiliative:* creates harmony and builds emotional bonds
4. *Democratic:* forges consensus through participation
5. *Pace setting:* sets high standards for performance
6. *Coaching:* develops people for the future

Different styles may be required to meet specific organization conditions. For example, if an organization is in a crisis, a leader may need to employ a coercive rather than the democratic style. It is important to recognize that a leader is capable of changing styles to meet the need. This does not suggest that solid management practices are abandoned. When style changes are implemented, leaders need to reflect on how such changes affect the management team and other stakeholders. A certain level of anxiety should be anticipated.

Currency

Executives are often blind in assessing their own professional currency. It is quite easy to slide toward professional obsolescence without recognizing the condition. Self-protective defense mechanisms can prevent executives from recognizing this flaw. Successful executives have learned to continually monitor their proficiencies against the challenges they face. As the environment changes, so do the professional requirements. One's ability to monitor change by accessing information from multiple sources, and then matching that information against one's competencies, is very important.

Motivation

The ability to put a career management plan together directly relates to the level of motivation. What are the drivers that motivate you? Drivers might include a social conscience to make things better, a personal desire to excel, or an interest in contributing to the body of knowledge. It is useful to try to identify the "why" factor.

For example, an executive may wish to attain fellowship in a professional society, a process involving a number of steps over a period of time. This goal requires significant motivation; therefore, the executive must understand from the beginning that professional recognition is one of the motivators involved and that attaining fellowship is one of the routes to achieve this goal.

Networking

Maintaining networking skills helps the healthcare leader stay informed. By keeping track of people, visiting with colleagues, staying current with the literature, and attending carefully selected continuing education programs, leaders can maintain professional currency. Executives must also consider themselves both as receivers and transmitters of information. They should transmit what they learn, whenever possible, to others. Successful executives work diligently to develop new professional relationships in other parts of the community, the region, and the nation. This requires a commitment of energy and effort, but the depth and richness it will bring to a career make it worthwhile.

Networking should not be limited to relationships with peers (at the same level of experience and responsibility) or superiors. There is considerable benefit in networking with younger associates and others who may be less experienced but who may possess unique skills. Networking in an organized fashion with colleagues possessing different skill sets than yours is also beneficial.

STRESS AS A BARRIER

Work-related and personal stresses represent major barriers to the process of building the plan. We all know individuals who have been stressed in the worst possible way, who have encountered great professional or personal tragedy and yet have survived and continued to flourish. Most of us also know those who do not handle stress well. Successful healthcare executives understand that stress is inherent in their profession. The individual who has really learned to cope with stress—who knows both how to reduce it and how to live with it—will usually stand out in a crowd. He or she has learned to put stress in perspective and move beyond the accompanying paralysis. The inability to understand and manage stress clearly detracts from career enhancing activities.

One concern in the current environment is job survival. Such worries and tensions naturally create stress of a higher order. Executives who become too focused on survival often begin to make decisions that may not meet either their organization's or their personal needs. For example, moving too cautiously and trying to please everyone may not be a smart course of action.

Some of the symptoms of stress might include:

- Expanding the workday at the expense of home life
- Failing to take time for recreation as demonstrated by the accumulation of unused vacation time
- Second guessing others and micromanaging business affairs, getting bogged down in details
- Shying away from difficult decisions accompanied by an increasing desire to please everyone
- Failing to complete projects and assignments on time
- Experiencing fatigue that never seems to go away
- Withdrawing from social contacts
- Accelerating home difficulties
- Being generally pessimistic about the future
- Feeling disconnected, anxious, and/or panicky

Strategy for Coping with Stress

Designing a personal strategy for recognizing and coping with stress provides the platform for managing one's career. An overarching strategy might include:

- *Staying in good physical shape.* Being physically fit helps one function better, providing that reservoir of strength and vigor needed for survival in volatile times.
- *Cultivating outside interests.* Finding activities and hobbies that you enjoy outside of work that fulfill and energize you helps maintain a balanced perspective.
- *Anticipating changes associated with aging.* For many, middle age is an uncomfortable experience. Not only are there physical changes, but emotional and personal ones as well. For example, many couples find that when their children leave home, their relationship becomes strained. Extra effort to maintain and enhance relationships becomes important because it affects both personal and professional life.
- *Managing time effectively.* It is not so much an early-morning meeting, working a major project through the board, or coping with the rebellious teenager at home that creates an overload. Most people can deal with problems one at a time—it is the cumulative effect that creates the problem. Managing time effectively requires being tuned into personal rhythms. To be creative one has to "go with the flow." Successful executives have learned to schedule down time and resist the temptation to fill every minute with activity, salvaging time for reflecting on the larger picture. Differentiating between those necessary immediate tasks and long-range assignments is important. Priority setting is key.

STAGES OF PROFESSIONAL GROWTH

Executives may experience three stages in their attitudes and managerial style. Young executives may worry about the inability of those around them to grasp their new ideas, yet they may be more willing to take risks. Midcareer executives may have been sorely tested, but are still unbowed. They make decision making look easy because of their reservoir of experience that provides them with a sense of what will work. Late-career executives have acquired wisdom and experience, which anoints them as elder statesmen. They may be more risk adverse and may be less inclined to make quick decisions; however, they also have that experience-honed instinct for what works.

During a career, competency needs shift, but core competencies are cumulative. The environment also dictates competency requirements. Basically, determination of core competencies depends on five factors:

1. The needs of the organization in reacting to the environment.
   Example: Stressed organizations may require different competencies.
2. The assignment of the individual within the organization.
   Example: The more senior the individual, the greater the focus on strategic issues.
3. The degree of specialty orientation of the individual.
   Example: The CIO has a special set of competency needs.
4. The extent of the individual's experience base.
   Example: Younger executives work first to develop basic skill competencies and then on their people skills.
5. The individual's personal goals and preferences.
   Example: The career goal helps establish the competence.

THE PLAN

Once competency needs have been identified, the executive must lay out a continuing education plan. Several plan-building suggestions follow.

- *Scan course brochures for applicable subjects.* Identifying specific continuing education goals by topic strengthens the process, while failing to match program content with a plan can weaken the process.
- *Identify current literature applicable to the plan.* Internet search engines make this task much easier.
- *Select mentors carefully for their competencies.* Mentors contribute to the design of a continuing education process.

- *Accelerate collegial networking.* Become involved in professional societies or other activities that provide opportunities to meet with peers.
- *Teach others to strengthen skills.* The preparation required to teach peers, colleagues, or students requires research and study, which helps build competencies.
- *Seek opportunities to make presentations to groups of colleagues.* It strengthens public speaking skills and contributes to a professional's reputation.

CONCLUSION

Actively managing a career requires recognition of the need to create and manage a professional development program based on continuing life-long learning. The process requires vigilance involving a constant assessment of competencies, a process of identifying and overcoming barriers to career development, and a significant commitment of time and energy. The rewards for aggressively taking responsibility for managing a career are immeasurable.

DISCUSSION

1. How would you go about developing your continuing education plan? (Be specific.)
2. Describe your leadership style and identify strengths and weaknesses associated with that style.
3. What specific steps are you taking to network with your colleagues?
4. Identify the methods you use to reduce your stress on the job.

REFERENCE

Goleman, D. 2000. "Leadership that Gets Results." *Harvard Business Review* 78 (2): 80–82.

Part IV: Leadership Competency Knowledge Areas

PART IV LOOKS at ten specific areas leaders must have knowledge of to effectively guide their organizations. Each knowledge area is introduced by a "Case in Point" and a question, then discussed in relation to its value for the healthcare leader. Specific competencies required for the knowledge area are listed, with practical application, followed by several questions to promote in-depth discussion. The ten leadership competency knowledge areas include:

1. Governance and organizational dynamics
2. Human resources
3. Financial management and economics
4. Strategic planning and marketing
5. Information and information systems
6. Communications and public relations
7. Community health and managerial epidemiology
8. Quantitative analysis and modeling
9. Legal and ethical issues
10. Organizational and healthcare policy

A leader does not need to be the technical expert in all of these areas, but the leader must have significant understanding of the issues in each area—both to know the capabilities to look for in the individuals they recruit, and to assess and evaluate the organization's competency need in each of these areas.

THE NECESSITY OF IDENTIFYING COMPETENCIES

Debate about skills and competencies is not unusual in healthcare organizations, especially in group practices where physicians hold a wide variety of positions. Professionals vary widely in their opinions as to what constitutes the necessary competencies and skills to lead and manage healthcare organizations. Those differences of opinion have frequently led organizations down a very treacherous path, where the leadership found that the only salvation was to be acquired by a practice management company or, in the case of a hospital, to be acquired by a larger system. While some of these moves have been successful, in many cases it was the beginning of the end. If one examines these situations very carefully it becomes clear that had the physicians and executive leadership known what kind of competencies their organization needed, then hired staff with this expertise and allowed them to lead and manage the organization, success would have been inevitable. The same is true on the hospital or system side, where the board of directors should engage in intense discussion about the necessary competencies and skills before attempting to bring in new leadership or consider a merger. This section identifies the necessary skills and insights into the practical applications to effectively lead and manage a healthcare organization.

The competency issue concerns not only the healthcare organization but academia as well. Faculties have long debated about the emphasis that should be placed on various skill and competence areas to prepare individuals for successful careers in the leadership and management of healthcare organizations. The debate has centered largely on those courses that emphasize human skills in contrast to those that are analytical in nature. Debate continues about emphasizing research without necessarily considering how that research might relate to the day-to-day management of a healthcare organization.

Rather than joining the debate, we will outline the competence areas—or domains, as they have been called—and describe the knowledge elements in each of these areas and how they will affect the success or failure of the organization. Emphasis will also be placed on the necessity for an intense study of the organization and its environment before a decision is made about what kind of competencies and skills are needed to lead and manage the organization. (To engage in this discussion, we will call upon those studies that were previously cited in chapter 2.) Each major area or domain will be considered in a somewhat different fashion than that considered by the authors of those studies. For the most part, however, they were the basis for the development of these cases and discussion.

This section will also consider the competence areas as described by the Accrediting Commission on Education for Health Services Administration (ACEHSA), which accredits graduate programs in health services administration. ACEHSA requires that an accredited program include the following course elements in its curriculum (ACEHSA 1997):

- Structuring and positioning health organizations to achieve optimum performance
- Financial management of healthcare organizations under alternate financing mechanisms
- Leadership and interpersonal and communication skills in managing human resources and health professionals in diverse organizational environments
- Managing information resources and collecting, analyzing, and using business and health information in decision making
- Statistical, quantitative, and economic analysis in decision making
- Legal and ethical analysis in decision making
- Organizational and governmental health policy formulation, implementation, and effect
- Assessment and understanding of the health status of populations, determinates of health and illness, and managing health risks and behaviors in diverse populations

- The development, organization, financing, performance, and change of health systems in diverse communities, drawing broadly on the social and behavioral sciences
- Business and health outcomes measurement, process/outcome relationships, and methods for process improvement in health organizations

The criteria state further that the students will not only be proficient in the areas outlined above but also that "students will apply management knowledge and skills in individually appropriate field settings." The curriculum section of the criteria concludes, "The curriculum will include integrative experiences, which demonstrate the student's ability to draw upon and apply material covered throughout the program of study and to demonstrate skills in continuous learning through information access, synthesis, and use in critical thinking" (ACEHSA 1997).

ACEHSA continuously evaluates the needed educational competencies and skills as well as the processes put in place by university programs to ensure that the students' preparation is meeting the needs of healthcare organizations. The criteria are updated on a periodic basis to ensure not only rigor but relevance as well. Input for this process is obtained from a wide variety of sources, including the university programs and the healthcare industry.

Governance and Organizational Dynamics (Behavior)

CASE IN POINT: Dr. Jane Walters is the CEO of a large academic health center that had merged a year and a half ago with a 200-doctor multispecialty community medical group. Attempts to consummate the merger were frustrated at virtually every turn by the cultural differences between the two organizations and the personal agendas of some of the leaders in both groups. A number of task forces were formed and significant progress was made at the administrative level; however, when it came to governance and the financial affairs of the organization, numerous roadblocks appeared at every turn.

Special task forces were formed to deal with the issues of governance, finance, and compensation. Each task force came up with a series of recommendations, which were to be presented to the board for consideration and approval. The governance task force made the first presentation and the proposal—to reduce the board from 28 members to 16—was approved by the board and then was moved on to the faculty for their consideration. Several influential faculty members who worked on the governance proposal opposed it and urged their faculty members to vote against it. Objections related to departmental differences in representation and key aspects of the terms of office. While the proposal received a majority of the faculty vote it did not receive the required two-thirds needed to pass. Dr. Walter considered the ramifications of the faculty vote and the possibility of bringing the matter back for another vote. She also noted that the community clinic voted almost unanimously in favor of the proposal and it was the university faculty who voted it down. She considered the alternatives.

QUESTION: Should the matter be quickly revoted or delayed? If delayed, what timeframe would you suggest?

GOVERNANCE AND LEADERSHIP BASICS

Governance and leadership are critical areas in the development of a successful organization. It takes a number of individuals in the organization with vision and a dedication to the mission of the organization. No one form of governance fits all organizations—governance must be tailored to meet the needs of the organization and the environment. One of the most difficult tasks is to have everyone in the organization understand that the principle concerns of governance are to chart the direction of the organization through its vision and mission and develop policies that will guide and govern the work of management. As discussed earlier in this text, governing bodies often become so immersed in the management and operational issues of the organization that they overlook the big picture and their policy-making responsibilities.

The organization depends on the development of strong leadership, which has as one of its primary competencies that of being a change agent. While change has always been with us, the frequency of the cycles of change and the height of each cycle seem to be increasing significantly. Even in the face of these changes a governance system must be maintained that keeps the organization on an even keel, even when it is challenged from both inside and outside on a daily basis. Leadership must be able to determine stakeholder needs to develop a governance system that will meet the needs of both the community served and the providers who deliver the services to that community.

Leadership must have all of the competencies and skills outlined in this section, and the organization must in some way possess those competencies as well. However, because one person cannot be competent in all of these areas, it is the responsibility of the leader to ensure that the organization has a staff to cover all of the needed competence and skill areas. The leader is responsible for the critical organizational systems and the range of strategies and goals that will help make the organization successful. The leader must also have a sense of vision; of how hard the organization can be pushed; of what the important issues are; and of the existing strengths, weaknesses, opportunities, and threats; and have the ability to focus and choose the right path. The leader must be flexible in style and know when to use the X or Y theories of management. Most of these attributes have been discussed earlier in this text.

Essex and Kusy (1999), in their discussion of "Fast Forward Leadership," suggest a series of trends driving change: "Technology links information to people; customers raise their expectations: more speed, quality, and cost effectiveness; talent becomes a critical competitive edge, yet hard to recruit and retain; speed goes beyond product development to include training and information utilization; staff members call out for balance in life; and workforce, work, and marketplace globalize." Let us remember these words as we continue our discussions of skills and competencies needed for healthcare organizations and their leaders and managers.

To be successful in leadership, governance, and organizational dynamics, healthcare leaders should:

- Possess leadership and change-agent skills
- Communicate effectively
- Develop and implement governance systems
- Evaluate and improve governing principles, policies, and processes
- Assess stakeholder needs and facilitate relationship development
- Facilitate staff development and teaming

- Facilitate physician understanding and acceptance of good business management
- Develop and implement both clinical and managerial quality improvement systems
- Understand the many aspects of both clinical and business operations
- Continuously monitor the organization and its delivery of services to ensure that the needs of the community are being met

PRACTICAL APPLICATION

On the practical level, what does this all mean, and is it possible to describe what it means to lead an organization in a successful manner? The Chinese philosopher Lao Tse was indeed correct when he said that the leader "must walk behind the people." A good leader possesses skills, knowledge, values, a social role, and self-confidence. What can be seen and evaluated on the surface are a person's skills and knowledge; however, motives, values, self-confidence, and self-image are more difficult to ascertain because they are buried deep within the individual.

The good leader or manager keeps a finger on the pulse of the organization on a daily basis without getting into a level of detail that obstructs the overall vision. The ability to listen is critical, and without this skill the leader or manager is soon out of touch with the staff and the organization. The other side of listening is communication—both verbal and written—and the ability to deal with internal and external audiences. One of the only ways to develop and improve these skills is to practice, formally and informally.

The importance of delegation has been emphasized by many authors and it should be reemphasized here. Leaders must know not only what to delegate, but how to do so as well. Many managers want to delegate, but simply do not know how. The leader must sincerely believe in participation and be able to enlist the help of others in such a way that they feel great responsibility and desire to deal with the delegated tasks. If communication is the door, then listening is the key.

An important question that must be raised is whether competence in governance and organizational dynamics can be taught or if only experience can provide these skills. Perhaps the answer lies in providing a firm academic foundation on the need for these skills and the ways that they can be developed and practiced. Experience must then take over, and the best approach is for the aspiring leaders to place themselves in the hands of a skilled mentor (see chapter 15). To do this effectively ego must be put aside and individuals must open themselves to constant inspection and critique. Such vulnerability is not easy in our competitive world.

DISCUSSION

1. What is the leader's role in governance system development?
2. Should the leader or CEO be a member of the board of directors?
3. How might the leader assess the needs of the key stakeholders?
4. Will the same governance system fit all organizations?
5. Describe the difference between policy and management.
6. Why is communication so important in leading and managing organizations?
7. What does it mean to be an effective mentor?

Human Resources

CASE IN POINT: The clinic had grown in size from 25 physicians in 1995 to 84 physicians through several mergers by 1999. Bob Clark, the executive director of the clinic, was preparing his case for the addition of a director of human resources for the clinic, a concept that he had been considering for some time. There were a number of physicians in the group who felt that this was just another layer of administration that would be in their way as they had for the most part been dealing with these matters with their own staff. A significant lawsuit involving a clinic and one of its nonphysician staff in a neighboring community caught their attention. There was an alleged sexual harassment charge against one of the physicians and it appeared as though the employee would win the case. Although Bob had laid out a strong position he knew that the case in the area clinic would have a significant effect on the executive committee's decision.

QUESTION: Do you think it is appropriate to have a full-time director of human resources in an 84-physician group?

HUMAN RESOURCE BASICS

Hudak et al. (1997) place human resources (HR) in the relationship management domain with communications, interpersonal skills, physician relations, networking, people skills, and team-building skills. These skills cut across a wide range of staff activity and emphasize the breadth of human relations in a healthcare setting. Managing human resources is a challenge for the leadership of the organization and is necessary to establish collaboration between the managers of the organization and the HR department. According to Robert D. Lenburg (2000), president of the HR Group and visiting professor of HR management at the University of St. Thomas, "It is important that the leader and manager study and understand the context in which HR management takes place, which is the nature of work in today's healthcare environment, the legal environment and workforce diversity." He also emphasizes staffing issues, how organizations can effectively recruit, select, orient, train, and, when necessary, phase out employees.

The leader, and most certainly the manager, must have a firm grasp of what can be termed the "three Cs" of HR: communication, compensation, and conflict resolution. Each plays a major role in an organization and their importance cannot be underestimated. These skills or competencies have their home in HR and, while the leader may not always be directly involved, it is important that the organization have significant competence in these areas. It is the leader's responsibility to see that this need is fulfilled.

HUMAN RESOURCES COMPETENCIES AND SKILLS IN BUSINESS VS. HEALTHCARE

The question is, are the competencies in HR are different in healthcare as compared to other businesses and industry? While there is great similarity in the necessary competencies, differences exist that must be appreciated, especially by those who are teaching HR in graduate schools of business. Certain situations in healthcare organizations staffed or owned by professionals are different from the usual business setting. Professionals in general believe that they have their own rules and they sometimes like to apply these rules to inappropriate situations. This can be especially true in HR when dealing with difficult employee situations. The leader occupies a most important position in dealing with other professionals in the organization when it comes to these kinds of difficulties. It has been suggested that a leader cannot really appreciate the need for a quality HR department until he or she has faced a sexual harassment situation with a physician and one of the members of the staff. Worse yet is when the physician is involved in an affair with a staff member.

The following are key concepts in HR that the leader should understand:

- The principles of HR management
- The key functions of effective HR management
- The legal and regulatory aspects of HR management
- Familiarity with the problem-solving tools of HR
- Communication as the central nervous system of the organization
- The value of the human side of the enterprise
- The significant investment the organization has in human capital
- The importance of the reward systems on both the professional and the nonprofessional side
- Acknowledging the role of the organization's culture, especially in times of change involving the staff
- The importance of a process for conflict resolution

PRACTICAL APPLICATION

Leaders and managers must engage in four key skill activities on the human side of the enterprise. Understanding the need an organization has for these activities is critical.

Recruiting

Hire people who are competent, who fit the culture you have or you want to develop, and, above all, hire people who want the job. Every job has its challenges. The people who want the job will see challenges as opportunities to show what they can do for the organization. Turnover is costly and it takes between three and five years for a management team to become fully effective. Retention begins with recruitment.

Orientation

The organization's leaders must orient new staff to "hit the ground running." This provides a valuable opportunity for the leadership to engage employees in the success of the company. It is important to describe the organization's culture, values, mission, vision, market position, strengths, and challenges. The leadership should ask the new employees to use their fresh eyes to identify opportunities to improve the organization as they learn about the culture and its idiosyncrasies. These activities will set the stage for regular, candid, and open discussions with groups of employees.

Performance Appraisal

The management should take the lead in describing the importance of both an individual's self-appraisal and a 360-degree review. A 360-degree review provides managers and leaders with an opportunity to receive an evaluation of their job performance from the people around them—those they report to, their peers, and the people whose work they supervise. Performance appraisals are an opportunity for coaching and will help the employee build on the strengths that they and/or others see.

Employee Meetings

Provide an opportunity for meeting with employee groups at least on an annual basis. The group should be kept as small as practical to provide an opportunity to build the culture with a strong participative element of the organization. This also offers an opportunity to recognize significant accomplishments and individuals and groups who contributed to those accomplishments. Management can also review organization performance, plans, and challenges facing the organization. At least a third of the meeting time should be open for questions. New employees bring their experience, knowledge, and paradigms from previous education and other experiences. Although the organization's paradigms are valuable—they outline how the organization has achieved its success—they can also be limiting. New employees are valuable because they look at the issues facing the company with a fresh perspective.

DISCUSSION

1. Can you identify the key HR competencies of your organization?
2. How should the HR department be involved in physician compensation?
3. What are some of the pitfalls in looking at HR in healthcare as the same as in a conventional business?
4. How should the HR department be involved in conflict resolution?
5. If you were the director of HR, how would you deal with issues of confidentiality?
6. What role do you see the HR department playing in the communication network of the organization?

Financial Management and Economics

CASE IN POINT: Dr. Thomas had been wondering for a long time about the financial condition of the clinic. He had been president for two years and had only minimal exposure to accounting and finance. He had taken a course in economics as an undergraduate before entering medical school. He looked over the financial statements at the close of the year and while he was not able to pinpoint any specific problems, he had the feeling that something was wrong. He consulted an accountant friend of his who also taught in a healthcare program at a local university. Together they reviewed the statements and discovered wide discrepancies in the information that was being reported. He commented to the accountant that he wished he understood more about the language of business and finance so that he could more readily understand the financial statements and financial reports of the clinic.

QUESTION: What level of financial knowledge do you believe a physician leader should have?

THE BASICS OF ACCOUNTING, FINANCE, AND ECONOMICS

Financial management and economics fall into the general category of resource management and include several competencies necessary for the leader or manager of the organization. The leader must be able to read financial statements and understand the principles of accounting and finance. It is not necessary to be an accountant or a financial manager; however, the leader must understand the language of business, the idiosyncrasies of accounting, and finance specific to healthcare organizations. Key aspects are accounting principles, cost accounting, reimbursement, capitation, capital and operational budgeting, reporting and control, and financial management. The individual must also be competent in dealing with database issues and have a working knowledge of information systems as applied to financial information management, which is also critical in the strategic planning process.

A working knowledge of economics and the theories and principles of supply and demand are also important if the leader is to place the organization in a position where it can both take advantage of and shape its environment. The delivery of healthcare is a complex business and knowledge of the economics of the marketplace is critical and essential. The leadership of the organization will have to deal with managed care and other types of insurance products. Because an understanding of both finance and economics is necessary, the individual should have significant competencies in these areas or develop a staff that does. Another competence involved in finance is contracting. Few professionals have had training or are skilled in contracting. Although it may seem that this is intuitive, it is as much an art and science as medicine itself and should not be underestimated. The leader should have enough knowledge of contracting to know when to ask for help.

STRATEGY AND FINANCE

Strategy, as it relates to finance, is perhaps one of the most important of the key competence areas for a leader in a healthcare organization, especially in a medical practice group. The success of the organization lies in its strategic positioning and the financial base upon which that strategic positioning is founded. There is no substitute for a strong foundation in finance to develop and implement a sound strategic plan. Important skill areas within this aspect of financial competency include evaluation of risk, value, cost of capital, and cash flow. The leadership of the organization should also be well-founded in the decision process for both for-profit and not-for-profit organizations. Together each of these elements will provide a sound understanding of the relationships between finance, accounting, strategic planning, and operations. Other skills are necessary to broaden the leader's financial perspective, including the time value of money, the valuation of stocks and bonds, the cost of capital, financial forecasting, capital structure, reorganization, and, in special cases, liquidation, merger, and consolidation. Although the leader does not have to possess the qualifications of a certified public accountant, the leader must understand and appreciate the language of business. The basic principle is to be able to read and interpret the financial statements and plan and evaluate the financial future of the organization.

According to the American College of Medical Practice Executives (1999), leaders must be able to:

- Understand and manage operational and capital budgets
- Oversee accounting control systems
- Read and understand financial statements and financial analyses
- Understand coding principles, reimbursement, and compliance policies
- Facilitate investment planning and management
- Establish business relationships in the community
- Choose financial advisers wisely
- Understand the complexities of compliance with tax laws and federal regulation
- Understand managed care
- Understand the principles of compensation formulae

PRACTICAL APPLICATION

The leader and manager must understand how to manage revenue and expense and to structure accountability for revenue and expense in clinical and management units for the entire organization. It is very important to recognize the dangers of considering revenue as the responsibility of marketing or contracting and cost as the responsibility of operations.

Formally reviewing the performance of all strategic initiatives at least annually as part of the strategic planning process is critical. There must be an acute awareness of operational and financial performance. Responsibility and accountability should be clearly delegated throughout the organization.

It is important to understand the use and misuse of the pro forma. Assumptions and conclusions that go into the pro forma should be evaluated against actual performance. This is a way to learn and improve the development of future pro formas.

The financials are a report card and should be regarded as such. There must also be an understanding of the underlying business to properly understand and interpret the financials properly. Benchmarks are needed to assess what good performance really is and to identify opportunities for improvement. Keep in mind, however, that one month's performance is not a trend.

DISCUSSION

1. Can you define the capital structure of your organization?
2. Can you define the time value of money and its meaning to the organization?
3. What is the relationship between strategic and financial planning?
4. Who is responsible for the overall financial health of the organization?
5. Describe the relationship between finance and economics.
6. What is the relationship of human capital to the financial health of the organization?

Strategic Planning and Marketing

CASE IN POINT: Mary Bass was asked by the CEO of her organization to lay out a strategic planning process for the annual clinic leadership retreat. Mary was the newly appointed executive director of the organization, and although she was familiar with the planning process in general she did not feel comfortable taking responsibility for the major planning effort that the CEO envisioned. She felt she lacked some of the competencies necessary to structure a retreat that would offer the clinic leadership a view of their own strengths, weaknesses, opportunities, and threats in a way that would paint a realistic picture of the organization. She discussed the matter with a friend who had just completed a course in strategic planning. Her friend urged her to take a strategic planning course even though the retreat would be held before she completed the course. When Mary discussed the matter with the CEO, he asked her why she did not already have that knowledge since she had a master's degree in health services administration. Mary admitted that the program she graduated from did not offer a course in either strategic or market planning.

QUESTION: What is the relationship between strategic and market planning?

STRATEGIC PLANNING

Strategic planning and strategic positioning represent one of the most important domains in leadership and strategic management. In this area competence is an absolute must. While analytic skills are of great significance, they will be of little value to a leader if they are not tied to a strong sense of the organization and its direction. To have a sound sense of the organization, it is necessary to have a clear vision of where the organization should be heading. The leader must also be flexible, be able to adapt to and manage change, be a critical thinker, be a good decision maker, be a manager of risk, and have a strong sense of ethical values. All of these traits must be present, as well as a strong awareness of the environment in which the organization and its leader find themselves. As stated earlier, these traits—unlike skills in finance and knowledge of the analytical side of the organization that can easily be tested and appraised—can be difficult to see and evaluate.

The leader must be able to lay out a vision for the organization, clearly define its mission, and then develop a series of strategies, goals, and objectives to move the organization toward its vision. One of the most critical competencies is the ability to develop a business plan that moves the organization toward the achievement of its goals and objectives. The business plan, in its simplest form, addresses what, why, how, who, where, and when. This process is most often preceded by an analysis of the strengths, weaknesses, opportunities, and threats facing the organization, and must be completed with a strong sense and appreciation of the environment in which the organization conducts its affairs.

The leader should be careful not to overlook the value of analytical skills in the strategic planning process. The decision process can be aided immensely by studying the issues using analytical models. These models have a sound foundation in decision analysis and are especially helpful to the leader as he or she chooses from a variety of alternatives. Therefore, because it helps estimate the degree of uncertainty, statistical analysis is also important for projecting future trends.

MARKETING PLANNING

Because of their similarities, it is difficult to tell where marketing planning and strategic planning begin or end. The competencies necessary for strategic planning are basically the same as for good market planning. If there is a difference between strategic and market planning it only lies in the application of the strategic positioning process. Sometimes it is difficult to determine which aspect comes first. Information and market research are useful in both processes. A strong sense of the environment and appreciation for the value of market research—together with a passion for meeting the needs of the target population—are the marks of an organization with a successful marketing orientation.

Marketing has a negative reputation with many medical groups and, unlike hospitals and large systems, groups have been slow to adopt advanced marketing research and strategies. If asked, "What is marketing?" the average physician would reply, "Advertising—and I don't need advertising because everyone wants to see me." Unfortunately, if budget cuts are necessary, the first programs to go are typically those in education and marketing—both critical for maintaining and gaining market share and retaining current customers.

THE ROLE OF THE LEADER

The leader must understand that marketing begins at home, that a need for market research exists, and that it is necessary to create an internal appreciation for marketing within the organization that is embraced by every single person in that organization. The "four Ps" of marketing—product, place, price, and promotion—play a key role in understanding the elements of the organization's marketing activity. The relationship between these four elements and the organization's strategic plan is vital. To evaluate these four elements, it is necessary to have a continuing market research program in place. The marketplace continues to change and only a sound market research program will keep the organization in sync with its environment.

Beyond supporting a solid marketing orientation, the leader must be a good judge of the resources needed to support the marketing activities. If the group is small, choosing the right consultant is critical. If the group or organization is large, choosing the right director of marketing will be key.

THE ROLE OF COMMUNICATIONS

The role of communications in the organization has already been introduced in the discussion of human resources. That communication focuses first on the internal environment and is part of the strategy that marketing "begins at home." Also of great importance is communication with the external markets or publics. While advertising plays a role in this process, it is not the most important activity. Communication through satisfied patients (customers) and image is a key aspect of the external marketing activity. The leader is responsible for ensuring that the patients see value in the services the organization delivers: Value = Quality/Cost. If the patients see value in the services they receive, they will happily communicate that information to the community at large.

To master the core competencies in strategic and marketing planning, a successful leader must:

- Understand the concept of the strategic planning process
- Have a keen sense of the environment
- Be able to vision and think strategically
- Be a cheerleader who can excite people to do the right things
- Understand the key factors that contribute to the success of the planning process
- Understand evaluation for process improvement
- Understand the role of marketing in healthcare organizations
- Understand the theories of the four Ps of marketing
- Know how to develop a marketing orientation in the organization

PRACTICAL APPLICATION

Before the strategic planning process begins, the leader must have a firm grasp on the vision for the organization and understand—but perhaps not necessarily articulate—the organization's mission. It is important to involve all the key players and stakeholders in the planning process from the very beginning.

Leaders who attempt to conduct the process themselves usually impose more of their own ideas on the group than is comfortable for the participants. It may also stifle significant discussion. The planning process itself should be facilitated by a consultant with expertise in planning for similar-sized organizations. The facilitator should be charged with committing the plan to paper for continuing reference by the leadership of the organization and its staff.

The planning sessions should be held in a comfortable environment removed from the day-to-day operations of the organization. The channels of communication should be open so that everyone in the group has an opportunity to speak and express their opinions freely. The leader should remain quietly in the background to observe the process and provide leadership only when necessary.

There should be ample time for social gatherings, which provide opportunity for informal discussions between the members of the planning group. It is often during these times that new ideas are first expressed for later development at the meeting itself. This is an opportune time for the leader to circulate through the group and listen to the ideas that are being expressed.

The development of a marketing plan or strategy should not be undertaken until the strategic plan is firmly in place. In order for an organization to have a marketing plan with significant effectiveness, it is important that the leadership understand who the customers are today, what services can and should be provided to these customers, what is the satisfaction of the present customers, and what they like or dislike about the services. Such key factors can only be determined through significant marketing research.

Market research should identify competitors and develop data comparing the organization's performance to that of the competition. It is also important to identify how services can be provided in a superior way to the competitors', and to monitor competitive response to new products, services, or programs.

The communication process should not be neglected and should be carefully crafted and made an integral part of the marketing plan. This process must involve both the internal and external publics if the marketing plan is to be successful. These processes are also necessary to tie the marketing plan to the organization's strategic plan.

DISCUSSION

1. Can you describe the elements of the strategic planning process?
2. What is vision and how does it differ from mission?
3. What does the phrase "marketing begins at home" mean?
4. What are the critical elements of a good business plan?
5. Why are the four Ps of marketing important?
6. Can you define market segmentation?

Information and Information Systems

CASE IN POINT: The physicians at the Jones Clinic had been discussing developing an automated medical record for the past two years. They asked the administrator, Sally Gray, to investigate the possibility of bringing the matter to closure in the next six months. Sally was unfamiliar with information systems and was not certain where to turn for information on the automated medical record. She called the Medical Group Management Association in Englewood, Colorado for advice and assistance. The association staff offered to forward the latest information on automated medical records, told her about meetings on the topic, and suggested consultants who might help her respond to the doctors' request for a system. They also indicated that a number of vendors would be pleased to discuss the matter with her.

She did her homework and, armed with this new information, made a presentation to the physicians on an approach to studying the issue. She recommended that a computerized medical record committee of physicians be appointed and that this committee work with her to investigate computerizing the clinic's medical records. The president responded by appointing the committee. One of the physicians reacted strongly, saying that this was the administrator's job and that if she did not have the system plan for execution in six months, she would no longer be at the clinic.

QUESTION: What is the most significant barrier to having an automated medical record?

HEALTH INFORMATICS

Jeff Hertzberg, M.D. (2000), stated in his syllabus for his informatics class: "Health informatics is a multi-disciplinary field with contributions from systems analysis, computer science, cognitive science, organizational/group dynamics, management science, and bio-statistics. As such it has often escaped clear definition, but I prefer Homer Warner's definition: health informatics is 'the study, invention, and implementation of structures and algorithms to improve communication, understanding, and management of health information.' By focusing on structures rather than computers, we recognize that business and clinical needs must drive technology choices, not the reverse. Health informatics techniques hold promise as a means to reform the healthcare delivery system based on scientific principles rather than intuition, politics, or perverse economic incentives."

The manager or leader must become conversant with the key technologies that are driving health informatics development, without ignoring the reasons for all-too-frequent failures of healthcare computer implementations. Relationships exist between the business of medicine and the delivery of healthcare services and the recording of data from these activities, which form the basis for medical informatics. The healthcare leader must understand the link between these two aspects of the healthcare system and work to bring them together for a common cause: providing the necessary information for high-quality patient care.

INFORMATION NEEDS

To understand the competencies healthcare leaders need, it is necessary to understand the information needs of the organization itself. The leader, in concert with the members of the organization—whether a medical group, a hospital, or an integrated system—must develop a very clear understanding of the information necessary to establish a high-quality patient care system, while at the same time providing a sound foundation for the long-term business and delivery of healthcare.

There was a time when it was necessary for healthcare executives to understand computers, systems, and the associated software. Although knowledge in these areas is important, it has been demonstrated that it is more important to understand the use of information and how that information can be developed on an ongoing basis within the organization. Systems must be linked, especially at the front end, and must be organized so the information gathered is available to the entire system. Doing so saves the time and effort of continuously collecting duplicate information.

By starting with the mission of the organization and moving toward the strategic and business plans, a leader can clearly define what information is needed to ensure the success of both the business plan and the strategy of the organization. If the organization is able to do so, there is no question about its performance in relationship to its mission and the movement of the entire entity toward the vision proposed by the leadership.

CLINICAL AND BUSINESS RELATIONSHIPS

A significant relationship exists between the business side of the enterprise and its delivery of clinical services. Most information systems were started as part of the billing process when organizations started computerizing the billing and collection systems in the early 1960s. These operations proved very successful and soon financial statements could be generated on a frequent basis, providing the management with a new tool to be used on a day-to-day basis. The management information systems that were born in this era have been used not only to plot the financial course of the organization but to establish its value as well. This was not possible prior to the introduction of the computerized financial systems. The importing and posting of data on a daily basis provided an ongoing financial update that was available to the managers at all times. Cost analysis of departments and services became a reality, and, more recently, the computer has allowed us to provide the information necessary for activity-based accounting. Because such abilities can revolutionize the cost side of the delivery of services, it is important that the leader be knowledgeable and possess competencies in this area of application.

Linking these business systems to the clinical systems of healthcare organizations has also become a reality. Because the same information base is used—the patient's account or history number—it is possible to develop clinical databases to be used in diagnosis, treatment, and research. The leader must understand the potential for these links.

E-HEALTH

While healthcare lagged behind other businesses in utilizing information systems across a broad spectrum of activities, the e-health era has begun. The growth of the business side of healthcare systems and of the electronic medical record has given rise to a number of different approaches that use information systems on an Intranet and an Internet basis. Two recent journals devoted a significant amount of space to e-health. *Health Affairs* (2000) ran a series of articles, "E-health: The Next Wave," which discussed networking health, health policy issues on the Internet, financing the healthcare Internet, and patients and physicians and the Internet. It is obvious that this new communication tool will change the way we think about healthcare and the way healthcare services are delivered. New kinds of communication competencies and skills are being described and defined so that this new mode of communication can be used to increase both the efficacy and the efficiency of the delivery of healthcare services. E-health is rapidly becoming a reality and an important part of the healthcare system. It will take great vision and leadership and all of the related competencies and skills to move this new communication tool in the right direction.

DEVELOPING INFORMATION MANAGEMENT COMPETENCIES

A number of ways exist to develop the needed competencies in information systems. The best way is to pursue a graduate degree that incorporates all of the aspects of leadership and management and ties them together with information management. If attaining such a degree is not feasible, then pursuing an educational program through a professional society is an excellent alternative. A number of these societies—the Medical Group Management Association, the American College of Medical Practice Executives, the American College of Healthcare Executives, the American College of Physician Executives, and the Healthcare Financial Management Association—provide courses on informatics to assist individuals who are working full-time to develop the necessary skills and competencies. Informatics has become a critical element in the language of both healthcare service and business.

To achieve competence in information management, a leader must:

- Understand the core concepts of medical information
- Understand the definitions used in information and information systems
- Understand the rationale for the field's existence and its current and future direction
- Broadly understand the technologies and processes that support the business and support systems in clinical and administration environments
- Appreciate the basics and complexities of computerized patient records systems
- Understand the process for system and vendor selection
- Understand the links between information and the strategic planning process
- Place informatics in the context of the organization's goals

- Prepare a high-level information technology plan for a health organization
- Oversee database management and maintenance
- Understand the need for security systems

PRACTICAL APPLICATION

Implementation of a new information system should be attempted only after careful study of the needs of the organization and should, if at all possible, be implemented in stages. To be most effective, process changes require system changes. While this was historically true for systems developed "in house," it is now even more necessary with the implementation of purchased software. Implementing systems in stages allows time for the process changes to be worked out and limits exposure of the total organization to possible problems with new software. Each stage should provide interim value and build support for the new system as the total system is implemented.

The electronic medical record can be considered the "holy grail" of medical management. Many challenges must be met to make the electronic medical record successful—not the least of which is the unqualified cooperation of the physicians. Electronic medical records call for careful standardization, which should be agreed upon before system development is attempted.

Vendor selection should be done with the help of an expert in the field. Although price is important when choosing a system, it should not be a sole factor in making the final decision—the least expensive system may turn out to be the most expensive system if it does not meet the needs of the organization. Although key stakeholders must be involved in the process, the final decision should rest with the leadership of the organization. Therefore, these individuals must be fully informed about each step in the process

The leadership of the organization must fully understand the implications of the need for continuing system development. The organizational change process continues at a high rate of speed and the informatics required to assist in this process are substantial. While most systems have their basis in the financial underpinnings of the organization, they must be expanded to include the clinical system as well to ensure that patient-care services are delivered and evaluated as efficiently and effectively as possible. Appropriate databases are necessary for these evaluations.

The information system is the central nervous system of the organization and should be treated as such. Constant refinements and upgrades can help to avoid significant conversions, which can cost the leader his or her position.

DISCUSSION

1. What does database management mean?
2. What factors stand in the way of the development of an electronic medical record?
3. What do you think about the future of e-health?
4. Is there more to information management than simply understanding computers?
5. What is the importance of information systems in daily operations?
6. How would you pursue informatics competence development?

Communications and Public Relations

CASE IN POINT: Bob Smith, the president of a growing health-care system, was preparing a presentation to the medical staff to outline his ideas for the development of a marketing and communications program for the system. He had given a great deal of thought to all of the elements involved, especially those relating to the organization's marketing efforts. He thought about how to impress upon the physicians the need for both internal and external communications. He felt quite sure that the physicians would be interested in external communication with the patients and the other publics served by the system. He was quite concerned, however, about internal communications because of the poor relationship between some of the physicians and the nonphysician staff. He thought bringing up the topic might open old wounds and some of the physicians would be so upset they would miss the communications message entirely.

He was pleasantly surprised to find that during his presentation the questions and discussion about internal communications were well received by the physicians. Several of the physician leaders pointed out the need for strong communications with both the patients and the staff. One of the doctors commented that "communications begins at home—we must do our best to communicate with our patients and our staff."

Bob was shocked, however, at the reaction of the physicians when he discussed external communications. He suggested that a marketing communications department could be beneficial. The physicians rebelled, grumbling about the proposed advertising campaign: "We don't need advertising. We are good and the community knows it."

QUESTION: What are the most important elements of communication?

COMMUNICATION SKILLS

We return to the issue of communications both inside and outside of the organization. Communication skills have already been alluded to in human resources and strategic planning and marketing as one of the critical competencies that every leader and manager must have in strong measure to be successful. Another competence that should be mentioned as part of communication is listening, which can be defined as the ability to concentrate on communications from others in a meaningful fashion. It has been suggested that in order to communicate, one must be able first to listen. Leaders and managers must concentrate on written and oral communications, body language, and one-on-one and group communications and interactions. Many people believe communication skills are inborn, which is simply not true. Communication is an activity that must consciously be practiced every day.

PUBLIC RELATIONS

Not only are personal communications important, but the communications from the organization to its many publics are crucial as well. Often termed public relations, it is important to discuss such communication within the context of marketing. A host of activities the leader must be aware of contribute to the communication between the organization and its publics. The image that the organization portrays to these publics is critical and can be developed in many ways. It is important for the leader to acknowledge what kind of image the organization wishes to present. Frequently aspects of the organization such as its research or educational accomplishments are emphasized to portray the desired image, even though the primary role of the organization is the delivery of healthcare services. Public relations is an important activity and should not be overlooked.

PLANNING AND DEVELOPING THE ORGANIZATION'S COMMUNICATION AND PUBLIC RELATIONS PLAN

Development of the organization's communication and public relations plan should be among a skillful leader's top priorities. Although a leader may not be skilled in the essentials of such a plan, it is important that they are knowledgeable of these elements so they can choose the individual or individuals to develop the plan. The leader must be constantly and consistently involved in the planning process because the communication plan develops from the organization's vision, mission, and strategic plan, becoming a crucial part of the process. Communicating this plan both internally and externally is a critical part of the overall communication plan process. It is interesting to note that this is not always cited in discussions about competencies for organizational success, as the topic is generally considered as part of marketing and is not extended to the very core of the organization. Overlooking the importance of communication may result in an organization that continuously struggles for success. In a recent study where groups of physicians were asked about the most important aspect of organization and business that should be taught in medical schools, the overwhelming consensus was communications—yet we seem to pay little attention to this most critical competency and skill.

ROLE OF THE LEADER IN COMMUNICATIONS

The leader must understand his or her role in the importance of communications both within and outside of the organization. Leaders rarely understand how each word they say or each announcement they make can be taken out of context. When speaking publicly, leaders must weigh their words very carefully. Although external publics may be forgiving in their misinterpretation of a leader's words, internal audiences may not be so gracious. Words may come back to haunt a leader if not well chosen.

Another important competence of the leader or manager is the ability to inspire and lead their respective staffs in the art of communication. Communication is one of the most important tools for conflict resolution, whether that conflict is inside or outside of the organization. The ability of the leader to articulate the issues that are in dispute and clearly define the differences of opinion is a key aspect of his or her ability to bring about a rational solution to the problem. The next step—resolution—is much easier if that foundation is in place.

The leader is also the spokesperson for the organization and as such must clearly state the vision and mission of the organization, especially to the external publics. When speaking on behalf of the organization, the leader must be sure that what is being said truly represents the consensus of the board and/or the physician staff. No matter how good a communicator a person might be, if they do not have the cooperation and full trust of the membership, the communication will lack the necessary elements to make it effective.

To be a successful communicator on both the personal and organizational level, a leader must be able to:

- Listen effectively
- Communicate orally and in writing to both small and large groups in an articulate fashion
- Oversee the development, implementation, and evaluation of a communication/public relations plan
- Understand the value of both internal and external communications
- Convince all staff of the importance of communication both externally and internally
- Listen to and understand what the marketplace is telling the organization

PRACTICAL APPLICATION

Communication to both internal and external publics is leadership's primary responsibility. Internal communications has been dealt with in the chapter on human resources and remains critical if the leader is to develop and maintain credibility with the staff. These communications must be open, honest, consistent, and constant. External communication with the publics that have an interest in or influence on the organization is also critical. Often leaders devote so much time inside the organization that they neglect communicating with these most important publics. Because those who hear the messages will judge the quality of these communications, great care must be taken to formulate these messages, especially when responding to criticisms or bad news.

Among the publics that the leader must be concerned with are members of the board, the staff of the organization, community leaders, local media, local government officials, state and national government, payers, and research- and grant-funding organizations. The leader must pay constant attention to the organization's publics if the organization is to grow, prosper, and maintain its competitive position in the marketplace.

Leaders must have a keen sense of how to influence issues that affect the organization, which begins with listening followed by careful thought and communication. Leadership must also anticipate and support common interests before the organization has specific needs, and understand how hard the organization can be pushed and act appropriately.

Caution must be taken with both internal and external statements. It is difficult to estimate the damage that can be caused by an offhand remark to a staff member or someone outside the organization. Such remarks are frequently taken out of context and a whole series of misunderstandings can ensue, causing the individual and the organization great difficulties.

When considering the best way to communicate with both your internal and external audiences, remember: there is no substitute for honesty and clarity in communications.

DISCUSSION

1. What is the most important competence in the area of communication?
2. What is the role of communication in conflict resolution?
3. Is the vision of the organization important to the external publics?
4. What must the leader remember when speaking internally?
5. What is the relationship between communications and the marketing plan?
6. Is oral or written communication most important?

Community Health and Managerial Epidemiology

CASE IN POINT: Jim Steinberg had just taken a new position with the Central City Clinic. As he looked over his appointment schedule he noted that he had an upcoming meeting with a group of representatives from the community. He asked his assistant what the meeting was about and she told him the representatives were concerned about the low immunization rates in the community and were wondering what the clinic intended to do about them. The Public Health Department had tried many different marketing activities to encourage parents to immunize their children, but with little success. Jim wondered what he had to do with immunizations and why this item was on his agenda.

He called Dr. Black, the medical director of the clinic, and asked for guidance since he was new to the topic and new to the community. Dr. Black explained that the community believed that it was the clinic's responsibility to do something about the immunization rates, and volunteered to attend the meeting with Jim.

This was Jim's first encounter with prevention and managerial epidemiology, so he quickly sought references on that topic. He also discussed the matter further with Dr. Black and by the time of the meeting he had some understanding of why management was involved in the topic that related significantly to the community's health. He concluded that the clinic and its physicians, under the leadership of management, could play a key role in dealing with the immunization issue.

QUESTION: Why should a leader be concerned with epidemiology?

THE IMPORTANCE OF EPIDEMIOLOGY

Historically, medical care has been oriented toward disease management, with the focus on the individual patient and the examination, diagnosis, and treatment. Insurance companies had little interest in the health of the communities other than seeking out healthy populations to stabilize their risk pools and were unwilling to pay for preventive services. Recently, however, there has been a resurgence of interest in moving toward a community focus on the population's health. This was first suggested in the early 1970s when the original health maintenance organization (HMO) legislation was passed. Even today students in graduate programs in health services administration wonder why they are taking community health and/or managerial epidemiology. The reasons become much more obvious when they realize the inroads into the economics of healthcare that have been made by keeping the population healthy.

THE SCIENCE OF EPIDEMIOLOGY

Fos and Fine, in their book *Health Care for Populations: Applied Epidemiology for Health Care Administration* (2000), state: "Common to all definitions [of epidemiology] is the concept of populations. Individuals are not the focus of the epidemiology but rather groups of individuals. Populations may represent large groups like the total population of the United States, as well as small groups such as employees of a factory, store or government agency. Central to the concept of populations is that groups of individuals exhibit certain commonalities. For example, groups of individuals who are related geographically, such as those living in the same city, represent a population. Also, groups of individuals who work in the same setting are a population. And groups of individuals who live and work together are populations, as in the case of military personnel. Groups of individuals of the same race or ethnic groups are also considered populations. This population-based perspective of epidemiology lends itself well to the objectives of healthcare management in the 21st century."

These new objectives give rise to the need for a specialized focus known as managerial epidemiology. Managerial epidemiology is the core discipline for designing and managing healthcare for populations. A functional definition of managerial epidemiology is: "the study of the distribution and determinants of health and disease, including injuries and accidents, in specified populations, and the application of this study to promotion of health, prevention of disease, treatment of disease, planning for health and disease, designing healthcare services to meet the population's needs, and health policy" (Fos and Fine 2000).

REQUISITE SKILLS AND COMPETENCIES IN EPIDEMIOLOGY

If the modern healthcare leader is to have a significant competence in the area of community health, what skills are important to ensure that an organization has a community focus? A number of issues quickly come to mind, such as those associated with statistics, strategic planning and marketing, quality improvement, informatics and information systems, and communications and public relations. Therefore, it is necessary for the leader to possess significant skills in each of these areas. It is also necessary for the individual to have a comprehensive knowledge of public health upon which to base an assessment of the community's health. Professor Peter Fos (2000) suggested the following in his syllabus for a course in community health: "The overall health status of the population is an important concern of the healthcare executive in the population healthcare management model. Understanding patterns of health and disease in the population allows for appropriate planning for services and programs to meet legitimate healthcare needs. Cost-containment and the resulting health promotion and preventive-services emphasis on portions of the delivery system promises to finally align social and economic objectives such that improving the health of the population has become a measurement of success for integrated providers in the healthcare system. Contemporary healthcare executives must be able to acquire data and understand the community by conducting their own investigative studies on the population served. Such knowledge will be essential to profitability in fully capitated, full risk assumption models of care."

Objectives of the population healthcare management model focus on the health of the population and cost-containment efforts to reduce utilization—which is not emphasized in the facility-based management model—and to shift utilization to low-cost facilities (e.g., outpatient settings or home care are critical executive concerns under conditions of population-based management). Another objective of population healthcare management is to organize and align providers in network schemes. Clinical improvement focuses on improving the health status of the population and the integration of care across all settings and all providers. Quality of care will be documented and studied, and efforts will be made to continually improve quality measures.

To be competent in community health and managerial epidemiology, the healthcare leader must:

- Understand the notion of population-based management
- Calculate and draw conclusions from epidemiological measures, including incidence rate, point prevalence, prevalence, case-fatality rate, proportionate mortality ratio, attack rate, secondary attack rate, and crude death rate, on a cause-specific, age-specific, sex-specific, maternal, and child health basis
- Understand the concept of risk adjustment
- Be aware of the sources for morbidity and mortality data as might be found in registries of reportable diseases, hospital records, morbidity surveys, and vital statistics

- Assess the usefulness of a test by observing the sensitivity and specificity of the predictive values of a positive or negative result
- Understand of outcome assessment and its relationship to epidemiological principles
- Use the above tools when planning for current health needs as well as be able to plan manpower and facilities to care for the ills of the population both present and future
- Understand the relationship between the concept of risk and causation
- Understand the decision matrix for evaluating risk, validity, reliability, and clinical effectiveness

PRACTICAL APPLICATION

The need to know and understand the status of the health of the community is critical for the leader. Without that knowledge he or she cannot effectively plan the strategy to deliver health services. The model so far has principally been that of disease orientation; however, in the future, health promotion and prevention will be one of the most important focus areas for the leaders.

Programs such as immunizations—especially for children—are critical to the welfare of the community and the leader has a responsibility to ensure that his or her organization promotes these activities with every opportunity.

Cooperation between healthcare organizations and public health agencies is also critical and the leader should take the time to investigate and understand these agencies and their purpose. This is one of the external publics with whom the leader should have a vital connection and a strong communication strategy.

The leader should also be concerned about the health and welfare of the disadvantaged and minority members of the community who may be missed in public programs. This is a social responsibility that should not be neglected by the leaders, managers, and professionals in the organization.

The leader should also be concerned about the health and welfare of the organization's staff and not only provide, but also encourage, health measures and preventive services for the staff. Healthy living styles are important and leadership can be a powerful example to the other members of the staff.

DISCUSSION

1. Why should the manager be interested in epidemiology?
2. Are system needs related to the prevalence of disease?
3. Describe how age and sex distributions might influence staffing in a multispecialty clinic.
4. Where can the manager find information on death rates on a regional basis?
5. Explain the differences between disease management and population management.
6. What relationship does emergency room activity have to epidemiological study?
7. Is there a relationship between direct contracting with employers, especially in large firms, and epidemiological principles?

Quantitative Analysis and Modeling

CASE IN POINT: The CHS healthcare system was faced with an unusual opportunity to acquire not only a facility but a delivery system as well. While the organization was in sound financial condition, there were a number of uncertainties about the proposed acquisition and the president, John Norman, wondered how he might approach assessing the risks involved in the new venture. He met with his staff and discussed the matter with them in detail. He told them about the system that was available and at the same time expressed his concerns about the probability of the long-term success of this new delivery system. He asked each of the staff members to prepare a memo outlining their thoughts and analysis of the situation. While due diligence had not yet been conducted, John provided them with substantial information on the history and background of the organization under consideration.

John asked a member of his staff, Bob Smith, to coordinate this effort and review all of the memoranda from the members of the senior management team. Bob had significant analytical skills and was well-informed about the financial condition of the healthcare system. He had also participated in the long-range planning sessions and understood the goals and objectives of the organization. The members of the senior staff had varying degrees of quantitative skills and analytical competencies. Bob was well aware of these differences and was wondering how he would deal with them and not alienate the staff members if they were headed in the wrong direction. He mulled the situation for some time and then decided, with the approval of John, to meet with the staff and discuss the various analytic approaches to the assessment of the risk involved in the new venture.

During the session, which was quite productive, the staff covered problem-solving techniques, the concepts of probability, regression as a tool for analysis, and the evaluation of risk through the use of confidence intervals as a measure of uncertainty. It was quickly apparent which of the senior staff members possessed skills that would be useful in the assessment of the project. Those members who did not possess significant competencies in the areas under discussion acknowledged their lack of skill and worked with the others who possessed the needed competencies.

QUESTION: Where can quantitative analysis and statistics have the greatest effect on the organization?

ANALYTICAL SKILLS

Analytical skills generally are unevenly distributed among members of the senior staff of most healthcare organizations. It is not unusual for the CEO to rely on members of his or her staff to provide this expertise for the organization. It is necessary, however, for the leader to have a broad understanding of the use of analytical and quantitative techniques, especially in the decision process. No matter what endeavor an organization undertakes, a degree of risk and a certain amount of uncertainty are always present. The ability of the organization to assess these risks and degrees of uncertainty is critical not only to seize upon unusual opportunities but also to protect the organization from getting into situations of high risk that could result in significant losses. A leader must have sufficient competency to assign problem solving to the appropriate staff and to hire staff who possess the needed analytical skills. Although leaders may not know every statistical approach and method of quantitative analysis, they must be familiar enough to ensure the staff is using these skills to the advantage of the organization. Included in these analytical areas are statistics, quantitative analysis, assessment of risk, sensitivity analysis, and decision analysis modeling. Decision analysis modeling is becoming a most important tool for the leader, who can now be assisted by the many software programs available.

KEEPING SKILLS CURRENT

Financial competencies are not discussed in this list of core competencies because they were addressed earlier. It is important to reiterate, however, that the leader must have sufficient competency in these analytical areas to understand the results of studies presented by the members of the staff. Competency is also needed if the organization is to use a decision modeling approach in its strategic planning process. Because this is a most difficult area for most leaders and managers, it is important that they continue their education and have the opportunity for graduate training with a strong emphasis on analytical skills. Few professional organizations provide ongoing education in this area; therefore, it is incumbent on the leader or manager to continually update their skills.

QUALITY IMPROVEMENT

Quality improvement is a most important area in both the managerial and clinical settings. Whether one is using process analysis or outcome studies, all of the analytical competencies come into play, especially those involving statistical variation. A direct link exists between statistics, statistical variation, and quality assessment. One of the best ways to approach quality improvement is the use of the determinations of statistical variation. When an aberration is discovered, it is followed by a thorough study of the process, an adjustment of the process, and a reevaluation to determine if the variation remains. These studies involve the use of analytical techniques and the leader and the manager must understand the use of these approaches.

To be competent with analytical skills, the healthcare leader must understand:

- Problem-solving techniques and decisions using numbers
- Concepts of probability
- Regression as a tool
- The use of binomial distribution probability
- The confidence interval as a measure of uncertainty
- Analysis for strategy determination and the evaluation of niche and sensitivity analysis
- The application of software tools in problem analysis and decision models

PRACTICAL APPLICATION

The leader must remember that statistics only measure degrees of uncertainty and should only be used for that purpose. Understanding the differences between information embodied in a series of numbers verses a random walk will serve the leader well as he or she wrestles with the many uncertainties facing the organization. It is important to understand whether or not a series of events are predictable or will occur in a random fashion.

When doing statistical or other quantitative analysis, it is also critically important to understand the underlying process. A high degree of statistical correlation by itself only means that two or more events coexist. The underlying process must be known to determine a causal relationship (i.e., a relatively low volume of production may mean that a physician is a low producer, or it may also mean the physician has a part-time employment status). The participation by people who may have no knowledge of statistics but who understand the process is invaluable in structuring the analysis and in interpreting the results.

The analysis of databases through the determination of probability or regression analysis provides the leader with the necessary information for predictions of success and the identification of the importance of variables found in the decision process. Problem-solving and decision analysis should use analytical techniques wherever possible to support empiric observations. Sensitivity analysis is especially useful in determining the risk of future opportunities. Statistical variations and their measurements should be considered when evaluating continuous quality improvement. Begin with a base of observations, be sure that they are not a random walk, and then use these statistical observations to evaluate process change.

Understanding the application of statistical analysis in both process and outcome quality evaluations is important for leaders if they are to direct their staff toward the rational approach to quality evaluation and improvement.

DISCUSSION

1. Why is statistics important in the decision process?
2. Is there a link between decision analysis and the effective management of the organization?
3. Is there a relationship between financial competencies and the quantitative competencies that have been described?
4. What is the relationship between quality improvement, statistics, and quantitative analysis?

Legal and Ethical Issues

CASE IN POINT: Jack Taylor looked out of the window of his office at the steadily falling snow. He found no answers to the dilemma he faced in the white blanket that now covered the vehicles in the parking lot below. He returned to his desk to contemplate the issues facing him and the associated problems. One of managers had just been charged with using his office to promote a product from a company in which the manager had a significant financial interest. Jack had known and trusted this staff member for over 15 years. Now it appeared that not only was their friendship at an end, but Jack would have the responsibility of discharging the staff member as well.

Jack remembered a managerial ethics course that was presented to the staff two years ago. He wondered what the staff member had been thinking about when he allowed himself to become part of an obviously unethical arrangement. He pondered what he would say when they met the next day. The law was one thing—but the ethical breach was another and it troubled him greatly.

QUESTION: Is there a fine line or a broad gray area between the law and ethics?

LEGAL ISSUES IN HEALTHCARE

The most important competencies that a leader must have are those related to the law and ethics. While law and ethics have always been significant issues, they have become paramount in the last several years. We find ourselves in an extremely litigious society and healthcare is not immune to the legal questions that can be raised in both the public and private sectors. Significant ethical concerns have been raised in both the managerial and biomedical areas. Leaders must not only realize the responsibility for the managerial ethical behavior of their staffs, they must also understand the bioethical issues that face all healthcare organizations. Legal issues of great interest to the healthcare industry include the litigation system and alternatives to litigation for resolving disputes; tort law and professional liability; contract law; product liability; administrative law; intellectual property; human resources law; compliance; agency and forms of organizations; corporations; and duties and liabilities of directors and officers. Not only is the law important in each of these areas, the regulations that follow the law are perhaps of even more relevance to the leader and the manager.

ETHICAL ISSUES

Ethical considerations are high on the list of concerns in both the managerial and the bioethical arenas. In the past decade we have seen a number of ethical breaches where it was apparent that the leader's ambitions were not totally governed by his or her ethics. This has led to the downfall of more than one organization. It is the leader's responsibility to ensure that all the members of his or her staff understand the role of managerial ethics and apply these principles to all of their activities. Most important is the ability to analyze a situation to determine whether the conduct was indeed ethical or unethical. This is a difficult task that requires significant competency and skill.

In the realm of bioethics the leader must know and understand the problems and difficulties of separating ethics, morals, and mores. Appropriate decision processes on ethical issues in the organization require significant insight into human behavior. It is the leader's responsibility to ensure that a process is in place for making the best possible decisions—especially for decisions as to "who will live," such as withdrawing life support for the sick, the elderly, or the unborn. Decisions related to withdrawing life support have both legal and ethical considerations and it is crucial that the leader understand the ramifications of these decisions.

PROFESSIONAL RESPONSIBILITY

Professional liability is one of the domains identified by the American College of Medical Practice Executives in *The Body of Knowledge for Medical Practice Managers* (1999). The text urges leaders to advance professional knowledge and leadership skills; balance professional and personal pursuits; promote ethical standards for individual and organizational behavior and decision making; conduct self-assessments; engage in professional networking; advance the profession by contributing to the body of knowledge; and develop effective interpersonal skills. These standards define the quality of leadership and the excellence of the management. While it is important that the leader pay special attention to the law and to regulation, it is also imperative that the individual incorporate those elements of behavior that have been listed above. Many issues arise that are not necessarily a question of law, but rather of ethics. Competency, knowledge, skill, and personal example are the principal ways in which the leader can demonstrate to his or her organization the importance of the law and ethics.

To be competent in healthcare law and ethics, leaders should understand the law as it is relevant to healthcare:

- The litigation system and dispute resolution
- Tort law and professional liability
- Antitrust considerations
- Contract law, theory, and practice
- Product liability
- Administrative law

- Intellectual property
- Human resources law
- Agency and forms of organizations
- Compliance
- Corporations and corporate law
- Director and officers' duties and liabilities
- Managerial ethics
- Bioethical concerns

PRACTICAL APPLICATION

The Law

Leaders must understand that unless they also practice law, the legal knowledge they possess is at best superficial—there should be no pretext of legal expertise, even if they have a broad knowledge of these competencies. Legal knowledge should be sufficient to enable the leader to recognize legal issues and be familiar enough with them to make the critical judgment of choosing the appropriate representation for the organization. If the organization is large enough, it may have a legal staff that assists the leader in making these choices. In this case the leader is responsible for hiring the legal staff and therefore must understand the competencies listed above. Choosing the right legal staff is just as important as choosing any other top-level management and professional staff.

The leader may also be involved in litigation as a representative of the organization and the listed competencies become a very important aspect of these legal relationships. The leader may also be called upon to serve as an expert witness in cases that do not involve his or her organization. The relationship of the law to like organizations becomes very important.

It is unfortunate that the leader must be able to detect litigation and always be prepared to protect the organization and its staff. If, however, there is a case of proven culpability, the leader is responsible to see that the individuals involved are treated fairly. In summary, the leader should have sufficient knowledge of the law to protect the organization and its staff and understand the need to manage the organization in such a fashion to keep it free of legal issues.

Ethics

Personal values are reflected in organizational values. The leader should pay attention every day to the ethical behavior of all of the members of his or her staff and serve as an example beyond reproach. Just as ethics should be taught across the curriculum in the academy, it should also be practiced across the organization.

Any situation that is questionable from an ethical perspective, whether managerial or bioethical, should be considered detrimental to the organization. All members of the organization—and especially the managerial and professional staff—should have a strong sense of values and ethical perspective that governs the action of the entire staff.

Leadership and management should balance ambition with integrity and always act in such a way that the highest ethical standards prevail. At no time should a leader compromise his or her values or principles. Trust is an asset that takes years to accumulate, but that can be lost in seconds.

Ethics committees in healthcare organizations should have community representation to best reflect community beliefs and standards. These committees should meet frequently, not only when an emergency arises. The committee should be the keeper of the ethical standards and policies of the organization.

It is important to discriminate between ethics and mores and be sure that ethical behavior is consistent with community standards. This may at times be difficult to determine; however, the leader should use every opportunity to evaluate the relationship between ethical behavior and the welfare of the community.

DISCUSSION

1. How much of the law does the leader have to know?
2. What is the leader's responsibility for compliance?
3. What does it mean to balance ambition and values?

4. What is the leader's responsibility in bioethics?
5. Is sexual harassment a breach of managerial ethics?
6. Does professional liability have ethical considerations?
7. Are there ethical considerations in all managerial decision making?
8. Where in the organization does the responsibility for ethical behavior lie?

Organizational and Healthcare Policy

CASE IN POINT: Bob Allen was thinking about the endless stream of managers seeking his advice on a series of personnel issues facing the organization. He realized that there was no statement or policy for the managers to use in their daily decision-making processes. At first it seemed an easy task to simply write a policy and send it to the board of directors for approval. However, the more he thought about it he realized that the management decisions on personnel issues were complex. It would be necessary to develop a policy that dealt with these issues and at the same time would be understandable to those responsible for its implementation.

As Bob considered the development of the policy he believed several criteria should be met, including accurate framing of the issues, provision of all necessary information, and weighing these factors carefully in making a fair and wise decision. He called in his coo to review the process with him and to discuss how they should approach sending the policy statement to the board of directors for approval.

After considering the proposed process, the coo suggested that the policy would be easier to implement if all of the problems and issues related to the policy were discussed first by the interested parties. She suggested that other elements for consideration might surface during the process of policy development. Bob accepted the suggestion—ownership of the policy for effective implementation—and proceeded to contact all those involved in carrying out the policy. He also discussed the matter with several of the influential board members before the board meeting.

QUESTION: What are the relationships between policy development and managerial practice?

UNDERSTANDING POLICY

The term *policy* is partially derived from the word "politeia" which means political sagacity; statecraft; prudent conduct sagacity; craftiness; or course of action adopted by government (*Merriam-Webster's Collegiate Dictionary* 1999). This definition relates not only to courses of action adopted by government, but those related to prudent conduct sagacity as well.

Policy formulation is often related to tradition, culture, and ideology. It is considered an active process where good policy is derived from a series of operating decisions. The policy is meant to guide management in the future as it makes decisions about issues that are covered by the policy in question. Organizations often attempt to develop policies de novo without having had the experience of operating decisions in the area in question. This can lead to a policy that does not fit with the later management decisions that must be made. It is imperative for the leader to know and understand what kind of operating decisions should be molded into a policy statement.

THE BASICS OF POLICY FORMULATION AND IMPLEMENTATION

Policies are best formulated when all questions are framed accurately, all necessary information is obtained, the problems or issues are discussed thoroughly with the interested parties, and all factors are weighed carefully. This task should not be undertaken by those who have not been well grounded—either through academic preparation or experience—in policy formulation. Unfortunately we frequently send individuals to our governing bodies at the state and national level with absolutely no experience or understanding of policy formulation or implementation. Part of the current healthcare crisis is a testament to that fact. It is of extreme importance that healthcare organizations and their leaders involve themselves with the development of health policy at the state and national level. As outlined in part II, chapter 9, the complexity of the healthcare crisis and the challenges of developing a public policy on healthcare are great.

Policy formulation is also directly linked with the decision process of the organization. Organizations that prefer a defined decision process find themselves reinventing that process every time a major decision has to be made. The result is that more time is spent on the process and less time is spent on the decision itself. To avoid wasting time recreating the process each time a decision is made, organizations should initiate the following:

- Thoroughly weigh or examine a wide range of alternative courses of action
- Survey the full range of objectives to be fulfilled
- Carefully weigh what is known about the risks and costs of negative consequences
- Weigh the benefits of each of the alternatives
- Search intensively for new information to assist in the evaluation of the alternatives
- Assimilate new information or expert judgment, particularly when it does not support the staff's preferences
- Reexamine positive and negative consequences of the alternatives, including those originally considered unacceptable, before making a decision
- Make detailed provisions to implement or execute the chosen action

- Give special attention to contingency plans to deal with known risks

The policies formulated must rest on a sound, clearly defined foundation. When disciplining a staff member, a manager often states that whatever the staff member was involved with opposes the organization's policy. Instead, the manager should explain the foundation behind the policy so the employee can understand what is necessary to change the behavior.

ISSUES AFFECTING POLICY MAKING

Special care should be taken when developing and implementing policies that involve ethical issues. These policies should address specific problems, issues, or concerns faced by the organization. They should not be written for just one or two persons; rather, a policy should determine and guide present and future decisions by the entire organization. If an ethics committee is involved, experts in areas of the specific policy from both within and outside the organization should be invited to participate in policy development. Input from the medical and nursing staffs is absolutely essential to the credibility of the policy.

Many aspects of policy formulation at the state and national level affect both the financial and clinical sides of the enterprise. A health policy framework should be in place to create an appropriate balance between patient care and the economics of the system. Many factors should be considered when developing health policy (Shortell and Reinhardt 1992):

- Explicitly consider the interrelatedness and interdependence of "incremental" policies.
- Consider the proposal from the patient's perspective. To what degree is the policy patient centered?
- Consider the policy from the perspective of the underlying process of how medical care is delivered. Does the policy promote active management of clinical care?

- Does the policy include or is it consistent with promoting both clinical and fiscal responsibility?
- Does the policy allow for flexibility and encourage innovation in approaches to meeting accountability criteria and incentives?
- Does the policy anticipate implementation issues, allow for mid-stream correction, and encourage policy development from those directly affected?

Healthcare leaders must be acutely aware of the environmental forces that are reshaping healthcare systems throughout the United States. The growing number of uninsured, access to care, the demand for greater financial and clinical accountability, and the financial pressures on healthcare providers at all levels are some of the issues of the healthcare debates throughout the country. A significant variance of opinion exists among the myriad of special interest groups who continue to pressure legislators at all levels of government. Many issues are influencing the healthcare system today:

- Growing number of uninsured
- Demand for greater accountability (fiscal and clinical)
- Technological growth and innovation
- Changing population composition: growth of elderly and ethnically heterogeneous population
- Changing professional labor supply
- Globalization of the economy
- Changing composition of the delivery system: consolidations and mergers, horizontal and vertical
- Information management

To the information management mix we could add the emergence of e-health as a factor. It is critical that the leader of the organization have a firm grasp on the latest developments—especially those related to how the professionals and the patients will interact in the future of the electronic age—which will have significant policy implications. One of the most important issues in the new electronic era is confidentiality. Policy formulation and implementation regarding confidentiality can either be a driver or a significant impediment in making new technological advances in communications work to the benefit of the patient and the availability of patient information.

The leader must be able to understand the following issues of organizational and health policy formulation and implementation:

- The need for policy to effectively lead a successful organization
- The basic principles of the organization, its functional relationships, and operating management principles
- The methods for policy formulation based on operating decisions
- Decision analysis and the operating principles of decision process
- How policy is used to direct management activities
- The key elements of health policy formulation based on community needs
- The relationships between healthcare organizations and those who make policy at the state and national level
- Ways in which the leader can affect policy development at the state and national level

PRACTICAL APPLICATION

The leader must be constantly aware of the managerial process and its implications on policy formulation. If good policies result from a series of operating decisions, then the leader must always be in tune with what is happening at the managerial level. It is obvious that most of this input will come to the leader from the managers for whom he or she is responsible. Listening is a key competence in this area. The leader will also need sensitivity for when a policy is needed or where managerial decisions can be codified at the policy level.

The ability to seek input from the many publics and stakeholders is a key process need based essentially on competencies and skills in communication. Often individuals in leadership roles are good communicators but not good listeners. Another important skill is the ability to consider alternatives objectively. Policy formulation based on operating decisions must consider a number of different alternatives. The leader should be able to examine these alternatives objectively while at the same time remaining acutely aware of both positive and negative responses from all who will be affected by the policy. This includes not only the staff but also the patients and anyone else involved with the organization.

Healthcare policy demands a good relationship with those who create healthcare policy at both the state and national levels. Leaders must be perceived as knowing and understanding the healthcare needs of the community they serve. They are also expected to understand the political process and the way in which laws and regulations are created because the laws can affect the healthcare organization and the way it delivers its care to the communities served. In short, the leader must maintain good relationships with lawmakers at all levels and understand the ways to communicate with them. This often means participating in fund-raising activities and actively supporting candidates who have expressed interest in the organization, without alienating those in high places where health policy is made. Being known to, and able to converse with, legislators is of significant importance and the leader should pay special attention to such opportunities.

DISCUSSION

1. What level of understanding do you have of the policy-making process?
2. Can you define a series of operating decisions in your organization that might need policy development?
3. Why do you think it is so much easier for a board to be involved in management rather than policy formulation?
4. Does your organization have a well-defined decision process?
5. Have you been involved in policy development at the state or national level?
6. How close do you think you should be to candidates in a political election?
7. How do you make decisions to contribute to political campaigns?

8. Do you think that the United States will one day have a unified health policy?

CONCLUSION

The ten competence areas covered in this section define the breadth, and to some degree the depth, of knowledge necessary to play a major leadership role in a healthcare organization. Knowledge in these areas may be thin, but it must be broad and the individual must have sufficient insights into each to properly assemble a staff that covers all the areas of competence, from finance to human resources. It is also critical that faculties in the universities have a working knowledge of what the competency needs are on both individual and an organizational basis. It is upon these needs that the curriculum for programs in health administration must be developed and maintained. The guidance for these needs must come from the field as they have been described by the two American College of Medical Practice Executives and the University of St. Louis studies in the area of competency determination. Studies such as these must be carried out by professional organizations and university faculties on a continuing basis, and university programs should continuously seek input from their graduates and the healthcare industry on what competencies are needed to meet the challenges of healthcare in this new century.

REFERENCES

Accrediting Commission on Education for Health Services Administration. 1997. *Accreditation Criteria*. Washington, DC: ACEHSA.

American College of Medical Practice Executives. 1999. *The Body of Knowledge for Medical Practice Managers*. Englewood, CO: ACMPE.

Essex, L. and M. Kusy. 1999. *Fast Forward Leadership*. Edinburgh, NJ: Financial Times-Prentice Hall.

Fos, P. 2000. Syllabus, "Community Health." MBA in Medical Group Management. University of St. Thomas Graduate School of Business, Minneapolis, MN.

Fos, P. J. and D. J. Fine. 2000. *Health Care for Populations: Applied Epidemiology for Health Care Administration*. San Francisco: Jossey-Bass.

Health Affairs. 2000. "E-health: The Next Wave." *Health Affairs* 19 (6): 1–328.

Hertzberg, J. 2000. Syllabus, "Health Care Informatics." MBA in Medical Group Management. University of St. Thomas Graduate School of Business, Minneapolis, MN.

Hudak, R. P., P. P. Brooke, K. Finstuen, and J. Trounson. 1997. "Management Competencies for Medical Practice Executives: Skills, Knowledge and Abilities Required for the Future." *Journal of Health Administration Education* 15 (4): 220–39.

Lenberg, R. 2000. Syllabus, "Human Resources." MBA in Medical Group Management. University of St. Thomas Graduate School of Business, Minneapolis, MN.

Merriam-Webster's Collegiate Dictionary, 10th edition. 1999. Springfield, MA: Merriam-Webster.

Shortell, S. M. and U. E. Reinhardt. 1992. "Creating and Executing Health Policy in the 1990s." In *Improving Health Policy and Management,* edited by S. M. Shortell and U. E. Reinhardt. Chicago: Health Administration Press.

Leadership Priorities
for the Year 2010

THE BIG PICTURE

We need not belabor the point that in the year 2010 we will have a health system quite different than today's. We may not know its structure but we know it will be complicated, information based, and highly technical, and that quality and the healthcare consumer will be very important factors in determining policy and decision making.

Three important questions to ask include:

1. What will be the leadership priorities of tomorrow?
2. Will leaders require a vastly different inventory of leadership and management tools or can they prosper with the same "old-fashioned" approaches?
3. Will value systems and the personal ethical bases erode, be the same, or improve?

Clearly caregivers will have responded to many technological changes. Hopefully a system for providing healthcare coverage to everyone will be in place and the merger mania of today will be history. Medicine will be practiced differently and include a good dose of complementary medicine. Executives at every level will continue to be stressed over the never-ending problems associated with reimbursement for healthcare services. The payment system may well have changed, but the shortages of adequate resources will continue to prevail.

LEADERSHIP PRACTICES

Based on collective thought and a bit of history, one might predict that executives of the future will still employ a number of traditional leadership techniques, including the building and sustaining of energy levels. As summarized by Katzenbach and Santamaria (1999), mutual trust, collective pride, and self-discipline are essential to generate the emotional energy executives need to lead. They suggest this energy can be generated by such practices as:

- Using processes that include transparent performance, measures and standards, and clear results tracking.
- Infusion of the entrepreneurial spirit path that includes personal freedom, the opportunity for high earnings, and a few rules about behavior. People choose their work activities and take significant personal risks.
- Fostering an intense respect for individual achievement in an environment with limited emphasis on personal risk and reward.
- Whole-hearted recognition and celebration of organizational accomplishments.

It is the responsibility of the leader to ensure that his or her staff has ample opportunity to continue to develop their competencies in the ten knowledge areas discussed in part IV. Senge (1990) has described the "learning organization," which can best be defined as an organization whose staff continues to develop their skills and competence to meet the challenges of their chosen field. There are many academic and nonacademic opportunities for education. These opportunities have been enhanced greatly by the introduction of distance-learning techniques. Advanced degrees are now available for working professionals who under previous circumstances would not have been able to obtain such a degree in healthcare administration or management. Physicians especially are taking advantage of university programs that have minimal on-campus commitments, where the majority of the program is conducted through distance learning. Computer conferencing has enabled university programs to bring the classroom to the student. It has also provided faculty with the opportunity to teach from wherever they happen to be at the time.

MANAGEMENT TOOLS

Will leaders require a new set of management tools? In 1915 on his extraordinary expedition to Antarctica, Ernest Shackleton had to apply leadership tools of the highest order to save the 27 men of his crew after they became stranded on an iceflow. From 1914 to 1916 they were 1,200 miles from civilization with no means of communication. During a lifetime of challenges, Shackleton developed a number of leadership skills. In the book *Shackleton's Way* (Morrell and Capparell 2001), a number of his suggestions are carefully documented.

- Cultivate a sense of compassion and responsibility for others. You have a greater effect on the lives of those under you than you can imagine.
- Once you make a career decision, commit to stick through the tough learning period.
- Do your part to create an upbeat environment at work. A positive and cheerful workplace is important to productivity.
- Broaden your cultural and social horizons beyond your usual experiences. Learning to see things from different perspectives will give you greater flexibility in problem solving at work.
- In a rapidly changing world, be willing to venture in new directions to seize new opportunities and learn new skills.
- Find a way to turn setbacks and failures to your advantage. This would be a good time to step forward on your own.
- Be bold in vision and careful in planning. Dare to try something new but be meticulous in your proposal to give your ideas a good chance of succeeding.
- Learn from past mistakes—yours and those made by others. Sometimes the best teachers are the bad bosses and the negative experiences.
- Never insist on reaching a goal at any cost. It must be achieved at a reasonable expense, without undue hardship for your staff.

- Do not be drawn into public disputes with rivals. Rather, engage in respectful competition. You may need their cooperation some day.

The lesson here is that much of leadership is constant and while the environment may change, the principles of leading endure.

ABOUT ETHICS AND VALUES

The importance and emphasis on ethical and value-driven behavior will continue to increase. Information technology will make comparative performance more visible. The fundamental relationship noted in chapter 6, "Ethics and Values"—that healthcare exists and functions as a trust relationship with patients and their families—will still be true. Healthcare will continue to be more than the typical business relationship of "we will do what we say." It will be based on the trust that we will do what we can to care for our patients and their interests. Amidst such trust, it will be increasingly easy to identify organizations where that relationship does not exist.

By 2010, the retirement of the Baby Boomers will be in full swing, placing large demands on the healthcare system. The baby boomers have demonstrated the ability, throughout their lives, to change social institutions to meet their needs. As noted in chapter 9, "Health Policy and Law," where the knowledge of consumers and market forces are not sufficient to produce ethical behavior, legislation is developed to produce socially accountable behavior. Legislation, however, has demonstrated itself to be a cumbersome way of ensuring accountable behavior. Therefore, we hope that access to information—by a large, sophisticated group of consumers who share knowledge—will reward the ethical, punish the unethical, and continue to produce a healthcare system that chooses ethical and value-driven behavior as the best way to ensure its success.

The opportunity exists to build successful healthcare organizations in the future, despite all the inevitable changes that will occur. It is our belief that the fundamental, human relationship of a caregiver and a patient will continue. The research of Arie de Geus (1997), noted in chapter 5, "Physician Relationships," identified the common characteristics of very long-lived companies, those 100- to 700-year-old institutions that he calls the "living companies." In summarizing his findings, he states: "Above all, in the living company, members know 'who is us,' and they are aware that they hold values in common. They know the answer to the definitive question about corporate identity: What do we value? Whoever cannot live with the company's values cannot and should not be a member." These are companies that value people more than assets. Patients, with knowledge of care and outcomes, will know if they are valued. They will choose organizations that provide demonstrably high-quality care, where the trust relationship with them and their families exists, and where it is valued and nourished.

CONCLUSION

So what are the competencies required for success in 2010, assuming the continuance of many practices and ethical and value systems from the present? The needed competencies will relate to a process of keeping current with technological and social change and continuing to fine tune leadership practices. Staying current will mean developing a professional and personal continuing education program. The executive of the future will need to be even more responsive to change. Understanding the importance of developing a continuing process to monitor and develop core competencies will make the difference for future executive leaders.

REFERENCES

de Geus, A. 1997. "The Living Company." *Harvard Business Review* 75 (2): 58.

Katzenbach, J. R. and J. A. Santamaria. 1999. "Firing up the Front Line." *Harvard Business Review* 77 (3): 109.

Morrell, M. and S. Capparell. 2001. *Shackleton's Way.* New York: Viking.

Senge, P. 1994. *The Fifth Discipline: The Art and Practice of the Learning Organization.* New York: Currency/Doubleday.

Suggested Reading

Andreasen, A. R. 1995. *Marketing Social Change.* San Francisco: Jossey-Bass.

Bagley, C. E. 1999. *Managers and the Legal Environment: Strategies for the 21st Century.* Cincinnati, OH: West Educational Publishing Co.

Barker, J. A. 1993. *Paradigms.* New York: HarperCollins Publishers, Inc.

Beckhard, R. and W. Pritchard. 1992. *Changing the Essence—The Art of Creating and Leading Fundamental Change in Organizations.* San Francisco: Jossey-Bass.

Bennis, W. and B. Nanus. 1985. *Leaders—The Strategies for Taking Charge.* New York: Harper and Row.

Berkowitz, E. N. 1996. *Essentials of Healthcare Marketing.* Gaithersberg, MD: Aspen Publishers.

Brigham, E. F., L. C. Gapenski, and M. C. Ehrhardt. 1999. *Financial Management: Theory and Practice,* 9th edition. Orlando, FL: Dryden Press.

Buckingham, M. and C. Coffman. 1999. *First, Break All the Rules.* New York: Simon & Schuster.

Clemmer, J. 1992. *Firing on All Cylinders—Service/Quality for High Powered Corporate Performance.* Homewood, IL: Business One Irwin.

Coddington, D. C., C. R. Chapman, and K. M. Pokoski. 1996. *Making Health Care Work—Case Studies.* Englewood, CO: Center for Research in Ambulatory Health Care Administration.

Coddington, D. C., K. D. Moore, and E. A. Fischer. 1996. *Making Integrated Health Care Work.* Englewood, CO: Center for Research in Ambulatory Health Care Administration.

Coile, R. C. 1997. *The Five Stages of Managed Care: Strategies for Providers, HMOs, and Suppliers.* Chicago: Health Administration Press.

Cunningham, B. M., L. A. Nikolai, and J. D. Bazley. 2000. *Accounting Information for Business Decisions*. Orlando, FL: Dryden Press.

Davis, S. and C. Meyer. 1998. *Blur: The Speed of Change in the Connected Economy*. New York: Addison Wesley.

Dawes, R. M. 1988. *Rational Choice in an Uncertain World*. Orlando, FL: Harcourt Brace Jovanovich.

Deal, T. E. and A. A. Kennedy. 1982. *Corporate Cultures*. New York: Addison Wesley.

de Geus, A. 1997. *The Living Company*. Boston: Harvard Business School Press.

Dick, R. S., E. B. Steen, and D. E. Detmer. 1997. *The Computer-based Patient Record: An Essential Technology for Health Care*, revised edition. Washington, DC: National Academy Press.

Drucker, P., P. Senge, and F. Hesselbein. 2001. *Leading in a Time of Change*. San Francisco: Jossey-Bass.

Dye, C. F. 2000. *Leadership in Healthcare: Values at the Top*. Chicago: Health Administration Press.

Essex, L. and M. Kusy. 1999. *Fast Forward Leadership*. Edinburgh, NJ: Financial Times-Prentice Hall.

Feldstein, P. J. 1998. *Health Care Economics*, 5th edition. Albany, NY: Delmar Publishers, Inc.

Flaherty, J. and P. Drucker. 1999. *Shaping the Managerial Mind*. San Francisco: Jossey-Bass.

Fos, P. J. and D. J. Fine. 2000. *Health Care for Populations: Applied Epidemiology for Health Care Administration*. San Francisco: Jossey-Bass.

Getzen, T. E. 1997. *Fundamentals & Flow of Funds*. New York: John Wiley & Sons.

Gomez-Mejia, L. R., D. B. Balkin, and R. L. Cardy. 2001. *Managing Human Resources*, 3rd edition. Upper Saddle, NJ: Prentice Hall, Inc.

Hanson, P. G. and B. Lubin. 1995. *Answers to Questions Most Frequently Asked About Organization Development*. Thousand Oaks, CA: Sage Publications.

Herzlinger, R. E. 1997. *Market Driven Health Care—Who Wins, Who Loses in the Transformation of America's Largest Service Industry*. Reading, MA: Perseus Books.

Hesselbein, F., M. Goldsmith, and R. Beckhard, eds. 1996. *The Leader of the Future. New Visions, Strategies and Practice for the Next Era*. San Francisco: Jossey-Bass.

Hopkins, B. 1999. *The Law of Tax Exempt Organizations*. San Francisco: Jossey-Bass.

Huang, C. A. and J. Lynch. 1995. *Mentoring: The Tao of Giving and Receiving Wisdom*. San Francisco: Harper.

Hurst, D. K. 1995. *Crisis and Renewal—Meeting the Challenge of Organizational Change*. Boston: Harvard Business School Press.

Johnson, H. and D. S. Broder. 1997. *The System: The American Way of Politics at the Breaking Point*. Boston: Little, Brown and Co.

Kaluzny, A. D., H. S. Zuckerman, and T. C. Ricketts, III. 1995. *Partners for the Dance: Forming Strategic Alliances in Health Care*. Chicago: Health Administration Press.

Kotter, J. P. 1996. *Leading Change*. Boston: Harvard Business School Press.

Kouzes, J. M. and B. Z. Posner. 1996. *The Leadership Challenge: How to Keep Getting Extraordinary Things Done in Organizations*. San Francisco: Jossey-Bass.

Kovner, A. R. 1995. *Health Care Delivery in the United States*. New York: Springer.

Litman, T. J. and L. S. Robins, eds. 1991. *Health Politics and Policy*, 2nd edition. Albany, NY: Delmar Publishers, Inc.

Lombardi, D. N. 1996. *Thriving in an Age of Change: Practical Strategies for Health Care Leaders*. Chicago: Health Administration Press.

Lorenzi, N. M. and T. R. Riley. 1995. *Organizational Aspects of Health Informatics*. New York: Springer.

Morrell, M. and S. Capparell. 2001. *Shackleton's Way*. New York: Viking.

Pearce, J. A., II and R. B. Robinson, Jr. 1997. *Formulation, Implementation, and Control of Competitive Strategy*. Chicago: Irwin.

Quinn, R. E., S. R. Faerman, M. P. Thompson, and M. R. McGrath. 1996. *Becoming a Master Manager: A Competency Framework*. New York: John Wiley & Sons.

Ross, A. 1992. *Cornerstones of Leadership for Health Services Executives*. Chicago: Health Administration Press.

Ross, A., S. J. Williams, and E. J. Pavlock. 1998. *Ambulatory Care Management*. Albany, NY: Delmar Publishers, Inc.

Rubin, I. M. 1991. *My Pulse Is Not What it Used to Be*. Honolulu: The Temenos Foundation.

Senge, P. 1994. *The Fifth Discipline: The Art and Practice of the Learning Organization*. New York: Currency/Doubleday.

Senge, P., A. Kleiner, C. Roberts, R. Ross, G. Roth, and B. Smith. 1999. *The Dance of Change*. New York: Currency/Doubleday.

Shortell, S. M., R. G. Gillies, D. A. Anderson, K. M. Erickson, and J. B. Mitchell. 2000. *Remaking Health Care in America*. San Francisco: Jossey-Bass.

Shortliffe, E. H. 2000. *Medical Informatics: Computer Applications in Health Care*. New York: Springer.

Simborg, M. J., D. W. Albright, and J. V. Douglas. 1995. *Healthcare Information Management Systems: A Practical Guide*, 2nd edition. New York: Springer.

Slavin, S. L. 1988. *Economics—A Self-teaching Guide*. New York: John Wiley & Sons.

Tichy, N. M. 1997. *The Leadership Engine: How Winning Companies Build Leaders at Every Level*. New York: Harper.

Williams, C. A., M. Smith, and P. C. Young. 1998. *Risk Management and Insurance*, 8th edition. Boston: Irwin/McGraw-Hill.

About the Authors

JOSEPH W. MITLYNG

Joseph W. Mitlyng is a principal in the Health Care Group of Larson Allen Weishair & Co., LLP. Larson Allen is an accounting/consulting firm with 700 professionals, 125 of whom are in healthcare practice. The firm has offices in Minneapolis, St. Louis, Charlotte, and Philadelphia. He consults nationally in the areas of governance, leadership, and management of physician groups and physician-hospital organizations.

Mr. Mitlyng was the executive vice president and COO of Park Nicollet Medical Center from 1986 to 1994, during a major financial turnaround period. Before taking his position at Park Nicollet, he was associate director of Marshfield Clinic from 1975 to 1986. In 1994, he was the president of the Medical Group Management Association.

He is the lead author of "It Takes More than Money—Keys to Success in Leading and Managing Physician Groups" and "Leaders as Combat Fighter Pilots" and is featured in *Trials to Triumphs: Perspectives of Successful Healthcare Leaders* (Health Administration Press 2001).

Mr. Mitlyng has a master's degree in business from Harvard Business School and is a Fellow in the American College of Medical Practice Executives.

AUSTIN ROSS

Austin Ross is currently professor emeritus in the School of Public Health and Community Medicine at the University of Washington. He was the first program director for the school's Executive MHA Program for physicians and clinicians. His teaching and research interests focus on integrated healthcare systems, group practice and ambulatory care, and leadership and management. Mr. Ross is also a senior consultant with Arthur Andersen's Health Care Division and has served as a project consultant with the Robert Wood Johnson Foundation and the W. K. Kellogg Foundation.

In addition, Mr. Ross is vice president and executive administrator emeritus of the Virginia Mason Medical Center in Seattle, Washington. After receiving his master's degree in public health from the University of California in Berkeley in 1955, he joined the Virginia Mason administrative staff and was with Virginia Mason until his retirement in 1991.

During his professional career he has been the recipient of a number of awards including the American College of Healthcare Executive's Gold Medal, the Harry Harwick Award from the American College of Medical Group Administrators, and the Administrator of the Year Award from the American Group Practice Association. He served as chairman of the American College of Healthcare Executives and president of the Medical Group Management Association, the Association of Western Hospitals (Healthcare Forum), and of other health-related organizations. He is an author or coauthor/editor of six books. The American College of Healthcare Executives named one of his books, *Cornerstones of Leadership for Health Services Executives,* the 1994 James A. Hamilton Book of the Year. He also has published over 50 articles with a special focus on leadership and strategic planning.

FREDERICK J. WENZEL

Frederick J. "Fritz" Wenzel is a distinguished service professor and was the academic director of the MBA program in medical group management at the University of St. Thomas in Minneapolis, Minnesota from

1976 to 1993. He was the executive director of the Marshfield Clinic and the executive vice-president and CEO of the Medical Group Management Association from 1993 to 1996.

He has an MBA degree from the University of Chicago and is a Fellow in the American College of Medical Practice Executives. He has served on the Accreditation Commission for Education in Health Care Administration for more than 15 years and was chair of the Commission for two years.

Mr. Wenzel has authored or coauthored over 120 papers. He has received numerous honors including the Harry Harwick Award from the American College of Medical Practice Executives (1993); the Administrator of the Year Award from the American Group Practice Association (1985); the Board of Directors Award from the Healthcare Financial Management Association (1993); and was named the Innovative Teacher of the Year in 1999 at the University of St. Thomas and the 2001 Alumnus of the Year at the University of Wisconsin–Stevens Point.

He lectures and consults widely and is a faculty member at both the University of Colorado and the University of Minnesota. He serves on a number of boards of directors, including the University of Wisconsin Medical Foundation and the Marshfield Clinic National Advisory Council.

Index

risk, 269–70
timing, 269–70
Consensus decision-making, 64–65
Consent agenda, 55
Continuous quality improvement
    (CQI), 148–50, 161, 232
Continuum of care, 175, 182
Control issues, 107
Control practices, 10
Core competencies. *See* Competency
County health commission, 180–81
CQI. *See* Continuous quality
    improvement
Credentialing process, 52–53
Credibility, 36, 230–31
Critical thinking, 32
Culture
    competencies and, 41
    ethics and, 121–23
    examination of, 111–12
    importance of, 109
    success characteristics, 9, 10, 76
    values and, 121–23
Currency, 291
Customer needs assessment,
    154–55
Customer satisfaction surveys,
    76–77

Dashboard model, 58
Debate, 253
Decision-making
    assessment process, 245–47
    credibility in, 230–31
    elements of, 244
    ethics in, 128–29, 133–34
    governing board's role, 57–58
    group thinking and, 267–68
    innovation in, 230–31
    leadership goals, 236–38
    organizational bureaucracy and,
        231–36

organizational stagnation and, 236
participation in, 104–5
physician issues, 107, 256–57
principles of, 235–36
process, 64–65, 229–30
responsibility, 238
risk in, 243–48
value in, 165–66
Delegation, 11, 234–35, 304
Democratic style, 291
Department chair, 99
Direction, 244
Disconfirmation, 151
Disenrollment rate, 53
Diversity, 286
Divine source, 126
Domain, 26–29, 31–33
Downsizing, 244

Early childhood services, 177–78
Economics, 313–16
Economies of scale, 5
Economies of scope, 162
Education, 102–3, 295–96,
    299–300
E-health, 326–27
Electronic medical record, 328
Employee meetings, 310–11
Empowerment, 155
Entrapment, 237
Entrepreneurship, 4
Epidemiology
    competencies in, 339–41
    importance of, 338
    science of, 338–39
Errors, 237
Ethics, 368–69
    audit, 130
    code of, 121–22, 130–31
    committee, 134–37, 353
    compliance programs and,
        123–25

Health informatics. *See* Information
 management
Health insurance, 192–94
Health Insurance Association of
 America (HIAA), 197, 200–202
Health Insurance Portability and
 Accountability Act (HIPAA),
 191, 197
Health maintenance organization
 (HMO)
 accountability, 53
 pricing, 83–84
 quality measures, 53
 stakeholders, 47
Health Maintenance Organization
 Act, 194
Health policy, 191, 356–61
 associations' role in, 200–202
 decisions for, 194–98
 development of, 199–200
 executive branch, 195–96
 grass-roots involvement, 202–3
 healthcare organization's
  responsibility, 198–99
 to law, 193–94
 legislative successes, 197–98
 lobbyists' role, 203–4
 mission and, 204
 need identification, 192–93
 political process, 196–97
 values and, 204
Health services advisory
 committee, 180
Health status, 20
Health system, 13, 61
Heir apparent, 52
HIAA. *See* Health Insurance
 Association of America
HIPAA. *See* Health Insurance
 Portability and Accountability
 Act
HMO. *See* Health maintenance
 organization

Hospital
 accountability, 53
 board composition, 60
 complementary medicine
  integration, 219–21
 physician group governance
  comparison, 67, 68
 physician practice acquisitions, 83
 physician relationship, 97–98
 quality measures, 53
Humanitarian service, 20
Human resources, 12, 307–11

Idea implementation, 283–84
Image, 237–38
Improvement, 9
Incentives, 245
Information management,
 323–29, 368
Information systems, 12
Information systems committee, 66
Initial organization era, 4
Innovation, 5, 230–31
Integration, 5
Integrative medicine, 209–10,
 217–19
Interests, 294
Intermountain Healthcare, 203
Interpersonal skills, 19–20, 136,
 254, 351
Intervention programs, 178
Isolation, 284

Job competency model, 25–26
Johnson & Johnson, 129

Kassebaum-Kennedy bill, 197
Knowledge jobs, 26

Leader
 challenges for, 103
 change issues, 90–91
 definition of, 24

Medicare, 194
Medicare Catastrophic Coverage
    Act, 194
Mental model, 49, 90–91
Mentor
    characteristics of, 278–79
    role of, 274–75
    suggestions for, 285
Mentoring
    activities, 285–86
    categories, 275
    pitfalls, 280–81
    program development, 275–77
    protege responsibilities, 279–80
    reasons for, 277
    relationship, 277–86
    special concerns, 286
    success and, 274
    team member orientation, 281–85
    value of, 274–75
MESH. *See* Measurable enhancement
    of the status of health
Michigan State University, 203
Mission
    community involvement and,
        173–74, 179
    development, 48
    ethics and, 121
    health policy and, 204
    public health issues and, 173–74
    team identification with, 253
Modesty, 11
Moral obligation theory, 125–26
Motivation, 291–92

Narcissistic leaders, 106
National Academy of Sciences, 274
National Center for Complementary
    and Alternative Medicine
    (NCCAM), 210, 215–16
National Federation of Independent
    Businessmen, 200
National health insurance, 192–94

National Health Insurance Task
    Force, 195
NCCAM. *See* National Center for
    Complementary and
    Alternative Medicine
Negotiation, 12, 267
Networking, 5, 284, 292
Noncustomers, 77
Nonvoting committee, 66
No-regrets moves, 88, 89

Objectives, 73, 75
Operational demands, 282
Operational effectiveness, 5
Options, 88
Organizational bureaucracy, 231–36
Organizational culture. *See* Culture
Organizational dynamics, 301–5
Organizational infancy era, 4
Organizational relationships, 282–83
Organizational will, 78
Orientation, 54–55, 310
Outcomes, 146–47

Pace setting style, 291
Park Nicollet Medical Center, 105
Participatory leadership style, 104–5
Partnership, 115
Partnership model, 107
Patience, 11
Patient
    care, 106, 109, 198
    dissatisfaction, 214, 215
    dumping, 174
    satisfaction, 53
    services, 12–13
Payment systems, 243
Peer relationships, 107
Perception, 10, 237–38
Performance
    appraisal, 310
    attributes, 23
    clinical, 115

CAREER RESOURCES FROM HEALTH ADMINISTRATION PRESS

Executive Excellence
Protocols for Healthcare Leaders, Second Edition
Carson F. Dye, FACHE

Technical skills do not ensure leadership success. This book describes the unwritten rules of executive conduct that are critical to your success as a healthcare executive.

Issues covered include:
- Establishing relationships and strengthening credibility
- Making ethical choices
- Interacting with the executive team and board members
- Enhancing relationships with physicians
- Supporting increased diversity in the workplace
- Strengthening communications skills

Order No. BKCO-1111, $50
Softbound, 176 pp, 2000, ISBN 1-56793-142-1
An ACHE Management Series Book

A Career Guide for the Health Services Manager
Third Edition
Anthony R. Kovner, Ph.D. and Alan H. Channing, FACHE

Learn the professional and personal skills necessary to succeed as a healthcare executive.

Topics covered include:
- Where health services managers work
- How to build an ideal career
- What skills make a good manager
- How to manage physicians, boards, and other employees
- How to advance within an organization and within the industry

Order No. CF21-1078, $43
Softbound, 203 pp, 2000, ISBN 1-56793-111-1

Prices do not include shipping and are subject to change.

To order these books, call (301) 362-6905. Or, order online at www.ache.org/hap.html